Rewilding

Rewilding

A Woman's Quest to Remember Her Roots,
Rekindle Her Instincts, and Reclaim
Her Sovereignty

KRISTY M. VANACORE, PSY.D

SACRED STORIES
PUBLISHING

Books may be purchased through booksellers or by contacting Sacred Stories Publishing.

Editor: Gina Mazza

Rewilding: A Woman's Quest to Remember Her Roots, Rekindle Her Instincts, and Reclaim Her Sovereignty
Kristy M. Vanacore, Psy.D.

Tradepaper ISBN: 978-1-945026-88-1
Electronic ISBN: 978-1-945026-90-4

Library of Congress Control Number: 2021949782

Published by Sacred Stories Publishing, Fort Lauderdale, FL USA

For the one whom I affectionately called "Ma"; my heart swells with love and boundless gratitude to you for inspiring me to find my voice.

Your life blazed the trail, showing me the way when I couldn't see one. Your memory lives on in my story and in the lives of all who will find inspiration in its pages.

I always believed you, and now your truth is finally set free. You are the reason why I will always be afraid not of the wild horses, but of the people who caged them.

Contents

PART 3: RECLAIMING MY SOVEREIGNTY

Declaration

I was angst, fear, jealousy, rage, depression, neurosis, confusion.
I was remnants of a protective ego lurking in the shadows of Earth's elements
that kept me shamed when I wanted to shine
caged when I wanted to fly
immobile when I wanted to dance
silenced when I wanted to sing
sheltered when I wanted to share love.
It was the cold harsh armor of steel that imprisoned my heart.
It was the toxic juice that fed my overprotective brain.
It was the punitive teacher who told me to color within the lines.
It was the overprotective parent who told me not to play outside in the rain.
It was the dominating boy who told me I was unworthy and told me not to
tell anyone when he touched me.
It was the trusted friend who held me and cut me with the same knife.
They have all been my greatest teachers, and it's now time to put
the lessons to the test.
It's time to become who I am truly am—who I was before
the world told me who to be.

—*Kristy Vanacore*

I read somewhere that domesticated horses hate the wind;
it makes them incredibly anxious and chaotic.
But wild horses thrive on it.

—K.V.

Part One

Remembering My Roots

The Heroine horse stands upon her pedestal after placing *Best in Show*. Smiling for the cameras with her shiny trophy on display, she examines her life. It is full of all that she set out to achieve, yet it has come with a price. She feels empty and devoid of purpose and passion; her inner landscape barren, her soul bereft and estranged from itself.

She hears a calling and knows she must go; yet fear is all consuming and she hides in her stall, clinging to the only life that she has known.

And then one day, she wakes up and discovers the gate has been left open…and the choice is all her own…

Domestication

I awake on a cold metal makeshift bed, my eyes immediately blinded by the worn fluorescent lights blaring overhead. Vague memories of the night before flood my consciousness. I'm eight years old and cannot comprehend why I am in a jail cell, surrounded by rusty bars and musty block walls.

"Kristy, I'm Sergeant Brandon."

The shadow of a man in uniform towers over me. I'm scared and confused. He hands me a Dixie cup of water. The name on his badge reminds me of the dog on my favorite TV show, Punky Brewster. I focus my mind on the image of the fiery-spirited girl Punky and her doting Golden Retriever, Brandon, who were abandoned by their mother at the grocery store and taken in by a sweet old man named Henry. *Had my parent abandoned me last night? Where is Daddy?*

As I sip the water, a woman sits down next to me.

"Hi Kristy, I'm Mary." She smiles sympathetically, brushing back my long strawberry-blonde locks. "Everything's gonna be okay, honey. We'll get you out of here real soon."

After a while, I hear the sound of Daddy's voice down the hallway as he emerges from the room where he was being questioned by a police officer. His face looks bloody and bruised. My mind flashes back to the prior evening; some sort of fight is all I recall. I'm suddenly frozen in fear.

"Come on, your father's here to get you." Mary takes my hand and tugs on me to stand up. "Uh oh," she murmurs, seeing that my pants are soaked.

I had urinated on myself. The tears come. I'm embarrassed and want to run and keep running—but I can't. In the car, Daddy doesn't say a word. He just stares out the window of his old blue Oldsmobile that smells smoky from the time the engine caught fire and burned a hole through the floor panels. When that happened, he made me smile by saying we could be like the Flintstone's cartoon—just put our feet through the floor and run. But today I can't find humor or *any* feeling. I'm numb.

The day prior started out like every typical Saturday. Daddy picked me up at four o'clock for his court-ordered weekend visitation. We drove to his apartment which he shared with his mother, my Grammie. I cooked in the kitchen with Grammie. Daddy stayed in his bedroom, watching TV and chain smoking.

"C'mon, we gotta go!" Daddy yelled to me just as I was setting the table for dinner.

"Johnny, what are you talking about? We're eating now," Grammie said. "What's so important? Don't tell me it's that girl again."

"Let's go! I said NOW!" I could see veins bulging in Daddy's head. Grammie had tears in her eyes. I felt nauseous, as I had many times before, being put in the middle between wanting to stay with Grammie and watch her favorite "Golden Girls" TV show and wanting to please my Daddy.

I put two-and-two together as to why Daddy rushed me out of the house. He had gotten a call from his girlfriend who was in some sort of trouble. I didn't understand it then, but she was in some crack den doing drugs, and one of the men there tried to hurt her. She was on the verge of overdosing. As we drove to her rescue, Daddy mumbled and banged the steering wheel. I just stared out the window, humming songs in my head. Something didn't feel right about the situation my parent was leading me into.

We arrive at the old, dank-smelling apartment building. The hallway is dingy and reeks of oil paint as I try to keep up with Daddy, whose brisk, purposeful walk leads us to a thickly-painted brown door with "Apartment 2H" on it. Smoke is wafting through the gaps in the door. It smells awful, almost medicinal. I am shaking, as I know something bad is about to happen. Being a man of few words, I'd gotten good at reading my father's facial expressions and body language. In these moments, anger is seeping out of his pores as he raps on the door repeatedly.

"Open the fucking door!" he screams.

Finally, a tall, muscular, bald black man cracks open the door until the safety chain catches. "Who the fuck are you?"

"Let her out of there!" Daddy demands.

"Get the fuck outa here." The man slams the door.

My heart is racing furiously. I want to run and hide but don't want to leave Daddy there.

"OPEN THE FUCKING DOOR, I SAID!" Daddy slams on the door.

"Daddy please let's just go," I plead timidly, but he doesn't acknowledge my request.

The intimidating man cracks open the door again and Daddy pushes his entire body into it, breaking the chain and swinging it wide open. The man raises his gigantic fist and repeatedly pummels Daddy in the head, blood spewing from every punch. I could faintly hear a woman moaning somewhere inside the apartment. Daddy struggles and slumps to his knees. I watch, absolutely horrified, as the hallway starts to spin. I scream so hard I can't hear my voice—only the sound of Daddy's body thumping onto the tiled hallway floor.

The next morning, after leaving the police station, Daddy takes me straight back to Grammie's apartment. She is there to greet me with a hug. I could see she had been crying. Daddy storms off to his bedroom and slams the door. Grammie helps me remove my soiled clothes and draws me a warm bubble bath. She sings softly to me while washing my hair. Once clean and clothed in warm flannel jammies, she holds me. I can't cry or even speak. None of it feels real.

Later, I hear Grammie reprimanding Daddy through the closed bedroom door.

"Johnny, come out and look at your daughter. She peed herself and you didn't even help her. That piece of shit woman has ruined you!"

I'm comforted that Grammie is my defender and at the same time, afraid that she might further upset Daddy.

That evening, when my visitation hours with Daddy were done, I took it upon myself to call Mommy to ask her to come get me since Daddy was nursing a concussion from the fight.

"Why are *you* calling?" she asks. "Where is he? Where's Grammie?"

"He has a bad headache. Just please come get me, Mommy."

I beg Grammie not to tell Mommy what happened because I knew she would never let me go with Daddy again. Instead, I make up a story about going to the park on Saturday and how much fun we had. This secret is one of many from my childhood that I lock away in a neatly organized cage in my heart, and one of the countless times when I abandoned myself in order to keep the peace. This self-betrayal accumulated over the years, little by little, unbeknownst to me, and oblivious to the damage it would eventually cause me.

Magical Gypsy Child

I was born with an untamed heart, an adorable little girl with eyes as blue as the sky and always full of wonder. I remember (not just the stories my family told me but somehow the feeling of) the mystical little gypsy of a child, always marching to the beat of her own drum. I saw magic everywhere. My eyes beamed with curiosity. My unbound flaxen locks thrashed in the wind as I ran free.

Yet this gypsy heart carried a burdened soul, a heaviness of responsibility that plagued her spirit. A baby who was entrusted with the responsibility of salvaging a fragile marriage between two people who were not destined to be. Right out of the gate, the circumstances of her life began to erode the beautiful landscape of her soul's innocence. With each blow, a fence was erected around her fierce heart. She felt as though she was born at the wrong time or place, a foreigner in a strange land. She always felt much older than her age and even loved talking with adults and hearing the wisdom of her elders. She had a mind and heart thirsty for knowledge and understanding of the ways of the world.

As she grew, people entrusted her with their stories, which she collected and preserved like precious relics from ancient, yet familiar, times past. She absorbed all of it; and whenever anxiety or apprehension consumed her as she attempted to navigate this strange land and adapt to its customs, she used each fiber of her collected stories to weave a cloak that she hoped would keep her safe in the midst of chaos.

The damage from that chaos started to manifest when I was four years old. The shaking, the crying, the nausea, the worrying. Fear was my first imaginary friend. It accompanied me when I'd sit at the top of the stairs and listen to the muffled sounds of my parents fighting. I had a mother eager to grow and explore the world, and a father who wanted to isolate because of depression. I heard it all and felt what was not spoken. Sometimes silence speaks the loudest.

Daddy came home from work one day when I was four, walked into the kitchen and swept me into his arms, sat me on his knee and with obvious sadness said, "I won't be living here with you and mommy anymore." After that, his lips moved but I didn't hear anything else. My world crashed down. I worried about who would take care of Daddy. He was obviously devastated by my mother's decision, and I took the blame.

From then on, all I ever saw was a man who was angry and depressed. He would share with me his shattered dreams of the perfect life: living in their semi-attached, brick duplex row house in the Bronx with tomato plants and fig trees in the yard, me riding my bike in the driveway, our dog playfully barking as it watched me going to and fro. The only thing he ever wanted was now lost. I heard these stories constantly from the moment he picked me up on a Saturday afternoon for visitation, to the moment he returned me back to my mother's house on a Sunday evening. He was a somber, lost soul.

I made him proud, though. Whenever we were out somewhere and he introduced me, he would boast, "This is my daughter Kristy. She is so smart."

So smart. That would end up being my claim to fame. I learned very quickly how to help him and help myself get the love I needed and craved: just keep making him proud by being a straight A student.

Neither of my parents ever spoke directly to me about the divorce. It was as if Mommy magically swept it under the carpet, wiped her hands of it, and moved on. I was left with no place to process my emotions about it. I developed separation anxiety when Mommy would drop me off at preschool. She would later share stories of how heart wrenching it was for her to drive to work after my teachers had to pry my arms off of her shins. I feared that something bad would happen and she would die and I would be abandoned. Eventually, I would run off and play imaginary games like "house" or "school" that allowed me to retreat into my inner fantasy world. In elementary school, anytime I heard a siren—living in the Bronx, that was several times a day—I got an immediate stomachache and would start to hyperventilate, thinking that something happened to my mother. The nurse would have to call her just so I could hear her voice and know that she was okay.

When I spent weekends with Daddy, he would ask me about school then spend the rest of the time unloading his burdens on me. It was usually the same story—he missed my mother, hated his life, argued with his girlfriend, and worked a lot. I offered a calm presence and listening ear as he entrusted his story to me. He always said how much better he felt after talking "with" me, even though I rarely said a word. I held onto that as if I had some special power to help Daddy.

Those weekends, Grammie would always cook for us, and by the time Daddy and I arrived, something was already on the stove and in the oven. Daddy worked the four-to-midnight shift at the Department of Sanitation and never wanted to eat that early so he would retreat to his room, his eyes glued to the 15-inch box that aired the Home Shopping Network. He would spend hours making hundreds of impulse purchases that he thought were sound investments, like diamond rings, Marvel comic figurines, and vintage appliances. Every Saturday he'd show me the gaudy, flashy bling he bought with money he didn't have.

"It's cubic zirconia, Kristy," he would beam, high from his shopping addiction. "They are clearer than the world's best diamonds for a quarter of the price. It's incredible! And it's for you!"

I always thanked him, yet never felt right accepting these gifts and I could never tell him that I didn't like it. I stayed quiet because it seemed to make him happy.

Saturday nights were almost always hamburger night. Grammie's hamburgers were unlike any burger I have had before or since. Her secret, she would say, is that she used her grandmother's octagonal-shaped griddle and greased it with lard and huge chunks of fresh garlic before putting the hand-pressed patties on the grill. They were always so big and perfectly round, yet thin and super juicy. After the burgers were cooked, she'd toast the buns on the same griddle after adding more lard and garlic. While the buns toasted, she'd stir spinach that she had sautéed with tiny chunks of diced white potatoes and more garlic and salt.

Like clockwork, just as we were plating the food, Daddy would appear in the kitchen all suited up in his uniform and ready to kiss me goodbye. Seeing him would cause my heart to sink into my stomach. Immediate panic. *You will never see him again. Something bad is going to happen to him.* The thoughts screamed at me and my body would tremble. I would run to the bathroom immediately after kissing him goodbye and sit there, rocking myself on the linoleum floor and focusing on the patterns and letters shaped by black and gold specks in the vinyl tile. As a compulsive ritual, I had to touch the letter "J" (for Daddy's name, John) three times, convincing myself that in doing so, I was preventing something bad from happening to Daddy. At bedtime, I would sneak my Grammie's crystal rosary beads out of her nightstand drawer and run back into my bed, holding them in my fist under the covers. Until I heard the turn of the lock on the door at 1am, I remained wide awake. The moment I heard Daddy come home, I was convinced that my ritual worked. Phew. I could exhale.

On Sundays, after breakfast and church with Grammie, Daddy and I often went to Woolworth's on Westchester Square, a busy central square in the old neighborhood lined with stores. We'd walk around for hours, really with no purpose. He always asked if I wanted anything to which I always responded politely, "No thank you." I never felt comfortable asking Daddy for anything; not even the time I got my period unexpectedly when I was 12. Not wanting to burden him, I wrapped toilet paper around my underwear multiple times creating a makeshift pad to absorb the blood.

On days when Daddy seemed to be angrier or more depressed than usual, we'd stay home. Daddy sat glued to the television from morning to night with his cigarettes while I sat in the background, bored, nothing to do and nobody to play with. I had toys and games but was more intrigued by quietly studying my father. He looked pathetic, like a lost puppy. I didn't understand why but I seemed to be able to feel things from him, as if I could read his thoughts and emotions. So much pain and sadness, yet his affect was flat as he stared at the items being hawked on the small screen—an attempt to fill a massive inner void.

"Go out with friends!" Grammie would say to interrupt his HSN stupor. "Go find a nice girl . . . go take your daughter somewhere . . . talk to your daughter!"

"Ah, go fuck yourself, will ya?" He'd curse his own mother as he raised his arm with the cigarette dangling between his fingers.

Grammie would slam her bedroom door and cry. In response, Daddy would raise the volume on the TV. I sat paralyzed and conflicted, wanting to run to check on Grammie, but not wanting Daddy to feel betrayed if I left him. Yet I didn't want Grammie to feel betrayed if I chose to stay with Daddy. I didn't know who I was supposed to be loyal to. I loved them both. This was always my dilemma, even with my parents. Who was I supposed to show my allegiance to? I felt pain in my heart because I didn't want to let anyone down. The confusion ate me up inside.

Eventually, when Daddy calmed down, I would sneak out of the room to go check on Grammie who I knew by that point would be having an asthma attack triggered by the stress. I would find Grammie with her head cradled in her hands leaning on her bureau, surrounded by her pill bottles and inhalers, rosary beads, and her statue of Mary the Blessed Mother.

"What's wrong with your father, Kristy? What happened to him? He was always such a sweet and loving boy. What kind of man is he now? Look, look at this beautiful boy! He's ruining his life!" She would reference his baby pictures that she had wedged under the protective glass topper of the antique wooden bureau.

When Grammie and Daddy argued, which was constantly, I would retreat to the covered porch in the back of the apartment and sit on the vinyl lounge chair with large, orange and green floral prints. I would lay there all day and listen to music, the only thing that calmed me. I loved to sing, as it seemed to be the only way I could freely express myself. I would also pretend to be a "radio announcer" and turn off the radio and have my own playlists in my head and I would sing each song. I'd close my eyes and escape into the world of music, allowing the melody, the rhythm, and the vibration to calm me and rescue me, cradling me like lullabies. I made up songs when tunes would appear in my head, mostly forlorn love stories. I didn't understand much about what I was imagining. Stories just came to me, the way they might when reading a book. Music drowned out the noise of the fighting, yelling or Daddy putting his fists through the walls.

On the drive back home to Mommy's house on Sunday nights, Daddy always complained, "I'm so aggravated…" while slamming his hands on the steering wheel. Not knowing how to respond, I would nod my head in agreement, and just close my eyes and imagine sending him beams of bright, white light and love from my heart and belly, like a Care Bear—one of my favorite stuffed animals. Daddy bought me the True Heart Bear for Christmas one year. She had light yellow fur with a rainbow star with a heart inside of it on her belly. Daddy wrote in the card, "For my Kristy, my daughter, the most caring creature there ever was." I always wanted the Wish Bear—the turquoise bear with a star on her belly. She was the dreamer. Mommy asked why I wanted that one so badly. "Because I want the power to make things change with just a wish." She laughed when I said it, but I was serious.

During weeknights at home with Mommy, I would lie awake and tiptoe to the living room where I would check on her lying on the couch, sipping hot water to soothe her nervous stomach as she waited for my stepfather to come home (she got remarried several years after divorcing my dad). Sometimes he would be gone for days. In the morning, I would hide behind the kitchen wall and listen to Mommy's telephone conversation as I wanted to be informed because I couldn't trust that I would be told anything.

During the days, after school or on weekends, I filled my time and distracted my mind like every other kid from the Bronx: hanging out with friends, riding bikes, walking "the avenue" or playing handball in the schoolyard, watching the boys we had crushes on play basketball or baseball. Growing up in the Bronx in the early 80's meant that we had freedom to roam the streets safely. We would leave the house in the morning and know to be home by dinner. We had a dollar in our pockets and that could buy us an eggroll and a "quarter water" or a "slice" and a soda for lunch. Sometimes if we had some extra change, we would pool our funds and get a three-pack of Fun Dip to share off the ice cream truck.

But most of the time, especially when I found myself alone—which was a lot being an only child—I would retreat into my own world of fantasy and imagination. I would find an area of grass or trees and pretend it was an enchanted forest. When I was in that forest, everything came to life in magical ways. Every blade of grass, every tree, every squirrel, every bug, felt like a mystical spirit. I would feel things that I couldn't see, yet were real to me. I was fascinated by this world that not only felt oddly familiar, but also felt safe.

But my wanderlust daydreaming quickly turned from seeing and feeling spirit everywhere to the conditioning of deeply entrenched Italian-Catholic values that limited my vision and muted my connection. Our family culture and religious traditions were so much a part of my life, and it was an anchor, something to believe and trust in. What I was taught in Catholic school scared me, the punitive God who was always watching me. But my maternal and paternal grandmothers would tell me different stories about saints who had our backs. My two grandmas always carried sacred medals in their pockets, pinned medals to their bras, and wore rosary beads coiled up their arms. They would call on these saints whenever they needed help. Although I couldn't see these saintly people, I believed I could feel them, and this gave me a sense of comfort knowing that at any time

I could go into my imaginary world and talk to them, and maybe, just maybe, they would help me.

Each night I had my ritual of getting down on my knees and praying, preferring to say my own words to God and the saints who I believed were listening. Mostly I prayed for the safety and protection of my parents. And I would always ask the saints to show me signs that they were listening.

One night in particular, I remember feeling so alone, so terrified, and I was desperate for divine intervention. I was at Daddy's girlfriend's house, and as usual the two of them were off in another room and me and her son Kevin were left on our own to sleep together in the same bed. I was about eight or nine years old at the time, and he was a few years older than me. He was scared, too, especially when we heard them fighting. Before we shut the lights, we built forts together to keep ourselves hidden and safe. But at night when it was time for sleep, we would lay in the dark together and he would pull out a flashlight.

"I have to check you to make sure you're okay," he would say.

As he would unzip my "feet-y" pajamas, I never knew what he was checking for, but I knew that it didn't feel right. After a while, it became familiar and comfortable, something I could rely on amidst the chaos that was ensuing in other rooms of that apartment. But one night, after my "checking" and after Kevin had fallen asleep, I heard Daddy's girlfriend run out of the apartment with him chasing after her. I was now alone in a dark apartment with Kevin. I had to go to the bathroom, but I was so scared to move and even more afraid to close my eyes. I prayed to every saint I had been introduced to. Minutes became hours and despite the fact that I was promised that if I prayed, I would be saved, nothing happened. So, I lay there in the bed, humming a song that seemed to come to me from out of nowhere; a hymn that I would much later in my life learn was the divine intervention that I had been waiting for and exactly what I needed.

As I grew older, I relied less and less on those prayerful rituals and let them fall by the wayside. As the veil of conditioning and imposed cultural paradigms clouded my vision more and more, I couldn't feel any connection to the divine, and the help never arrived. Late at night when I couldn't fall asleep, I would sit up and wonder. *Is God real? How did human beings get on this planet? How did people get a soul? What really happens to our souls when we die?* I had memories of things that I didn't even know had happened yet. I wondered why I felt like I had been a different person or even an animal in another lifetime. I wondered why I felt feelings so deeply. Why I was so sensitive to everything, seemingly more so than everyone else. I wondered why I could somehow feel what other people felt. I also wondered about my parents and their feelings and whether they loved each other or not. I would brainstorm ways to fix their marriage so that my father wouldn't be upset anymore. Enough people told me that I worried too much or was too sensitive. My parents were always dealing with their own struggles, so I didn't want to burden them with mine. I couldn't confide completely in my friends about my deepest feelings because I wasn't confident that they would understand. And anyway, I felt I had to be strong for them. My friends always came to me with their problems. I would happily listen and give them advice and feel so grateful to be entrusted with their secrets. But my secrets and thoughts and feelings—I kept them caged.

When I was in fourth grade, I decided to entrust my thoughts and feelings to a diary that I named Missy. It was an ivory hardcovered book with an adorable cuddly brown teddy bear sitting in a white wicker rocking chair on front. It was a Christmas gift from my grandmother. It had a small combination lock on the side, and I felt privileged to create a "secret" code to something that nobody else would know. I continued to write in Missy throughout my teens and right up until I got married, and then added to my collection of journals. Writing became my escape, my therapy, my mentor, and my friend. I wrote about my burdens, including my parents. Daddy was barely taking care of himself; and adding insult to injury was his poor judgement and insight with respect to subsequent relationships; dysfunctional patterns that were so obviously unhealthy, even to a young child! He ended up marrying a highly unstable alcoholic diagnosed with bipolar disorder who showed up at my mother's apartment one night with a steak knife. She held it up to my mother's throat right in front of me and threatened to kill her if she had any contact with my father ever again.

Daddy put me in danger continuously and exposed me to things that I shouldn't have been exposed to. *How could he have brought me to a jail to bail out his girlfriend?* Seeing him cry in the car time and time again. Seeing him yelling at my Grammie and uncle and putting his fists through the walls. He scared me. I didn't see a man who could be vulnerable enough to stand with his feelings, or strong enough to cope and take responsibility for himself and the needs of his child. So how could I trust him to protect me?

Similarly, when I was about six years old, Mommy had started dating and eventually married my stepfather, who became an angry tyrant when he drank, which was frequently. One night he got so angry he chased Mommy through the house with a broken cabinet door. Seeing my mother victimized in that way, not able to defend or advocate for herself made me view her as weak and ineffective. How could I trust her to care for me if she couldn't care for herself? So, I became the parent while a bitter resentment accumulated within me for my parents' choices that threatened my safety.

Desperate to Fit In

Into my teenage years, my anxiety continued to grow like a weed. The heaviness in my chest, knots in my stomach, constrictions in my throat, incessant feelings of dread and obsessive what-if thoughts. I constantly questioned *What is wrong with me? Why do I always imagine the worst possible outcome?* Even when everything was calm, I was always waiting for the other shoe to drop.

When I was 12, my stepfather's 17-year-old son, Brian, came to live with us. I was so excited as I had always wished for an older brother who could protect me and now was my chance to have it. He was so handsome, and all my friends were completely smitten with him, so I felt proud to call him my brother. When he got his license, he would drive me around in his cool red sports car with the windows down blasting Freestyle music. I felt important and popular.

I didn't realize initially that the catalyst for him coming to live with us was that he had fallen in with the "wrong crowd" and had started to experiment with drugs. His mother hoped that living with his father would straighten him out, but things got worse. He would go out and not come home for days. I would be woken up in the middle of the night to get in the car so that we could drive around through sketchy parts of town to search for him. We never knew whether we would find him alive or dead. I would sit in the backseat in my pajamas and hum a song in my head, praying he was safe, and sending him love from my belly and heart just as I did with Daddy. Brian must have had a guardian angel watching over him because he always made it out alive. He threw himself through glass storefronts to steal money out of cash registers, drove cars while high as a kite, used all kinds of needles and paraphernalia, and yet somehow survived. He stole money from Mommy's pocketbook, stole my radio and some toys, all for drug money. I was never angry, as I always felt enormous pain in my heart for him, and I felt everyone else's fear. I wanted so badly to help him, but I didn't know how. So, I just prayed and sent him love. I felt like I was the one who needed to protect him.

Brian would remain on my mind during the school day, and though my academics didn't suffer—if anything they improved because I managed anxiety by diving into my studies—I couldn't navigate the social scene. In my mind, my school was divided into four social classes: 1) the very unpopular girls, 2) the slightly more popular but still unpopular girls, 3) the girls who got along with everyone and didn't really belong to a clique and 4) the most popular, well-liked beautiful people. I didn't know where I fit in. I was terrified that if I put myself out there, I would not be good enough. I was different than most of my peers. I rarely spoke so I was endlessly ridiculed for being shy. Because I was short, I was never picked for teams in Phys. Ed class. One summer when I attended a fancy day camp, all the snooty girls nicknamed me "Pond Scum" because I loved nature and the color green. Girls can be so cruel.

By the time high school rolled around, I was tired of being invisible. I wanted to be noticed. I wanted to be popular. I desperately wanted to fit in. So, I began to pay attention to how I dressed and the company I kept. I watched intently how the popular girls acted and carried themselves. I liked the attention that I got. Boys started to notice me, and it was finally for my looks and not because of my brains. I was over the moon when I discovered that the "hottest" boy in our friend group, Charlie, liked me; so much so that I ignored my intuition that told me that I shouldn't go to his house one day during summer break. His parents were working, so he and his friend had the house to themselves. My stomach hurt and a voice from within told me to leave as the four of us sat on the couch in the living room listening to music. Charlie went into his bedroom and called me to follow. "Come in here I want to show you something." I looked at Leah, who by that time had already locked eyes with Charlie's friend and the two of them got up to leave to "go for a walk." I shouldn't have gone into the room. Leah shouldn't have left me.

I said no. He told me I was so pretty and that he would make me feel special. I said no again. He got angry. As he ripped my shirt and bra, and scraped my shorts down my legs, his nails dug into me but scathed a lot more than my skin. It reached into my soul somewhere so deep that the wounds still bleed from time to time. When I eventually got away, rather than be angry at Charlie or Leah, I was upset with myself; upset that my desperation to fit in and be liked and feel like a "normal" rebellious teen caused me to override my intuition.

Despite Charlie's desire for me, and others' interest in me, I felt even less confidence in myself. I was full of shame and the persistent sense that something was inherently wrong with me. I always carried the core fear of *If I am my true self, will I be abandoned? If I am myself, will I be loved and safe? If I am carefree and let go of the control so tightly, will everything fall apart?* But by this point, I was no stranger to fear, or insecurity, doubt, dread, and depression.

Parentified Child

In fact, I had become adept at serving my father's needs and being a secret-keeper for him. Being a "parentified child", I would later learn in my college psychology class, comes with a deluge of responsibility that a kid isn't ready for. But at the time, I was up for the challenge, or at least I didn't feel that I had much choice. Being my father's confidant was a role that just happened naturally, and there were so many times that I was grateful I could be that for him. Looking back, he was my first "client."

Caring for the emotional and physical needs of my parents, of course, caused me to suppress my own childhood needs. They assumed that I was fine because I wore the mask of a smile, maintained my straight A+ average, and never complained. I was invisible because they needed me to be. Not surprisingly, data on the long-term effects of childhood parentification show that a child is at increased risk for anxiety, depression, eating disorders, and substance abuse as an adult. I remember becoming offended by the term "parentified child" in my psychology classes and I immediately defended my parents. I also convinced myself that it made me more mature and self-sufficient and gave me a stronger work ethic. I never trusted anyone to do anything as well as I could. So even friendships were plagued by distrust, which sometimes translated to a friend believing that I thought I was better than them. Working on a group project in school, for instance, was a nightmare because I couldn't bear the thought of relying on anyone to handle any part of the project. I needed to micromanage it all.

These actions were reinforced because others saw that I was responsible and hard working. I could be relied upon. However, this also added to my pressure because in my mind there was little room for error. Having to be responsible ("perfect") all the time reinforced my crippling anxiety, inability to trust and incessant overworking.

Living a Double Life

By the time my twenties rolled around, I was living a double life. There was the face of Kristy who I showed the world and people loved to see—the smart, organized, prepared, always smiling, helpful, woman who always seemed to have her shit perfectly tied together in a bow. She was a diligent

21

college student on an academic scholarship, with her eye glued to her goals; engaged to marry her high school sweetheart; working two jobs to pay her own way. She "had it all." Yet if anyone had taken the time to really *see* her, to look deep within her wide green eyes, the other face of Kristy would have revealed itself—a tangled mess of fear, anxiety, sadness, self-doubt, and self-loathing.

And yet I knew how to manage my fear by burying my head in the books and taking on every intellectual endeavor that I could get my hands on. Besides working in a bakery and internists office, I was offered a position as an ABA therapist to provide in-home therapy to children with autism. I was also invited into the honor's program at my college which required additional credits that were to culminate in an honor's thesis, similar to a dissertation. I worked nonstop, fueled by insane amounts of caffeine and fast food. A solid 4.0 GPA, promotions at work, awards at school, and a size 2/4 waist. And now with a handsome devoted man on my arm and a ring on my finger that would soon seal the deal, I could rest easy knowing I would never feel alone again. I felt on top of the world and on track, but like any train moving erratically at lightning speed, derailment is inevitable.

It became increasingly difficult to manage my full honor's level college coursework, three jobs, and a long-distance relationship. I had intense palpitations, constant outbursts of crying and rage, refusing social invitations, and plummeting into a cesspool of disordered eating patterns. Most of my nights were spent lying on the floor of my shower banging my head until it bled to try to get my mind to stop racing. While sitting in my classes during the day, I would be blindsided by debilitating panic attacks that caused me to hide in the bathroom sobbing and hyperventilating while layering wet paper towels on my neck.

I knew I needed help. So one day, I walked into the college counseling center on the 3rd floor of Dealey Hall, reluctant yet curious. I always wondered what went on in there. I was studying psychology and by that time was fairly certain that I wanted this to be my profession; but seeing the world from the perspective of the proverbial therapy couch seemed so scary. Growing up, I had no idea what therapy was. In our family's culture, you wouldn't dare trust an "outsider" with your problems. You brought your problems to family. Everyone was enmeshed in each other's business because it was believed that what affected one affected the whole. *La famiglia* was the therapist. Therapy was also believed to be for the "richie's"—the silver spoons with fancy clothes, vacation homes and the luxury of cash to pay someone to listen to their woes. But us blue-collar, hard-working-class folks from immigrant European families, we sucked it up and forged ahead without complaining.

What motivated my interest in psychology in the first place was a book I read in my 12th grade Introduction to Psychology class, *I Never Promised You a Rose Garden*. It's a semi-autobiographical novel from the Seventies about a teenager hospitalized for delusions and other "schizophrenic-like" symptoms. The character Hannah Greene experiences an alternative world that she believes to be real. And despite the poor prognosis for schizophrenia around that time, she had the privilege of meeting one particular doctor who saw past the labels to see her innate genius, creativity, intuition, and gifts; and for those reasons believed that she was healthier than anyone. Reading that book affirmed my early childhood belief in my purpose of helping others and my mission of serving the world. From the moment I read this book, I knew that I wanted to be someone who saw the inner gifts in people and empowered them to believe in themselves against all odds.

And here I was walking into that counseling center, hoping that someone could be that person for me.

Dr. Jeffrey was exactly who I needed in that moment. His compassionate smile, genuine warmth and easygoing demeanor created a safe space for me to begin my long healing journey. In those earliest sessions with Dr. Jeffrey, our conversations always circled back to Daddy. One day, doc asked me why I defended Daddy. I didn't realize I was, but I knew that talking about Daddy in an accusatory way felt wrong. I believed that talking about him in a blaming way would make something bad happen to him; and one month after my sessions began with Dr. Jeff, my worst fear came to fruition.

It was a beautiful, warm Sunday morning on Mommy's birthday, May 16, 1999. I was 21 at the time. While Mommy and my stepfather were still asleep, I was up at the crack of dawn preparing to defend my honors dissertation that would be happening two days later and just a few days prior to my graduation from Fordham University. I was startled by the ringing of my seashell-shaped telephone that lit up in blue when it rang, a Sweet 16 gift from Daddy.

"It's your Dad ... rough morning .... struggling to breathe.... it's his heart .... on the floor of the bathroom .... paramedics working on him .... you better come here ... might not make it."

I threw the phone, shouted for Mommy, grabbed my keys and raced out the door to my car. Apparently, she had been awoken by a call on her bedroom phone. She screamed out the door for me to come back in.

I shouted back, "No, no I have to go quickly!"

She was crying and distraught, begging me to come back in the house and finally she shouted, "It's too late! There's nothing you can do. He's gone!"

Saving Daddy had always been my job. And this time, I was too late.

In the three months that followed Daddy's sudden heart attack suffered while smoking a cigarette during a nebulizer treatment, I mustered the strength to bury my father, defend my thesis, walk across the stage to receive my college diploma and awards, start a new job, hospitalize my future mother-in-law for what they referred to as a "psychotic break," get married, move out of my childhood home, and fly cross-country for the first time for work. It's amazing how resilient the human spirit can be when given no other choice. That had become my normal.

During a gap year between college and graduate school, I continued to work as an Applied Behavioral Analysis therapist for autistic children, as well as a full-time marketing director and office manager for a psychological software company. I was making something of my life. On the inside, I was unraveling. I was consumed with guilt that I couldn't save my father. As life carried on, my anxiety began to surface in the form of intrusive and obsessive thoughts, which led to compulsive behaviors and even more neurotic tendencies to bulldoze through life. Dr. Jeff continued to meet with me in his private practice and had proposed the idea of medication "just to take the edge off." I was invested in trying to "fix" myself and intuitively, a pill didn't seem like the answer. I somehow knew that I was supposed to feel what I was feeling. My work with Dr. Jeffrey was invaluable in helping me to make some important connections between my behaviors and underlying fears; but after several years, I was exhausted from rehashing memories and started to feel worse, not better. So I stopped my sessions and busied myself even more, trusting in the protection of the loyal bodyguard by my side: my fiancé.

Meeting Dominick

Dominick and I met at a high school graduation party. After exchanging numbers, we had a four-hour phone conversation on a Monday night, May 16, 1994, during which I was pretty sure I was falling in love. Yet that same week, Jesse (my best friend and secret crush) and I admitted our feelings to each other. Ah! Those teenage years! One evening, after spending the day together on a class trip to an amusement park, Jesse formally asked me to be his girlfriend. Yet as he leaned in to kiss me, there was this other "voice" that emerged in the darkness as if it were coming from the heavens, whispering *NO!* I'd never heard a communication so loudly, and I didn't understand it. *Pursue the new boy, he is the one.* I just knew I had to listen.

Dominick and I went out on our first date that Friday night, and have never left each other's sides since. We were married five years later. At age 22, though in wedded bliss, my phobias persisted. For example, Dominick had to work long hours, sometimes overnight, in his career as a technology engineer. He worked for a financial firm and was responsible for their computer networks, which could not be worked on until after trading hours. When he would prepare to leave for an overnight shift, a huge knot would manifest in my stomach, the same feeling of dread that I would feel as a little girl when Daddy left for work. I was convinced each day when Dominick left the house that I would never see him again, so I would call him every 10 minutes of his commute. I would compulsively watch the clock and on the exact minute I had to call or else I was convinced something would happen. If he didn't answer, I was flooded with panic and terror; shaking, trembling, hysterical crying, hyperventilating, profuse sweating, vomiting, and diarrhea. This happened all day every day. I would leave work and eventually my graduate school classes every 10 minutes to make the calls, and nobody noticed because I got my work done. I would always stay later at work than expected so that I didn't have to be home alone. My bosses loved me because they saw my behavior as dedication.

At night and most weekends when Dominick had to work, I would travel into the city with him because it was easier than having to call him every 10 minutes. I would sit in our car and do my graduate schoolwork for a solid 48 hours. I would freeze in the car with my computer on the console, books all around me, and just work through the night, with few breaks sprinkled in to hit Dunkin' Donuts or McDonald's to pee, grab food, and get warm.

By then I had developed a fear of leaving the house by myself. I'd lie to friends and family about why I couldn't go places, always blaming school and work, and they believed me. My whole life had become consumed with managing feelings of dread that people I loved would be taken away from me. Every thought, feeling, and action was tied to that.

I managed my obsessive thoughts with compulsive actions that became a numbers game. Especially after 9/11, which had a devastating effect on my psyche because Dominick had been working several blocks from the Twin Towers, my rituals became more extreme. I would check every 10 minutes to the second; making sure the radio station was set to an even number; making sure the heat and air conditioning in the car was set to an even number, except for the number 6 or 16; making sure to say, "Bye, I love you, be careful" in that exact order each time I hung up with a loved one; never taking the first or second item on a shelf in the store but reaching for the third one. All of these algorithms that I created were done in an attempt to keep myself and loved ones safe. I had convinced myself that if I didn't engage in these rituals, something bad would happen. So, these carefully executed equations were my preparations. I would never have the rug pulled out from under me ever again. I just wanted to be prepared. And all of this control and micromanaging was happening while working as an education administrator at a learning center, managing my course load at a prestigious doctoral program filled with externships, internships, and fellowships; and eventually in 2006, about seven years into my marriage, I graduated and opened my private practice working 80-hour, six-day weeks.

By the time I was 30, Dominick and I were talking about starting a family. I'd always wanted to be a mother and imagined that I would have sons. The year before we started trying, I began my preparations. I made a commitment to living a healthier lifestyle. Motivated by my experiences of working with autistic children, and severely mentally ill adults and children, I had started to understand the connection between the mind and body, and the influence of our world on the health of that connection.

When we learned that I was pregnant, I committed to ridding our home of any toxic substance from plastic to pesticides to fluoride to formaldehyde. I vowed to take care of myself the best I could; to eat only the best food; to use only the best products. I was basically on a mission toward a perfectly prepared pregnancy. I fully embraced my pregnant physique and didn't obsess over how much weight I was gaining. I felt free. Not bound by restrictions of any kind, I was like a completely different person. I attributed it to doing everything "right." Growing a healthy family became my new obsession.

I had created what I entitled "My Birth Plan Manifesto," a carefully researched list of do's and don'ts for the staff and my family at the hospital for how I was going to birth my baby. Everything from no epidural, to meditation music playing, to no IV, to immediate skin-to-skin contact, to no bottles and exclusive breastfeeding, the list was exhaustive and covered all my bases. I went into labor two weeks beyond my due date. From the moment I entered the hospital, my freedom to advocate for myself was swiftly taken from me. I was instantly hooked up to IV despite my adamant refusal because the nurse thought I looked dehydrated. As my labor progressed, I must have been asked 16 times if I wanted an epidural. Despite the contractions increasing in frequency and intensity, all the mantras, deep breathing, and essential oils were not helping me to dilate. The doctors and nurses couldn't figure out why. By the next morning, I was exhausted, but still adamant about sticking to my plan to have natural childbirth.

Somewhere in the midst of listening to the Regis and Kelly morning show blaring from the TV, Mommy nervously commenting on the weather outside, and Dominick compulsively chewing his 10th pack of M&M's, I heard the fetal monitor beep and saw the red-digit numbers going down. My heart sank, literally, as my blood pressure started to plummet, and I felt woozy and sleepy. Mommy leapt up to call for the doctor. Dominick turned sheet white. Next thing I knew, a new doctor I had never seen before was standing at my bedside.

"We need to get you in the operating room immediately! You are losing oxygen and so is your baby! We are losing you both. It's an emergency!"

Dr. Gannon tossed Dominick a set of green scrubs and I was immediately shifted to a gurney and rushed down a long hallway. I stared at the ceiling, blinded by the bright lights racing by me, and I heard my mother crying. Dominick looked down at me and all I could see was the redness in his eyes, as the rest of his face was covered by the surgical mask.

"Mommy, I'm so scared," I cried out and instantly felt her hand brush mine. I looked at Dominick and shouted what should have been the last line of my manifesto: "If you have to choose me or the baby, choose the baby ..."

And then everything went black.

What I came to learn one year later—yes, it took a year to find out exactly what had happened to me and my baby—was that trauma had caused my pelvis to tilt in response to the pregnancy. Apparently, the baby was trying so hard to descend into the birth canal, but he was literally hitting a wall and couldn't. The umbilical cord had wrapped around his neck three times, causing him to lose a significant amount of oxygen.

As for my post-labor hours, my manifesto had not accounted for waking up alone from an emergency C-section, completely anesthetized, feeling like a semi-truck had hit me, and frantically searching the room for my baby. *Is he alive? Is he dead?* Then Dominick walked in holding the most magnificent sight I had ever laid eyes on. Antonio, my baby boy. As Dominick placed him on my chest, the crisis leading up to this moment disappeared. I was enamored with this little angel in my arms, and truly felt my heart expand in ways I never could have imagined. As he latched onto me and nursed for the first time, filling him with nourishment felt most fulfilling for me. My heart and soul felt bathed in love and I was completely overjoyed.

All was blissful for the following two weeks until Dominick had to return to work. I had a full-blown panic attack at the thought of being home alone with this baby. I cried louder than my newborn and clung to Dominick's leg the same way that I had clung to my mother's leg in preschool. My fear surprised me. *What if he cries and I don't know what to do to calm him down? What if he chokes while nursing and dies? What if I get sick or fall down the stairs while carrying him?* I saw the pain and confusion in Dominick's eyes as he gently peeled me off his leg so he could leave the house. He knew I was a hot mess, but didn't know the "right" thing to do in response. I eventually calmed down enough to sit in my cozy armchair and nurse Antonio. I allowed the oxytocin flooding my cells to soothe me, to the point where my eyes became heavy. What happened next was totally unexpected and bewildering. As I dozed off with Antonio in my arms, everything went black except for flashes of light and the sound of blood-curdling screams inside my head. And someone demanding, *Choose the baby!*

Hunger Pangs

That was the first of many trauma flashbacks that would haunt me for years to come. The word "trauma" is rarely associated with childbirth, and nobody prepares you for it in the prenatal classes, OB visits, and *What to Expect When You're Expecting* books. It's not something you talk about at dinner parties. No one wants to hear about it, and I was too ashamed to share my experience. For years after Antonio's birth, I hid the fact that I had a C-section, the result of my "faulty" body, or so I believed. In my circles, the women would talk about their labor stories like they'd just run the New York City Marathon. Their perfect babies were their gold medals at the end of the race. I had my beautiful prize, but I felt as though I cheated my way across the finish line because of a handicap.

Birthing Antonio was yet another experience that impressed upon my psyche that the unthinkable can happen. Every day with my newborn brought increasing what-if thoughts causing paralyzing anxiety. By the fourth week, I was having regular palpitations, shortness of breath, profuse sweating spells, crying spells, nausea and stomach pain, and I was losing chunks of hair. My OB/GYN chalked it up to fatigue and a "touch of post-partum blues."

"Kristy, you just had a baby," she counseled me. "You aren't sleeping well, you're nursing round the clock, you're tired, and you don't know your limits. Hire a nanny so that you can sleep. There is nothing wrong with you." She agreed to run some bloodwork then wrote a script for Prozac. "Here. This will keep you happy and calm while you're working on hiring that nanny."

Though relieved to get lab results that validated my symptoms of hyperthyroidism (a condition of having too much thyroid hormone in the body), the nurses and doctor continued to treat me for the next year as a depressed new mom by pushing meds that I continuously vehemently refused. I was furious that my OB's "temporary solution" was turning into a long-term salve. I knew it was wrong and they didn't hear me. I could no longer trust my medical team.

Meanwhile, my life as a new mother went on. During the day, I lovingly held Antonio, played with him, fed him, talked to him, sang to him, washed dishes, did laundry, cooked dinner—until it was nighttime when I would crawl into bed and cry. Nobody knew I was dying inside with anxiety, sadness, and worsening physical symptoms. Not my husband for whom I dutifully made dinner and asked about his day at the table. Not my mother who visited and babysat when I went to work. Not my friends who would happily come over for coffee and to see the baby. Not even my doctors when I had my 15-minute post-natal checkups.

Days turned into weeks turned into months turned into years. I watched Antonio grow, though I realize now that I wasn't always present. When Antonio was almost two, I became pregnant with my second child. Excited yet terrified about how this childbirth experience would compare to the first, I was eager to try for a VBAC. Two months before my due date, my new OB Dr. Shaw broke the news to me.

"I'm sorry Kristy, but it looks like your pelvis tilted again. Your body turns in, like it's trying to protect you. Let's get you scheduled for a C-section. This time around you will have a much better experience, I promise."

Body turned in to protect me. What does that mean?

On the morning of April 12, 2011, I kissed Antonio's head as he slept in my Mommy's arms, and Dominick and I started our drive to the hospital. In the operating room, Dr. Shaw lovingly explained that I would be given a subarachnoid block ("spinal") instead of an epidural because it works faster. Dr. Shaw knew I was terrified so he consoled me by promising I'd be safe and that everything would be okay. The needle penetrating the layers of tissue and bone in my spine made me scream. Dr. Shaw softly rubbed my head through the process. His fatherly demeanor caused my mind to flash to Daddy and how I wished he had been the one to make me feel safe in my life. As tears streamed down my face and my body went numb, I hummed a song that appeared in my consciousness.

"Okay Kristy, the next sound you will hear will be your baby."

And there he was, my precious angel Gianni. My heart expanded as I heard his first coos. *Everything had gone okay, or had it?* As I was wheeled to the recovery room, I suddenly became nauseous and started to vomit. Then came severe head pain and an itchy feeling all over my body. I was having a reaction to the anesthesia. For almost a full week, I was violently ill. I struggled to hold the baby, have visitors, or keep down food. All I could do was close my eyes and hear Dr. Shaw's nurturing voice, and pretend it was Daddy's, and somehow, that mystery song in my head that calmed me like a lullaby.

The birth of these babies made me feel a love I've never felt before—comfortable and familiar, yet heavy and foreign at the same time. Most days my heart exploded out of my chest with enough ammunition to annihilate me; but feeling so much felt burdensome, as I'd never allowed myself to feel this much. It was exhausting on top of the exhaustion of mothering a baby and toddler. I never felt that I was doing enough. Or doing it right.

Nursing my babies gave me comfort and joy and fed my need to feel needed. Cracked and leaky nipples, stretched out bras with clipped cups, warm cabbage leaves layered on my breasts to heal mastitis, an impeccable diet to ensure quality milk production—all of it was a welcome tradeoff for the sense of purpose I felt nourishing my babies. Keeping up—that was the goal. Keep up with laundry, cooking, the frozen breastmilk stash, work responsibilities, school responsibilities. Despite knowing that there were billions of mothers in the world doing the same things, I felt alone. Despite the fact that my dreams of having two boys had come true, I felt incomplete, fractionated, ripped apart.

During the middle of the night, in the stillness of the dark, I questioned the meaning of my life. *Is it to just be a mom? Why did I want to be a mom in the first place? Was I just going along with societal expectations? Was it the pressure from an Italian mother and grandmother who wanted grandbaby cheeks to squeeze? Was it feeling like I owed my husband offspring? And how did these babies' souls make their way to me? Why the emptiness? Why do I feel like there is something else I have to give birth to?*

I started having bizarre dreams about living in a desert as a Native woman. Sometimes during the day, I would have these "feelings"—a sense of having been somewhere else or that something was "out there" waiting for me. As strange as these visions and feelings were, they were oddly comforting, especially through the waves of anxiety and panic I felt due to flashbacks I'd begun to consistently have about my childhood and earlier adult life. I had no time to deal with them, which made me feel more and more disconnected. After a while, I no longer recognized myself. I loved my boys and I loved being their mom, but I wasn't sure how I felt about being a mother. My life as an incredibly successful overachiever with my dream career that I'd worked so hard for was now pushed to the back burner. *But shouldn't it be? Shouldn't my children come first?* Somewhere deep inside, in places we don't like to talk about, I felt resentment.

Something else was brewing and percolating, like I was still pregnant but with ideas. I was agitated, restless, and starving for something that I couldn't identify. It was the same feeling I got as a child that I was in the wrong place and time, yearning for a place that I wasn't even sure existed. I felt like a ravenous and encaged wolf detached from her pack.

These hunger pangs continued; and despite feeling like I should be able to fuel myself given that I was a psychologist, I put my egoic pride aside and decided to seek help. I contacted my colleague Sheila Pearl; a clinical social worker, certified life coach, bereavement counselor, family therapist, retired cantor, and author of several books about love, relationships and spirituality. I had referred several clients to her but now it was time to make a self-referral. Sheila's more "alternative" and spiritual approach resonated so deeply with me by that point, and I trusted that she was the one who I needed to help me now.

Midway through rambling my history to Sheila, she interrupted.

"Oh, sweet love, you are experiencing an awakening!"

She identified three aspects of my life that were in need: sense of self, intimacy with self and others, and reparenting the inner child.

Awakening? What does that mean?

"You are getting glimpses of who you *really* are; that there is more to your life than what meets the eye; that your life is bigger than what is even possible to imagine! Follow the Shamanic way as that will be most valuable as you come into your power. That's just who you are. The answers you seek are already in you. You are looking into your mind, but it's your heart that needs healing and what will set you free. This isn't personal development; it's a journey of spiritual development."

I was already confused by "Shamanic way" and how I would heal my heart, but something about this powerfully resonated. During our next session, Sheila guided me through a practice of talking to my body, visualizing the organs, seeing their colors, listening for any messages they might communicate. Afterwards, Sheila invited me to do a mind-mapping activity. As I dutifully drew the circles and lines, I felt agitated and frustrated. I didn't see how mind-mapping was going to help me heal my illnesses and anxieties, improve my marriage that was becoming increasingly strained by my anxiety, or make me a better mother or a more powerful psychologist.

"Sweetie, you have choices. Ask yourself: How do I want to feel? What actions do I want to take? What feels good to me? How can I allow myself to do what feels good? Spiritual growth is about understanding yourself and cultivating your inherent ability to make choices by following your intuition. All of life is choice. YOU get to answer those questions. You came here as a healer for others. You are the medicine. Work on healing yourself so that you can eventually step into that power."

Admittedly, the words "awakening" and "spiritual growth" aroused some skepticism. My brain swirled with preconceived notions of spiritual people as perpetually blissed out, evolved to the point of perfection, radiating blinding light that made them appear ethereal, while levitating during meditation in ashrams. Though my life looked so radically different, *something* was undoubtedly happening to me that was bigger than me, and I just knew that I had to trust this process. I concluded that session knowing that my task was to sit, listen and rediscover my truth buried under the façade of adaptations that was keeping me alive but not allowing me to thrive. It was time to unveil and release all that lies beneath.

Letting Go

When you grow up in chaos, stillness is a terrifying place to be. Meditation is a practice that I had taught to countless clients yet had avoided doing myself. With Sheila's encouragement, it was time for the teacher to become the student.

I enrolled in an eight-week course on Mindfulness-Based Stress Reduction (MBSR) with a lovely teacher in my professional network named Matilde. MBSR is a structured program developed in the 1970s by Jon Kabat-Zinn at UMASS Medical Center. This evidence-based intensive mindfulness training assists with reducing stress, anxiety, depression and pain. Kabat-Zinn's goal was to offer a practical approach that helps people cultivate awareness with open-hearted curiosity, noting all sensations, internal states, thoughts, emotions, and memories without judgement. It results in the ability to see possibilities and take wise action, minimize suffering, manage illness, and improve one's quality of life. Matilde integrated MBSR with breathwork, body scanning techniques, basic yoga postures and more—all practices that were new to me and that I admittedly used to shun because I didn't understand them. But now I was ready to go to the places that scared me…or so I thought.

Body Scanning

Body scanning is a guided practice of systematically bringing attention to areas of the body, starting with the feet and eventually ending up at the top of the head. Pausing at each part, Matilde guided us to simply notice, with curiosity or "beginner's mind," any sensations, whether it be tingling of the toes, the creak of a knee, the churning of the stomach, or the twitch of the neck. Then simply allow it to be there, without questioning or striving to do something about it. Matilde explained that when we pause, stay in the present moment, in full awareness of what is happening around us and within us, we become an objective witness of these circumstances; and rather than reacting in preconditioned patterns, we learn to respond thoughtfully. In doing so, we break the vicious cycle of worrying about the future or ruminating about the past.

The first time Matilde guided us, I felt anxiety like I had never felt before. I fidgeted constantly and couldn't settle myself as my heart raced in panic. Initially, nothing "happened." I didn't feel any sensations. I thought about how this was only the first of eight weeks, and that this training was to culminate in one full day of a silent meditation retreat. *If I can't even feel my own fucking feet, how am I going to meditate for seven hours?* During the two months of the course, I did the body scans faithfully each night, only growing more annoyed that I was wasting my time. Once weekly, I returned to Matilde's lakeside cottage for in-person instruction. One night, I had flashbacks of the hypnobirthing class I took while pregnant with Antonio. I had been so deeply invested in it—the mantras, the breathwork and meditations, the playlists, the essential oils. A feeling of rage overtook me during the body scan that night, and I screamed out: "IT DIDN'T WORK!

HE ALMOST DIED! I ALMOST DIED! I won't let anything happen again. Not to me, not to my kids! I'm done!"

Matilde tenderly responded, "Kristy, what if your birth with Antonio wasn't a failure at all? Have you considered that this birth experience was exactly as it was supposed to be so that you, and your son, could grow from it? It must have been particularly difficult for you, being an empath."

"An empath?" I had never considered this.

"Your birth experience with Antonio was exactly what you both needed to evolve. And now, this is your chance to be born. Stop allowing your brain to judge it. The discomfort is nothing more than a sensation. Notice it, welcome it in, be curious about it, and let it teach you what it's supposed to. Don't micromanage your own rebirthing like you tried to manage your son's birth. Let it unfold in natural time."

Meditation

Micromanaging everything, desperately seeking control, had been the only way I had ever known how to live since childhood. But now as I struggled to get through my days with children of my own, ravaged by palpitations and racing thoughts that propelled me into a biochemical tsunami of flight-or-fight energy, I knew it was time for me to break the cycle of running on the fuel of fear.

The documented scientific and medical benefits of meditation cannot be disputed. Just 10 minutes per day benefits the mind, body, and spirit. Meditation, as a practice of mindful awareness, is our training and support for how to stay with our vulnerability rather than run away from it. Pema Chodron, a widely influential American Buddhist Nun whose teachings have had a tremendous impact on my spiritual growth and evolution, describes meditation as a stance of loving-kindness and compassion. By learning how to sit with the thoughts, feelings, and bodies, and allowing whatever to be, we cultivate an unconditional friendliness toward ourselves, as well as a sense of connection to all beings.

Early in my daily mediation practice, I had some misconceptions about it and was inadvertently using meditation as a scapegoat. I learned to label any thought I had as "thinking" and then to immediately return my focus to my breath, forcing away all mental chatter. But the goal of meditation isn't absence of thoughts. It's to bring awareness to those thoughts so that we can begin to see what we care about, what we want, what we are craving, what stirs us up. It's an opportunity to witness the thoughts and actually allow them space to exist. I had also erroneously assumed the purpose of meditation to be physical and mental relaxation, and to be happier and calmer. True, but this isn't *why* we meditate. I began my practice with an intention to fix myself. I wanted to be less anxious, fearful, and sick and hoped meditation would be the panacea; but that expectation just reinforced the belief that I was damaged and struggling, which created more discomfort and self-deprecation.

Pema's teachings helped me to understand meditation as a practice in being compassionately loyal and steadfast with myself regardless of what comes up. As someone who dissociated for years whenever I experienced discomfort, meditation was about to teach me how to relate to all sensation with neutrality. It would eventually show me that my lifelong pattern of being maniacally driven was a fear-based adaptation to trauma that helped me avoid pain. Just "being" in meditation allowed me to lovingly acknowledge and confront the underlying pain even when it was uncomfortable. Over time, as I'd come to experience, the longer we go without giving into our habitual trauma-infused patterns and adaptations, the more the brain sees that we can stay with discomfort and still be safe. For years, I gave power to, and felt compelled to act on, thoughts that were incredibly intrusive. I left meetings, checked my car doors, called loved ones to make sure they weren't dead. To learn that it was possible to be a witness to thoughts without participating in them was astounding.

The Buddhists teach that under every thought is a pulsating energy that carries inherent wisdom. Rather than trying to stop thinking, we learn to welcome thoughts so that we may see clearly what they reveal about our limiting beliefs, self-destructive tendencies, defense mechanisms, expectations, needs, desires, and wishes. In the words of Robert Frost, "The only way out is through."

Just weeks into my consistent meditation practice, I noticed my dreams becoming more vivid, as they had been during my early life, and each one was rich with symbolism that I would write about each morning. I was also sleeping much better every night. During the day, I began to have "visions" that were glimpses of animals and people. It was strange at first, admittedly, and I didn't understand why, for example, I would see horses and feel as though I was seeing the world through their eyes. I saw Native American women dancing in the desert. I saw what felt like the energy of creation in shapes, like triangles and circles. Over time, the visions became calming and comforting, and easily accessible in meditation.

Warrior Training

About a year into my work with Sheila, she commented one day, "Kristy, now I see your inner warrior." Sheila's words blew me away. "A fighter who has shown courage, vigor, strength, and fearlessness. A spiritual warrior is one who manifests power, confidence, integrity, chivalry, accomplishment, honor; one who is disciplined in their focus on life and its 'opponents.'

With persistence, you face difficulty, pain, discomfort, discouragement and the prospect of failure without quitting."

As I listened to Sheila, visualizing an image of a warrior, she continued.

"Warriors never blame or fault their opponent. A warrior doesn't take the actions of her opponent personally. She respects and honors the presence of the opponent as a great teacher and welcomes the lessons learned from their sparring. Surviving the battle grows the spirit stronger and deeper. A spiritual warrior embraces the journey of self-discovery to enlighten the self and to benefit others. The real battle is the mastery of oneself. In Buddhism, the true warrior is not a fighter; instead, it's one who has the courage to look at oneself. She knows that the only threatening opponent is that of the self."

I continued to make a daily meditation practice part of my self-discovery. It became a sacred ritual that some mornings I was excited about, and other mornings dreaded. Some days, my mind was messy and scattered. Other times, it seemed empty. Regardless, I surrendered and listened into the parts of me that had been shut tightly away. Subtly, the more I let go, the layers began to peel open. More flashbacks and memories came to speak to me.

One flashback was to the time when both of my boys needed emergency surgery as undiagnosed allergies caused both boys' tonsils to fuse, obstructing their airways. At the time, Antonio was three and Gianni was just shy of his first birthday; and both Dominick and I were hesitant to agree to the tonsil removal surgery. Our logic was that if you are born with a body part, you must need it. Yet their conditions worsened. Antonio snored all night and was exhausted during the day; and Gianni choked while nursing, struggled to breathe, lost a significant amount of weight, and was failing to thrive. One night, I dozed off while lying in bed nursing him, and woke up moments later to see my baby turning blue. So, we gave in to the surgery.

In my meditation flashback, I recalled all the details of the day of the surgery: the dingy blue hospital walls, the dark hallway outside the operating room, the image of nurses and doctors restraining the boys, me trying to pin a religious medal to their hospital gowns, the doctors asking me to force the oxygen mask over their little faces that were covered in tears, and being forced to leave the operating room, ripping my heart right out of my chest. Thankfully my boys recovered, but clearly the experience left an impression on me that was subconsciously still affecting me.

The more I courageously sat in stillness, I recognized just how much bravery it takes to go deep into the trenches of unpleasant memories. I had a renewed sense of compassion for the many clients who I have had the privilege of guiding through this process of excavation and recovery, one that we must tread carefully and lightly. Healing old wounds means that we are rewiring our brains and training them to see the world through a lens of love and trust instead of fear. Healing happens by feeling, even if it's not always a comfortable process.

With consistent practice, I was slowly changing my relationship with my thoughts and belief systems—now seeing them as separate from my essence, and no longer the identity that I was tethered to. I was discovering an entirely new inner landscape—one that was expansive and bright, instead of constricted and dark.

Nevertheless, at that point in time, I was at war with my body, battling every symptom and illness. I seemed to have a new diagnosis each week for which I had to try a new supplement, treatment program, book, or practitioner. In the midst of my frantic search for the holy grail of health, while trying to parent my young boys, I was becoming increasingly worried about my mother-in-law, who had become seriously ill. I felt responsible for her care, yet so many aspects of it felt out of my control.

"I'm failing in all aspects of my life," I bemoaned to Sheila at our next appointment.

"The guilt and the shame are consuming you, Kristy. This self-created 'torture' is a byproduct of trauma." Sheila's words resonated. "You have to be willing to let things die in order to let the most important things live. Begin to take control by letting go."

Sheila made me realize that I was full-on "in recovery," which means "to retrieve what was lost." I thought about my experiences in healthcare, both as an administrator and medical assistant, and my time working at St. Vincent's Hospital in the Dual Diagnosis Unit in which patients were diagnosed with co-occurring psychiatric illness and substance abuse. At the time, I was trained in the then-innovative Harm Reduction treatment model in which "recovery" was a loaded and misunderstood concept. It implied some obscure place in which the patient was making progress towards being mindful, establishing connections within themselves and with others, and making a commitment to practices and a lifestyle that enhanced inner growth. In that model, a person could reasonably be in recovery—living a healthy new life, while still using substances.

But what did that mean for me? Was I going to be "cured?" What did I need to retrieve that had been lost?

Who Am I?

"And now . . . it is my honor to introduce . . . for the first time as husband and wife . . . Mr. and Mrs. Vanacore!"

The ornately shellacked, wood-stained glass doors fling open as Dominick and I make our grand entrance into the banquet hall. Scanning the roomful of 200 guests, I spot six empty tables where my paternal family should be sitting. Not only was Daddy not there to walk me down the aisle, but 60 of his family members decided to abandon me, too, because they didn't agree with my decision to proceed with my wedding so soon after Daddy's passing.

Tears poured out of me as I relived that bittersweet day during a session with Annie Samojedny, a physical therapist who specialized in Integrative Craniosacral Balancing. In my professional circle of holistic providers, Annie is known simply as a "magician," able to access the root causes and unreleased pain and trauma in the physical and energetic bodies.

Though my coaching work with Sheila was invaluable, I knew that simply talking about trauma from an intellectual and analytical place was still leaving me disconnected and dissociated. If trauma was first felt in the body, as I was learning, then that's where it needed to be healed. And I just knew that Annie's expertise could help.

This first session would be the first of many releases that day, and the years to come, that would allow me to heal. As I lay down on the heated massage table that was covered in soft fleece sheets and blankets, I clearly felt Annie's hands on me. Other times I could feel something—a sensation, a tingling, warmth, buzzing, in one part of my body yet her hands were seemingly in another part. I distinctly recall exhaling in a way that felt like I had been holding my breath for my entire life up until that point. I started to cough afterwards, saliva dripping from my mouth. I could feel "stuff" moving in my throat, chest, and stomach, and later learned that what I was feeling was energy. When Annie encouraged me to put words to the experience, I spoke about feeling devoid of spirit.

"I used to have this feeling as a little girl, like I wasn't alone, like I was connected to every tree and animal. I could transport myself to a happy place. When I prayed, I spoke to them . . . the horses, the birds, the bears, the fairies, the angels, the saints. I saw things; but it went away."

"What went away?"

"The ability to go there. I've been longing for it. Every now and again I swear I could hear something, like a whisper, barely a voice, but it comes to me as a melody of a song that seems to emanate from the chamber deep inside my heart or someplace over my head. And then it's gone."

"Where does it go?"

"It's blocked. If trauma is the portal, that means it's both the cause and the cure."

Annie held space as I felt a surge of immense sadness and grief rising to the surface. This was too big to force back down. Before my mind could interject, I heard a voice roaring from within me.

"Free her! Let her run free! Let her sing! Let her dance! Let her rage with the fires and flow with the ocean. Let her live!"

And then almost immediately I felt like I was going in and out of dreams. Various memories from the past kept popping up like a flipbook or a photo album. First, an image of the day Dominick and I returned from our honeymoon. We had a disagreement, and I was so angry I hurled a huge marble vase across the room. He ducked and it slammed through the kitchen window, crashing down into the backyard where the landlord's children were playing. I was horrified at what I had done, and I didn't know where it came from in me.

Flash to a new page: The day Daddy died. I walked into the kitchen looking for my mom. My stepfather was there; he and I had a tenuous relationship. He touched my arms, looked into my eyes and said, "Go ahead, you can cry. You need to cry!" I was trembling and desperately fighting back the tears, terrified of being vulnerable. I whispered through a forced smile, "I'm fine."

Another scene: Standing in a stuffy, dimly lit funeral parlor, scented with the strong perfume of white lilies, carnations, and chrysanthemums, people mumbling and milling about the room paying their obligatory respects. Standing as still as a Buckingham Palace guard, as my two half-sisters clung to me: five-year-old Lily on my left, and 13-year-old Sara on my right. I kept a stiff upper lip that entire day so the girls could rely on my strength. We peeked at Daddy's casket from the back of the room, and after all the guests left, together we approached the pine box that held his lifeless body. His face looked noticeably different, as if the deeply ingrained lines of stress and tension were magically erased. I wanted to scream but remained stoic.

Another image: The day after Daddy's funeral was my wedding shower; and in between ripping open boxes of ivory and silver Lennox china, I ran to the bathroom to cry, reapply mascara, and return to smile for the cameras. Two days later, I defended my undergraduate honors thesis, going through the motions of explaining theories and statistical data.

Memories flooded me as I lay on that table, my body tremoring, my heart palpitating, my limbs quivering, and my skin sweating with Annie's hands on me as I wailed guttural tears that had never been released. The grieving tears quickly turned to raging screams, and my wounds finally found words.

"I AM ANGRY. I AM SO FUCKING ANGRY!"

I felt like I had been run over by a truck, yet when I was eventually able to lift my head and my body from the table, miraculously I felt lighter, clearer, grounded, and I could actually breathe. Looking out the large windows of her office, the world appeared so different. It felt like months had passed.

"Kristy, do you even realize who you are?" Annie asked in a gentle voice.

"Who I am?"

"You are an empath. It's what makes you a powerful healer. But there is more for you. You have barely scratched the surface of knowing your power. You are having a healing crisis. As you evolve, you will step more into your power so you can share your gifts with the world."

That was now the second person I trusted who told me this on the healing table. To reach my full potential, I had to understand what it means to be an empath.

It's Not Easy Being an HSP

The scientific term for empath is a "Highly Sensitive Person" or someone with a sensory processing sensitivity. An estimated 15 to 20 percent of the population carries this trait. Having sensitive neurological systems, HSPs are like sponges soaking up energy in their environment and in the world, feeling everything to an extreme. Lights, smells, sounds, large groups of people, chaotic environments, and even people with big personalities and intrusive energy all may easily activate the HSP. This is why they require time alone and become easily fatigued. Neurologically it has been demonstrated that HSPs have a more active mirror neuron system in the brain, meaning that we fire the same set of neurons as the people we are around. Having a more activated emotional brain makes it more difficult for us to access our thinking brain, oftentimes leading to overanalyzing, difficulty making decisions, and big reactions to small triggers. We possess an advanced ability to notice subtle facial expressions (being most affected by angry or sad expressions) and read and interpret nonverbal cues and moods.

Early on, I questioned whether being an empath is a byproduct of nature or nurture. *Was it an inherited trait or a consequence of life experiences?* I remember my mother telling me the story of how I came out of the womb immediately alert and aware of sounds, lights, voices, the temperature in the room. Yet research has consistently demonstrated that empathic gifts are most strongly correlated with childhood experiences of trauma.

It is not easy being an empath in an overstimulating, fast-paced world that not only does not value, but does not have time for, sensitivity and depth of processing and feeling. Like me, many HSPs struggle with anxiety, chronic fatigue, insomnia, feelings of being different or weird or out of place, like black sheep. We tend to have gastrointestinal issues, body pain, weakened immune systems, obsessions and compulsions, and increased sensitivity to pain. I was beginning to understand my poor self-esteem, feelings of inadequacy, propensity to take everything personally, an overly excessive need to please others at the expense of my own needs, social anxiety and difficulty with large crowds, depression and rumination, perfectionism and seeking order, excessive expectations of myself and others, difficulty handling change, constant agitation, and difficulty focusing and concentrating. This new insight also brought clarity to my tendency to always see the good in people even as they were stabbing me in the back, why I always felt different and misunderstood, and why I was always so drained and depleted after being around certain people.

So many of my early life experiences came flooding back as I was able to now witness them through this empathic lens. Like the time in summer camp when the group of girls who incessantly bullied me threw me into the deep end of the pool knowing that I couldn't swim; and rather than feel anger towards them, I felt their inner wounds and conflicts. Or the many times I could sense the feelings and emotions that weren't even conscious in my best friend Hailey, and make them my own without boundaries, and then feeling incredibly emotionally and physically drained and exhausted after spending time with her. And then there were the times when, like a chameleon, I could become what I believed others needed me to be— shifting my energetic frequency to match theirs so they would feel validated and supported, and I could feel safe and connected to someone.

Through continued meditation practice and eventually Shamanic practice and somatic bodywork, I would learn how to embody these empathic gifts responsibly by establishing healthy boundaries that would fiercely protect me from energetic intrusions; as well as practices for cleaning, clearing, and detoxifying my energy fields so that I could remain strong and resolute in those boundaries. I would learn how to be incredibly discerning with who I allowed into my circle. I would learn how to avoid absorbing the emotions of others; how to avoid adapting to the energy of a room and instead influence it; how to let energy move through me without holding onto it; and how to remain in my own energetic frequency. With good energy hygiene, I could begin to honor my gifts with reverence and compassion, instead of seeing them as a hindrance. It required a strength that I didn't know that I had—to be true to myself at all costs—even if that meant people would be disappointed in me.

Ironically, the more I learned about myself as an empath—both in the sense of having such strong empathy, and this more "spiritual" empathy of sensing others' feelings—I was seeing more and more HSP clients—both adults and children. Everyone has empathic capacities to some degree. Because we are energetic beings, we are always absorbing and emitting energy all the time.

What I would eventually come to understand is that being an empath is something *I am*, not something that *I do*. Now I believe that empaths come into this world to share light with the planet. They are here to show others that empowerment and evolution of the soul comes from experiences of sharing love and truth in the world and in doing so, offer humankind the possibility of the highest level of transformation. As Annie taught me, the only thing that empaths are asked to do is to work on themselves; however, like most empaths this was quite challenging for me because I am a natural giver. I was learning that my life's purpose is simply to learn how to take care of myself.

By this time, I was beginning to explore managing my psychotherapy practice more holistically, and had begun integrating alternative modalities into my work as I was learning about and experiencing them. I began to see how I was called to help others not as a practitioner in the way I had been formally trained and instructed to do, but instead as a guide and mentor to support others' self-healing journeys led only by the instruction of my own life experiences and accumulated inner wisdom. I was beginning to see the major difference between *helping* and *empowering*.

Annie's words of caution reminding me to "stay in my business" and not immerse myself in others' stories now resonated. I could witness without attachment. I didn't need to try to fix or understand everything and everyone. My only responsibility was to show up authentically— radically committed to remaining in my frequency of love, gratitude, and compassion, allowing that authentic expression to ripple through me and radiate out into the world. That's how I could help others transmute and transform.

My authenticity was my medicine.

I was embracing the fact that my sensitivity is a gift for navigating the world, and my intuition, my compass, was with me all along. I now realize all the times in my life when turning off this sensitivity GPS allowed me to be taken advantage of, physically and emotionally. I also now realized that my formal education had been another barrier to hearing the voice of my intuition, as it kept me in my head, and away from my truth. My mind was so strong for safety and survival and I was programmed to fearfully and incessantly seek ways of feeding it with information from external sources. I was beginning to understand that I'd spent my life overfeeding my brain, while neglecting my starving heart and soul.

Hiding in the Shadows

Traversing my inner energetic and physiological architecture with Annie unveiled more layers of the illusory cage that entrapped me. The more layers I shed, the more I remembered my roots bringing me one step closer to reclaiming my sovereignty. I had to keep going; and I knew it was time to explore the deeper realms of my shadows, quite literally.

Intrigued by all the memories that were effortlessly surfacing through this journey, I decided it was time to venture through the dark cobweb lined corners of my attic; finally feeling ready to excavate the actual stories of my past that had been safely locked away inside Missy's sacred vessel. I was ready to discover more about who I was before the world told me who I should be.

Nov. 6, 1990
Dear Missy,

I have never felt like a 'Kristy.' Mommy told me that Daddy wanted to name me Kristy. "Daddy loved that name. He said it was 'unique' and 'different' and that he felt there was something magical and important about that name. He said you would be a pretty big deal to all who would know you. And Kristy felt like the right name for a person with that much power."

Missy, this might sound crazy, but my name is Allegra Topanga. Allegra has a smile as bright as the sun. She dances creating rainbows wherever she goes. Her golden locks fly in the wind as she dances, sings, holds hands with all the kids and together they form hearts and circles on the ground. Her joy is infectious. Her liveliness wakes up the Earth and all its inhabitants. She is so strong that even the fiercest storms can't knock her down. She wears feathers in her hair, and a burgundy and white flowing cloak that sways as she glides effortlessly on the land. A large bird perches on her shoulder, for she is as regal as the most majestic of trees or mountains. She is a creator, and whatever her hands touch is a masterpiece. She is confident, believing in who she is and her purpose in being here. She sits under a big beautiful oak tree and thinks about the meaning of life, and nobody bothers her. In fact, they watch her as though she is a mystical being for whom they have respect and admiration. She is quite lovely, captivating in fact, and carries herself with grace, poise, and ease. She is fearless with the courage of a warrior. She is emotional and feels everything so deeply and profoundly. She cries during movies, can feel what others are feeling without even being in the same room as them. She sees visions that nobody else can see or imagine. She sees relationships as objects and shapes, that look like ancient symbols, and she communicates with people from other times and places. She can *even speak in foreign tongues, some languages that nobody has ever even heard of! She is independent, takes care of herself, and says no when she means no.*

She doesn't care about grades, or school, or religion. She cares about freedom. She has her own style of clothes and the more unique the better. Sometimes she doesn't even wear clothes, as her beautiful pure skin shines and her natural curves mirror the most stunning of landscapes. She wears a golden ring around her arm, her ears are never naked, and the jewels adorning her neck are powerful amulets. She colors outside the lines. She laughs at her own jokes, and she cries whenever she wants to. She doesn't care who likes her or who doesn't. She dances and sings and blazes her own trails. She is perfect. She is free. She is a legend, and like black beauty, she will heal the world.

As I read those innermost musings of my 13-year-old self, rivers of tears cascaded down my face, a physical sign of a heart swelling with grief as I mourned the loss of the abandoned and wounded child within me; while at the same time the startling revelation that I had remembered Allegra Topanga before she was imprisoned in the shadows by her own two hands. I finally understood what I was searching for, and it was time to retrieve it.

Shadow Work

"Shadow work" has become a popularized concept in the field of psychology and spirituality and yet it is often a bit misunderstood. As Carl Jung taught, the shadow is what you perceive to be dark or weak about yourself and therefore what you keep hidden and denied. It represents all the repressed emotions, desires, fears, impulses and instincts, perversions, and ideas; feelings such as anger, aggression, and jealousy; all the parts of ourselves that we don't want to admit to having.

Though it is widely accepted that this dark side represents chaos, passions, and recklessness—the more negative parts of the self—Jung noted that the shadow may also be positive aspects such as personal power, emotional sensitivity, creativity, and independence. If we learned early on that those aspects of self were not valued or respected, or would not contribute to our survival and get us the care and unconditional love that we sought from the adults in our lives, we would deny those parts of self in an effort to keep ourselves safe. Jung believed that these parts of self can be a rich source of creative energy if channeled healthily.

The shadow self is undeniably a part of us, but very early in life, we are shown who the adults in our world need us to be. We are taught about "bad" versus "good." I was taught by family, religion, and society that it wasn't ladylike to be angry, or to be jealous, or to run "wild," or to have desires. Anytime I got angry, I was told, "No, no, Kristy, don't upset your mother, or your father." Anytime I got scared I was told, "Don't be scared, that's silly!" Anytime my free spirit ran wild, my grandmother would say, "No, no, Kristy, simmer down, just simmer, act like a lady." Anytime I was too sensitive, I was told, "Get a thick skin, that's silly to have feelings about." Anytime I asserted myself, I was told, "Apologize and just behave." These messages were internalized, and I learned to separate parts of myself into the categories of "good" and "bad."

The ego develops by adapting itself to what is compatible with and acceptable to our family and the world that we are living in for safety and survival. The parts that weren't valued or determined to be "bad" are split off to protect itself. The ego develops coping mechanisms, or defense mechanisms, to keep those parts in hiding so that we can feel safe, comfortable, and loved. This becomes the primary way that we interact with the outside world. This is the formation of "personality" or who we refer to as "I."

The ego relates with the outside world through personality. Persona means "mask" in Latin and represents all the social masks that we wear when we are out interacting with the world and in relationships. It's the way we wish to be seen in the world. When the ego decides what it needs to be preserved and safe, so as to keep us detached from true self so that we don't experience pain, it creates the socially acceptable mask. The mask preserves the ego, but it's highly inauthentic and limits the depth of our relationships with ourselves and others. Disconnected from our true essence, relationships become nothing more than reenactments and reinforce defensive patterns of behavior, and we never reveal our true authentic being.

The primary mechanism used by the ego to protect itself is repression. The uncomfortable feelings, memories, and sensations are blocked from our consciousness, but they still influence our actions. To protect ourselves and preserve the ego, we rationalize behaviors, and may even laugh them off by attributing them to personality. For instance, "That's just me, I like things in order," or "That's just how I was raised," or "I don't cry," or "They mean well, it's no big deal, they didn't hurt me." Or there may be a complete lack of feelings around a particular topic or situation. That's when we intellectualize, hide behind the facts and data, not allow ourselves to feel or minimize our feelings. But those expressions are nothing more than a façade covering the emotion hiding in the shadows.

Denial is another mechanism by which we refute and reject parts of ourselves that are so readily apparent to others. And typically, when people in our lives call us out on it, attempting to shine the light on those shadow parts, the ego shouts, "No, that's not true, I am not like that!"

Projection is the mechanism by which we displace the parts of self that we find unacceptable onto others. In relationships, this plays out through scapegoating, blaming, and gossiping and criticizing traits that we see in others that we don't want to accept as true about ourselves. Addiction is also a mechanism of the ego. To numb feelings of discomfort, the ego seeks to engage in behaviors that produce positive feelings to counteract those negative feelings. These defense mechanisms are actually in and of themselves not entirely unhealthy. We do need protection at times when overwhelmed and flooded with painful feelings. However, defense mechanisms are only temporary solutions because the underlying thoughts and feelings do not disappear. Jung stated, "What you resist, persists."

Over time, when the more mature psyche can handle them, the feelings that had been percolating behind the scenes resurface and intensify because they want to be uncovered, recognized, and felt; and this typically takes the form of reactivity when triggered by circumstances or relationships.

The ego isn't inherently bad. In fact, we need it to navigate this human life. But left unchecked, it can wreak havoc. The real work of healing comes from expanding our consciousness so that we are alerted to what activates the ego and develop an awareness of how the ego handles its fears and pains, understanding the defense mechanisms that were created for the underlying feelings, and learning how to face the feelings head on without relying on patterns of coping and defense. When we can witness the thoughts without judging them, then we can reconnect with our true selves. The inner child is what becomes the shadow, as its desperate to get our attention. The entire journey of spirituality is reconnecting with, repairing, and reparenting our inner child so that we can align with our true self.

The Inner Child

The ego is just the way that the fearful inner child demands attention from us. For me, those were the times I burst into tantrums (as a child and as an adult), the times I became overly neurotic, the times I decided not to return a phone call, slips of the tongue, became angry at friends for what I found deplorable about their choices because I secretly wished I could make those same choices. These such instances triggered the unhealed experiences of my inner child who did not get her needs met. And when her needs weren't met, she formed beliefs about why—she was not worthy of love, her needs were not valid or important, she was too needy, she was a "bad" girl who couldn't obtain love because that love was conditional. With unmet needs, she could never learn healthy ways of expressing her needs even as an adult. My inner child was creating those grumblings that I heard from within, as she desperately needed safety and freedom to be herself.

It became clear to me now that I didn't need my parents to apologize or give me any support now (and more than likely they would be unable to anyway because of their own wounds that they still carry); I could give that to myself as an empowered and awakened adult who knows better now. I am in a position now to provide my inner child with unconditional love, validation, and safety. That's how we are psychological self-healers, through this process of turning inward, offering to our inner child what only we could know she needs.

To reparent my inner child, she had to feel safe and secure enough to come out of hiding. She had to trust that she could reveal all of herself and that I wouldn't respond with shame, judgment, contempt, or control, and instead would offer her trust, support, and unconditional love. Nor could the conditions of my life be filled with chaos, turmoil, and neuroses. Those were all the conditions that made her hide in the first place. And when she did have the courage to emerge, and she shared her feelings and emotions about all that happened to her, I had to validate her experiences. Not make excuses for the people who hurt her or make her feel badly for reacting to them.

The parts in hiding were the missing pieces to my story; and excavating them lovingly and compassionately as sacred relics was essential for healing and living authentically. Integrating my light and darkness was the only way for me to achieve the balanced whole of love. I remembered the words spoken by Pat, my acupuncturist at the time: "When we lack wholeness, and only operate from parts of ourselves, we can never achieve stability, and we will always feel off-center."

I was learning through shadow work that being "awakened" had nothing to do with muted opinions, tempered emotions, and proper movements. Through this initiation, I was waking up from the deep slumber that kept me enslaved by illusion, manipulations, imprinting of outdated and oppressive dogma, cultural norms and belief systems, and trauma bonds, now ready to unlearn my absorbed conditioning that told me that anger, jealousy, lust, desire, shame, and fear, are wrong. This healing journey wasn't about becoming anything new—it was about removing all that was in the way of me accessing the true undomesticated parts of me that were already there. This journey was a reclamation.

Inner Child Acts Out

I was beginning to realize that one of the most prominent places where my repressed inner child acted out was in my relationship with Dominick.

I spent the first 10 years of our marriage feeling lonely, isolated, invisible, disconnected from myself, and blamed Dominick for not giving me what I expected him to give me to make up for what I didn't receive as a child. The more he failed to live up to my expectations, the more I resented him. I accused him of neglecting me, of not loving me "hard" enough, of being shut down and affectless and cut off from emotions. I became needier and more dependent to get his attention. And we became the quintessential trauma-bonded, co-dependent couple.

When I got sick, it was good to have something "wrong with me" to make me seem vulnerable so that he had an opportunity to take care of me. But the needier I became, the more he pushed away, feeling stifled and suffocated. Yet my dependency on him fed his need to be needed and to provide. Nevertheless, he continuously pushed me to find myself. And the more that we engaged in this dance the more we experienced a roller coaster of feelings and emotions that created intense chaos in our home. The more I continued to betray my own needs and desires to try to get the love that I felt I desperately needed in order to complete me. Other times, it felt good to be pushed away because it validated how rejected my inner child had always felt. Ironically, Dominick would come to discover that my dependence on him actually met some of his needs; and eventually as I healed and extricated myself from the co-dependency, his inner child was terrified.

None of this was Dominick's fault. He could have all but smothered me and it still wouldn't have been enough to satisfy an inner child who felt unloved, abandoned, misunderstood, invalidated, lonely and scared. This was all an inside job. And I had been trying to outsource it. All that created was frustration and insecurity for Dominick, as he felt that he couldn't meet my needs, which triggered his insecurities and caused him to shut down, leaving me feeling more isolated and alone. It was a vicious cycle that persisted for years.

What I was experiencing with Dominick was what so many couples experience—trauma bonding as opposed to bonding in authentic unconditional love. I was motivated by an inner child needing desperately to be saved, fixed, held, and rescued; and who also needed to fix and rescue others to feel useful, needed, and important. And Dominick had a similar need to save, fix, and rescue. It was a perfect catalyst for co-dependency. I thought about what I told so many couples with whom I had worked for years---when trauma is what binds you, the resulting relationship is almost an exact carbon copy of the earliest relationships in our lives. Our history gets projected on to our partners, and we develop expectations for them to fulfill the roles that are a part of the story. In this recreation, there is no opportunity for a new script. All that exists is a recycling of old storylines and characters.

My shadow and inner child work was showing me for the first time that nobody else completes me, because I am already whole. In relationships of any kind, knowing this is critical. We are walking parallel paths with another person, not an enmeshed intertwined path. It is vital that there be space and freedom for each person to be who they are, without any expectations imposed upon them. Togetherness is important, but so is space and freedom. I can be okay with being wrong and owning when I hurt someone. I don't have to get defensive or run and hide when conflict arises, because I now see conflict can be a huge invitation to grow and evolve both individually and collectively. And when I feel triggered by a person or situation, that informs me that I am bleeding from a wound that is still open and raw. If I curiously examine the wound, treating it tenderly and lovingly, I can acknowledge the discomfort and also cultivate gratitude for what it has to teach me.

It's still not easy to discover aspects of myself that I don't really like very much. Parts that have been tucked away in neat little boxes tied tightly with barbed wire and pushed into the deepest darkest corners of the walls of my inner cave. When hidden there I can pretend they don't exist. And I can mold a mask out of the very desirable parts that I want the world to see, and put on that mask every day. We all do this. It's just what we believe we need to do in order to be loved, accepted, to feel good enough, to please others, to feel worthy of our existence and our place in this world. To not feel afraid.

You can't just read a quote about love and miraculously become love. You can't simply hire a "mindset coach" or read the latest-and-greatest guru's book or podcast on optimism and positivity and truly make lasting changes in your life. You can't just will away the parts that you don't like. I was learning that it doesn't work that way. You have to enter the cave. Get on your hands and knees. Get dirty. Be brave enough to seek what ultimately is seeking you.

I believe now that a true warrior is a hunter of shadows, knowing that she must seek to shine her light into the dark corners to excavate what's hidden, even with fingers bleeding from ripping open the barbed wire covered boxes. Knowing that her shadows hold the essence of who she really is—her most treasured gifts—and only when she finds them, creates space for their existence, admires them lovingly and compassionately regardless of how ugly they once appeared to be, can she experience the glorious totality of her being. Only then can she reclaim her power and her purpose. I know this now.

Nevertheless, around that time, I had many sleepless nights in contemplation about my marriage. Having to unlearn all that I thought was true about love and relationships was terrifying and overwhelming. *If I had been clinging to my husband out of fear, and the marriage was based upon the fragility of two egos, then did we really love each other, after all? Could we stay together? Were we supposed to stay together? What did true love really look like or feel like?*

I knew I cared about him and I did love him deeply. But the relationship was depleting, and I was finally understanding why. It takes a lot of energy and effort to maintain a false sense of self. Dominick and I were physically inseparable, yet worlds apart. We were lost; and for the first time I was beginning to wonder if we could make it back.

The more work I did on my own healing, the more that the co-dependent patterns of our relationship became glaringly obvious; and seeking to extricate myself from the entangled web that we co-wove became imperative. I had spent the last 20 years only feeling whole and complete in the context of the enmeshed relationship. I knew no other identity. And the only way I knew of relating to Dominick was no longer working for me. I didn't know how to navigate this, but I knew that something had to change. And I also knew that the changes had to come from within me. At times it was tempting to consider separating from the marriage, but I realized that this wasn't about Dominick. It was about me; and if I didn't do the inner work of healing, then I would continue to play out unhealthy adaptations and coping patterns in new relationships. They had become my universal default. And given my expertise in child development, I also knew that my inner work was vital to ensure that I didn't pass these unhealthy patterns to my boys.

So, I trudged on with my journey, trusting in the organic unfolding of it all, as my fiery spirit continued blasting away outdated belief systems and fear-based conditioning. Some days it felt like ecstatic fireworks, and other days it looked and felt like utter destruction. I trusted that as the veil of shame and guilt was lifting, unapologetic fearlessness and authenticity could bloom so palpably. And the energy that I expended into hiding those shadow parts would then be available to creatively craft a life that was authentic and all my own. I was working towards unbecoming what I wasn't in order to become who I came into this life to be.

A Portal Appears

enter the grassy, flat forest path. Panda greets me with a loving smile and leads me towards an opening. The portal looks dark and I am afraid, but Panda's presence reassures me. Venturing into the dimly lit cave with rough reddish-clay walls, I see a huge brick-like tomb with Daddy's body inside. I outstretch my hands, lift the tomb easily and walk towards the portal. Even from inside, I can still see the sky. A giant hawk and eagle come and wait for me to climb up. I toss the tomb into the sky and the hawk catches it in between his feathers and flies off with it. The eagle soars above them like a guardian. I'm left with lightness, joy, and freedom. Panda and I rejoice in an ecstatic dance.

Trusting now that I was on a journey to remember my roots, and still hearing Sheila's words from several years prior, *Follow the Shamanic way,* I was called to a course called "Healing for the Healer." It was designed to help health professionals focus on their self-care in order to work safely and more effectively with others. At the time, I was still working with Sheila and Annie, was an on-again-off-again yogi, and was still having vivid, confusing dreams and visions while in the throes of some medical issues. I was beginning to shift the scope of my clinical practice by weaving in spiritual practices that I was encountering in my quest to manage my own physical and psychological illnesses. I didn't yet completely understand the spiritual nature of my symptoms, and I was still bulldozing through life more times that I would have liked to admit, but I felt prodded by a power much larger than myself.

I walked into the workshop to find a woman sitting cross-legged, eyes closed, with a drum by her side. A tingling feeling came over me and I could swear she had a halo and wings. My eyes darted to the coiled snake inked on her arm and hand. When I got close enough to see her eyes, I dove right into them. I felt like I had known her my whole life and tears welled in my eyes with this "recognition."

Natalie would be teaching us shamanic journeying— traveling into different realms of our own consciousness. She asked each of us in this small group of six women to think of an animal that had special significance in our lives, and a vision of a panda came to me immediately. Pandas had always attracted me since I was a child, though I never understood why. I studied them extensively while in graduate school, fascinated by how the attachment patterns between mothers and their cubs mirrored human attachment patterns. I even traveled to Washington, DC to see a cub being born!

Natalie guided us to journey somewhere out in nature, a familiar place or not, in which our animal was to lead us down a path into a portal that might look like an opening on a tree or in the brush. Natalie began to drum very slowly at first and instructed us to pay attention to the sound. Almost immediately, tears came to my eyes. The captivating drumbeat brought on a euphoric trace state . . . and then I heard only silence. Panda appeared and I was in another dimension for an unknown amount of time. As the journey ended, the sound of the drum once again flooded my consciousness. When it stopped, we were instructed to return to our physical bodies and open our eyes. I noticed that my mat was saturated with my tears. My brain re-engaged yet I couldn't comprehend what had just happened. I felt incredible. I felt changed.

When it was time to share our journeys in the circle, I struggled to speak, not trusting that it would all make sense. That night, I woke around 3:00am and sensations of swirling energy in my stomach sent me running for the bathroom. The room spun as I vomited and had diarrhea. Visual images flashed quickly in front of my eyes, like someone was flipping through a photo book at lightning speed. I legitimately thought I was going crazy. I was terrified. The next morning, I called Natalie.

"Something is happening to me… and I'm scared… and I don't know what to do or what it means."

"Oh Kristy, I'm so happy for you!" Natalie responded. "This is amazing! You released and purged so much of what is in the way of answering your calling."

I hung up the phone that day confused and blown away by all this. It defied logic yet a voice inside me said *this feels right.* Nevertheless, my skeptical scientist-trained brain was triggered into overdrive, and I felt compelled to study all that I could get my hands on that would make sense of this experience.

I learned that weekend that Shamanism is the oldest universal, cross-cultural spiritual practice dating back more than 100,000 years. It remains alive and vibrant today, as it offers us much critical wisdom and guidance necessary for navigating these modern times. In indigenous cultures, it is believed that the shaman is first initiated through a profound encounter with his own helplessness and fragility that leads him/her to feel completely shattered before assuming the role of healer or medicine woman/man. The shaman journeys through ceremony to invisible realms to connect with spirits and guides that can take form of an animal, angel, plant, landscape, or ancestor. These spirit forms convey healing wisdom and guidance for both individuals and the planet. From the shamanic perspective, all physical illness is an expression of energetic imbalance. The shaman explores causes of imbalances in the energetic, spiritual, emotional, mental and physical realms and is shown how to heal the issue. Drumming, rattling, plant medicine, song and mantras, dance and trance can all be used to bridge the physical and spirit worlds.

According to the shamanic view, traumatic life events cause our conscious awareness to withdraw from parts of our bodies and our lives. A piece of our soul dissociates so that we can survive and not have to experience the full impact of the pain. According to Sandra Ingerman, a renowned teacher on Shamanism who focuses on healing traumatic stress and illness, these holes create a "soul loss." Left in the body, the mind and spirit attract disease, misfortune and other issues. People often report that after experiencing a traumatic event, they are never the same. These holes—the root causes—are what need to be healed before physical symptoms can be resolved. The guides show what has become spiritually out of balance, causing the person to lose their power—a process that manifests on the surface as depression, anxiety, suicidality, chronic health problems, or constant "bad luck." They offer wisdom for moving through these problems with ease while creating lasting healing.

To do this, the shaman utilizes the process that Natalie took us through called journeying. The journey is a portal into oneself that allows you to access your innate wisdom and healing intelligence. These divination trips are commonly facilitated with the use of drumming. Drumming itself carries an array of health benefits, including opening and aligning the chakras and energy meridians, facilitating the release of emotional blockages and ingrained patterns, stimulating creativity, and enhancing our natural healing abilities. During a shamanic healing session, the drummer communicates with the spirit world, as well as the person being treated, and discovers the right rhythm for that person.

As I studied this topic of "soul loss" in the months following, I reflected on the countless times throughout my life when I experienced time lapses when I was dissociated. I learned that issues such as chronic immune issues, addiction, and physical pain can be a result of dissociation because in blocking out visceral sensations, the connectivity between the body and brain is shut down. Being unable to detect areas of the body, the brain sounds an emergency alarm that sends signals to those areas of the body to get us to notice them. I wondered how this related to my growing list of physical symptoms. If I wasn't fully connected with my body, I would betray myself, feel empty and lost, and inevitably search for fulfillment outside of myself.

I was enamored with this journeying practice that felt so natural to me and was reacquainting me with aspects of myself long forgotten. Each journey was a portal through which I got a glimpse of a long-lost world that I had been longing for. I continued to participate in weekly journeying groups facilitated by Natalie and I continued to meditate on my own. Sitting in stillness I would see images of animals, plants, and trees. I went to nearby hiking trails and parks, and once amongst nature, I was propelled into a calm, peacefulness trance. It took me back to being a kid from the Bronx, pretending that my backyard patch of grass was a forest, and the trees were my playmates. With city streets filled with cars and buses and sirens, nature and quiet were hard to come by; but on special weekends, we visited the New York Botanical Gardens, an iconic wonderland of lush gardens and plant conservatories where I could spread my arms and feel free. Amidst the green, it was as though the world came to life. Animals and spirits and fairies would come out of hiding to greet and communicate with me. And here I was as an adult, starting to reestablish that connection with the natural world through shamanic journeying. It's no wonder I took to this practice like a bee to a flower.

So many of the visions and dreams I'd been having for months and years leading up to my first shamanic experience now began to make sense: shapeshifting into horses and seeing the world through their eyes; seeing myself in a warm, rocky place somewhere out West doing yoga on a mountain, walking through a village, or harvesting plants and talking to them; dancing around a fire in ceremony; feeling a connection to something larger that I couldn't explain. And recently, I had begun consistently hearing, seeing or reading about New Mexico. I recognized now that all of these things were signs, not coincidences. I had never been to New Mexico, yet I felt like there was something of significance there for me. *Was it a memory of having been there in a past life? Was it a foreshadowing or premonition of some kind? Was it a wish or a dream?* I couldn't be sure. I decided to ask Natalie.

"Signs are about seeing the extraordinary in the ordinary, the magical in the mundane," she shared with me. "Whether they're real or not doesn't matter. It's your brain that doubts what your heart already knows. Your ability to see the magic—that's the important part about it all. They are guided by our interpretation of the world, and what we choose to allow ourselves to see. Signs appear when we are open and ready to receive."

The Dismantling

Though I was having these incredibly magical journeys and remembrances while in Natalie's office or in the woods, my daily life felt dull and overwhelmingly pressured. By this time, Dominick's mother, whom I affectionately referred to as "Ma", was significantly deteriorating in her physical health. A frail 78 pounds at the age of 65, we decided that we needed to head out to her home in Long Island and take her to the hospital for tests.

I knew that I had to be strong for Dominick and Ma, as she needed me to advocate for her. Yet, I was starting to get sick again. I had a fever and I couldn't swallow so I figured I probably had strep for the eighth consecutive time that year. I was beginning to recognize the latent anger I had towards my husband for not having taken care of his mother sooner, but I didn't feel safe enough to express it. The drive to Long Island gave me time to reflect on the countless times I had wanted to help Ma and was told by the family to "mind my business." I obeyed just to keep the peace in my marriage. I felt shame for letting her down and contributing to the problem by not listening to my heart or my intuition. She never had a voice, and in that moment, I realized that I never had a voice, either.

At the hospital, I calmly spoke on her behalf and stayed with her in the emergency room all day. I wish I could share more of her story here, because it affected me so profoundly, but it isn't mine to tell. I will say that Ma's life was sacred to me. I saw gifts in her that most others couldn't see. What others believed to be crazy, I recognized as all that was lucid and true. She and I shared a deep connection that transcended what could be witnessed on the surface. I knew that she and I were here to help one another, yet at the time I didn't realize how.

My efforts to help Ma mirrored my own downward spiral of overextending myself, trying to fix everything for everyone, judging my efforts as not good enough, and stifling my needs and feelings. It was no surprise that my physical illnesses worsened by the day. Especially painful were PMDD symptoms and significant digestive issues that made eating challenging, along with recurring bouts of strep infections, and autoimmune disease. Faced with life responsibilities, I reverted back to my conditioned "medicine" of choice: dissociation, which anesthetized me so that I could keep bulldozing through life.

By that point, my boys were ages five and seven and dealing with some health issues of their own. We still had concerns about Gianni's growth patterns and now he was getting impetigo infections on his face (which we later learned was a result of strep infections.) He was also preparing to transition to first grade and experiencing anxiety around that. Antonio was still, like me, getting strep throat on a consistent basis and had even had scarlet fever. My marriage was in a weird undefinable "funk" as it was clear that we were both changing, though not sure how or why. We seemed to both have an undercurrent of resentment for one another. Everything felt messy.

But I forged ahead, and when I wasn't taking care of my boys or Ma, I drowned myself in work with my clients. My business soared as a result, and many were attracted to my holistic approach. I expanded my offerings to include empowerment workshops, mindful parenting programs, and had started an initiative called Be the Change, a charity organization to support a local children's hospital that served families of children with chronic illness or terminal cancers. I organized a fundraiser that summer of 2015 and also initiated a campaign to donate books and money to children in India displaced after a hurricane. Working in this way meant continuing to cultivate the courage to do things my way, going against the grain, and letting go of providing services that no longer felt authentic. It felt right to move in this direction, yet at times financial pressures created strain about whether I was contributing enough to my family. I was still driven by fear.

Our house at the time reflected what we were all experiencing. We had constant leaks and floods, causing us to take down our kitchen ceiling multiple times, gut out a bathroom twice, and endure mold rehabilitation for a flooded basement. Yet the greatest demand on my time was managing Ma's healthcare. Although Dominick was finally on board with the idea of helping his mother, he clearly didn't have the emotional bandwidth to support the efforts. Towards the end of summer, she was ready to transition out of the hospital and into a rehabilitation center. Unable to live on her own due to heart and lung issues, she required constant medical support. She was still incredibly frail and her mental faculties were variable. I spent every spare moment researching facilities and many sleepless nights praying for her pain to dissipate and for the right facility to become available before her hospital discharge date. Catching up at the office one morning, apologizing to my client, Janet, for not returning her call sooner, I never expected what she was about to say. Within minutes after hearing that I was seeking a rehab facility for Ma, Janet called the director of the Byram Rehabilitation Center.

"Kristy, they have a bed for your mother-in-law and are arranging transportation from the hospital in Long Island," Janet reported. "They should have her transferred by Wednesday. You have helped my family so much. I wanted to offer help in return."

I was speechless. I knew that spirit had worked to manifest my prayers and intentions. Byram Rehab was the perfect place for Ma. I was there every day, sometimes multiple times a day, attending weekly care plan meetings with the social workers, closely monitoring her medication and symptoms, labeling all her clothes, bringing her favorite foods and treats, and having the boys there to spend time with her as that always made her smile. All the while I continued to get one strep infection after the other. Often burning with fever, I'd force myself to get dressed and leave the house. I realized how "off" I felt but would muster every ounce of energy I had. Stopping wasn't an option.

To help keep my balance, I resumed my work with Sheila and Natalie; both of whom showed me that my inner child was hiding due to the noise and chaos in my life. I was still assuming the role of my adaptive self; the frenetic, overly anxious adult still acting out the defenses that kept me safe as a child. But by now my spiritual practice helped me understand that this persona and the life created around it was a grand illusion. In journeys, I saw myself clairvoyantly as a wise sage who exuded calm, grace, regality, confidence, strength, and pure love. She is my truth, and I heard the message of my guides loud and clear: *Unless I choose to align with my truth, my Higher Self, the noise will never stop. The fear will keep me locked in a cage.*

My guides showed me the way to choose love over fear through journaling, painting, being with animals in nature, and meditation. They encouraged me to cultivate self-compassion and shed the old skin of conformity.

As much as these communications were exciting as they revealed all that was changing internally, I saw my external world as still fraught with chaos and suffering. I was consumed with confusion, as the new parts of me co-existed with the old, with neither one feeling completely secure. My moods were erratic as my old ways of thinking no longer worked. I found myself increasingly distracted and forgetful. I had moments of intense insights, clarity, and memories, followed by moments of nothing and emptiness. I felt increasingly lonely and distant even when surrounded by people who once brought security. In these uncertain moments, I relied on Sheila's words as a reminder to lean into the void instead of running from it: *Silence is a doorway to much greater knowing. Not knowing is the only way we ever come to know.* I had to love myself through it and trust that new possibilities awaited. I had to have faith that eventually, my newly discovered undomesticated parts could not only be integrated into my modern world, but would be exactly what was needed to navigate my life healthfully.

A month after moving Ma, I scheduled a session with Natalie to focus on the obvious tension between Dominick and myself. I did not understand how he could be angry at me after all I was doing to help his mother.

"Dominick IS angry, you're right. He resents you!" Natalie's words hit me like a punch in the gut. "He feels unheard by you." Dominick's process with his family was his karma to work through, yet here I was sabotaging that process to do what made me feel good. I resented him for having boundaries, yet he resented me for having none; and these sharp shards of truth pierced my core. Natalie also helped me understand that Ma was on her own journey, not mine. This was the experience her soul needed, and it was not my place to intervene.

In another session with Natalie, I cut all energetic cords tethering me to Dominick's family. Until then, I had worked so hard to fortify my entanglement with everyone else, while unknowingly severing my connection with myself. I woke up one morning feeling the most desolate I have ever felt. Drained, hopeless, and in agony yet simultaneously numb. I didn't want to live like this. I didn't want to live, period. The next thing I remember, I was in Natalie's waiting room.

Apparently, I had called her and asked if she could see me as an emergency, though I had no memory of calling. Natalie scooped my lifeless body off her waiting room chair and laid me down on her table inside her office. I don't remember everything that happened in that session, except for drums, and feathers, and rattles, and lots of smoke, and Natalie yelling and rattling and throwing my body around. I felt like I was in and out of consciousness. After some time, I woke up and sat up on the healing table. I felt like a completely different person. I had no words, just a profound feeling of gratitude that spirit had taken the wheel that day.

Natalie explained something about black, snakelike attachments coiled around my heart that were siphoning my life force. "They were killing you," Natalie explained. "We cut the cords. Now that they are released, you can effectively take steps to live your sacred life without these energies impeding your progress. Surrender and allow whatever happens to be." Though I knew that cutting the cords was necessary, it was still terrifying to consider setting boundaries and severing energetic bonds that by now felt like bondage. I began considering all of the people, places, and things I kept myself tethered to for fear of letting them go; for fear of the unknown;

for fear of who I would be without them. I was beginning to trust that I could allow my old ways to die to make space for what was waiting to be born.

Unraveling

"Mommy please don't make me go to school."

It was 7:30a.m. on an early September Monday morning. I was running around the house in a towel with wet hair, making school lunches, cooking breakfast, doling out supplements, preparing my work bags, and fighting with a paper jam in the printer so I could print the permission slip for Antonio's class trip that day. That's when I heard Gianni scream. I ran upstairs to find my five-and-a-half-year-old on the floor in a massive pile of vomit, a look of sheer terror in his eyes.

What transpired that morning was just the beginning of a long journey into the world of PANDAS—an acronym for Pediatric Autoimmune Neuropsychiatric Disorders Associated with Streptococcus—but we wouldn't have this diagnosis for some time. Basically, strep bacteria infiltrate the system because, molecularly, they look like our own body's natural molecules. Eventually, the immune system sees them as foreign and produces antibodies; but because the bacterial invaders are still causing confusion by appearing like the body's own molecules, the antibodies attack the body's tissues. The areas most affected are the gut and basal ganglia of the brain, hence many of the neurological symptoms of the illness. Symptoms can present both physically and psychologically and can range in severity. Common symptoms include intense anxiety, obsessions and compulsions, panic attacks, depression, suicidal thoughts, irritability or rage, tics and involuntary movements, sensory sensitivities, changes in appetite and sleep patterns, trouble with concentration or memory; hallucinations, bedwetting, stomach pain and more.

PANDAS certainly wasn't new to me, as I had worked with many families who experienced it. I had seen children become so rageful that they did things like throw chairs through windows. One put a knife in the family cat. But watching my own little boy suffer for the coming few months took it to a whole new level—cyclical vomiting, bouts of diarrhea, terrified to leave the house, unable to eat, no interest in playing, barely leaving my side.

That morning before school, it was like someone had flipped a switch and over the coming weeks Gianni became a different child. My once funny, outgoing and charismatic kid became sullen, morose, terrified, withdrawn, and isolated. He refused all activities that he once loved, including school and friends. At the pediatrician, he tested negative for strep and his bloodwork showed an elevated white blood count indicating an infection. Tests showed that he was anemic and dehydrated, but otherwise everything was normal. My intuition told me this was PANDAS, but nevertheless I sat up each night terrified because I knew these symptoms could also mean a brain tumor. As his condition worsened with each passing day that we waited for lab results, I felt myself slowly unraveling.

In the meantime, we tried a variety of remedies, but nothing was working consistently. We couldn't do a trial of antibiotics because his stomach was so fragile and weak due to the consistent vomiting and diarrhea. He had some good days—attending school for half the day; and more bad days when he wouldn't leave the house. My life became a waiting game and a juggling act of caretaking responsibilities for my son, Ma, my clients and Dominick. I struggled to prioritize. During the worst moments, I thought of what I had learned at a Kripalu workshop entitled "Yoga Off the Mat" and asked myself: *Is it possible to just be with this feeling, to just stay in it, to allow it? Can I just breathe into it and hold on just another moment longer knowing that it won't last forever? And when I'm ready, can I just get back up and realign?*

From Bad to Worse

On a chilly, dreary morning in November, things took a turn with Ma. Gianni woke up easily, said he felt great, had no vomiting during that night, and no diarrhea so far that morning, and he was amenable to going to school. We left the house on time, they were early to school, and I arrived at the office with a few minutes to spare.

As I prepared for my first client, my phone rang.

"Good morning Kristy, its Patty from Byram. Your mom had what appears to be a heart attack. The ambulance just got here. They're going to take her to the hospital."

I grabbed my purse, texted my client to cancel, and flew out the door. On the way, I called my sister-in-law to tell her what was happening. She arrived at the hospital before me and was scared to go in alone. I suggested she go in and talk to someone about Ma's status. I reassured her that Patty said Ma "has a heartbeat and is conscious."

As I turned into the ER parking lot, my sister-in-law rang again, this time hysterical. "She's gone. It's too late. She isn't alive!"

Seeing her standing in the pouring rain hyperventilating and inconsolable, I took her in my arms and jumped into action to handle the logistics. When it was my turn to go into the room to say our final goodbyes, I stared at Ma's body that, ironically, looked more alive than it had in a long time. There was a peacefulness to her, a liberation, and a sudden calmness that washed over me despite the tears and words that flowed as I spoke to her while holding her hand.

"Ma, all I ever wanted to do was empower you to see your strength, find your voice, your joy, your freedom. I made a promise to you that I would save you, Ma, and I let you down. All I can do now is promise to save myself. Maybe that's how you can help me now. I was your voice, Ma, and maybe now you can help me find mine."

My heart was broken, but in true fashion I sidelined the pain so that I could be strong for my family. That evening with the boys, they were visibly shaken by the news of their grandmother's death. My heart dropped into my stomach when one night after vomiting, Gianni whispered, "Mommy, am I going to die like Grandma Marie?"

The days that followed were tough. Amid managing my grief, holding space for the entire family and dealing with funeral arrangements, I felt tremendous guilt, like I didn't keep my promise to save her. Three days after her funeral, Gianni's condition worsened. He woke up at midnight vomiting as usual, but this time he was screaming and lying on the floor in excruciating pain, unable to move and struggling to breathe. We rushed him to the children's hospital. Once stabilized and in a private room, Gianni was lying on the bed watching a cartoon. Dominick sat up in a chair next to the bed with Antonio in his lap. I paced the floor, silently praying to Ma, asking her to watch over Gianni. I felt her all around us. When I could lean into that, I knew he would be okay, even amidst moments when I feared the worst possible outcome.

"Mr. and Mrs. Vanacore, I'm ordering a brain MRI to rule out a tumor."

In a flash, a radiology technician wheeled in a gurney and transferred Gianni off the bed. He looked so exhausted, almost too tired to be scared. Racing down that hallway took me right back to my emergency delivery of Antonio all those years earlier. I tried to stay in the moment, watching the bright lights above and sensing the warmth of my baby's squeezing fingers around mine. Once inside the MRI room, I panicked as my brain immediately recalled an event that had happened at that very hospital years prior in which the magnet of the MRI machine broke and smashed a child's head and killed him. When it happened, I didn't have kids of my own yet, but the news story was traumatizing nonetheless.

Trying to control my shaking voice, I reassured Gianni that he would be okay. I praised him for how calm he had been. On the ride back to the ER room, I even managed to get Gianni to laugh about how we were getting a ride as we cuddled together. Back in the room, I could tell that Dominick had been crying. Once Gianni was back in his bed, I walked out to the bathroom. One of the nurses stopped me.

"I'm so sorry about your mother-in-law. Your husband is scared. He lost his mother and now he is scared he might lose his son."

So many emotions passed through me, yet I felt numb. Suddenly every sound became magnified . . . the beeping of the heartbeat monitors, the overhead pages on the loud-speakers, the elevator, every pump of the hand sanitizer machines, the laughter of nurses on their breaks, the phones incessantly ringing. I was on complete overwhelm. I felt faint. And as I caught a glimpse of a sunflower in a vase on the nurses' station, it seemed to call to me. I removed it from the vase, touched its petals, and rubbed it on my cheek. I inhaled the scent and imagined its energy filling me with hope. I thanked the sunflower, returned it to the vase, and went into the bathroom. I sat on the floor, closed my eyes, and immediately went into a journey. There was Panda, with Ma. He brought me bamboo to eat and told me this is all part of the plan to teach me to surrender to my instincts and intuition. I walked out of the bathroom calmer and with clarity, knowing what needed to be done. I went right up to the nurses' station and asked for the resident in charge of Gianni's case.

"Listen, please, you need to take more lab work," I asserted. "The labs you drew were not enough. Please check him for PANDAS. Please check his ASO levels and Mycoplasma levels immediately."

Next, I walked up to the chair where Dominick was sitting. "Gianni is going to be okay. He doesn't have a tumor. I know it. This is PANDAS. Your mother told me. My guides told me. I just know."

I laid on the bed next to Gianni, cradled him in my arms and sang the lullaby that I made up as a kid when I was scared. He dozed off in my arms and it was the most peaceful he had looked in months. A little while later, the doctor appeared.

"I have good news and bad news. The MRI is completely normal. There is no sign of any abnormalities. The bad news is that Gianni's ASO and Mycoplasma levels are significantly elevated. You were right, Mrs. Vanacore, Gianni likely has a strep-induced infection."

I wish I could say that this resolved things overnight, but the coming weeks continued to be rough. We couldn't treat the PANDAS with antibiotics due to Gianni's gut inflammation. He was treated with a cocktail of homeopathic and herbal remedies, craniosacral therapy, sound healing, and behavioral interventions. Thankfully he healed a little more with each passing day to the point that by Christmas he was back to his old self again.

As for the rest of us, we threw ourselves back into the hamster wheel of life. I know now that regardless of how much we have evolved, stressful and traumatic life events often bring us right back to our tried-and-true coping adaptations. For me and for Dominick, that meant deep diving into work, and shuffling the kids to school, hockey, cub scouts, and music lessons. I had days where my energy was sky high and I felt like I could accomplish anything. And then some days where I felt complete inertia and had to peel myself up off the floor. I was either binging or starving myself most days; not intentionally, there was just never time to stop to eat and I never felt hungry. Then I would have a moment in which I would feel ravenous. I was uncomfortably overweight and disgusted with myself. I was tired all the time but wouldn't allow myself to rest. I knew I was depressed but something even deeper had been triggered by Ma's death: a surfacing of every wound I still carried. Most days, I drowned myself in my business so I didn't have to deal with anything else. Yet I felt my inner and outer worlds dismantling right before my eyes.

"You're all masculine energy, Kristy. Your alpha dog ego is trying to protect you," Natalie said in one session. "It believes you to be in danger, so instead of being here and now, it brings you memories of the past and premonitions and fears about the future, giving you a big picture view so that you can be prepared to take action quickly to be safe. It tries to protect you by ushering you out of the moment, because in the moment you feel pain, and it doesn't want you to feel pain, so it moves you fast, so you can transcend it, never stopping to feel. And so you focus on all these other things—growing your business, becoming super mom, super wife."

I couldn't stop sobbing.

"And part of that pain is so much guilt. You feel responsible for your mother-in-law and for Gianni. When you want to be recognized, when you want people to see you, and to listen to you, and validate you and your choices, it's because you want to hear that it's not your fault. You need to hear that you're good enough. You need to hear that you're worthy. You need to feel redeemed for the things you believe you have done wrong. Your ego seeks validation of what your soul already knows."

"No, that's not true. I just want to know. I just need to know at all times."

"Maybe that's just what you need—for your brain to NOT know."

"Kristy, you say you're done with trauma. In the last two months you have buried Ma and watched Gianni become incredibly sick. That's trauma! Right in this moment! This reopened past wounds that were only partially healed. Feel it! Reconnect with the divine feminine energy within you who is a beautifully complex being who feels deeply, who sometimes feels chaotic and fiery with emotions, who is a beautiful intuitive warrior and healer who brings softness to the edgiest of places. Kristy, that's who you are. YOU aren't the frenetic neurotic over-achiever that your ego told you that you had to be to get love in the world and protect yourself. The world needs to see all of you, with all of your complicated parts. No more books and courses and health programs. Those are still a way for you to run away and hide. There is deeper work to be done to remove all that is in the way of you being who you really are."

That night, I decided to revisit my meditation and journaling practices that by this time had fallen by the wayside. For structure, I followed Oprah Winfrey and Deepak Chopra's 21-day meditation program called "Shedding the Weight: Mind, Body, and Spirit."

The day's theme, "Healing Your Hidden Issues", was about working through old traumas and dealing with the "sleeping dragons." In his distinctively calm, melodic voice, Deepak spoke about meditation as the antidote to unhealthy patterns of avoidance and repression. He cautioned that we can only experience freedom, confidence, and joy when we illuminate our dark corners with awareness. When we go to a place of stillness and sit with darkness of the unknown, we gain access to the answers that lie within and the confidence to trust what we hear. The soul always knows what to do; it's the mind that must be silenced.

When it was time to meditate, I called upon the mantra "So Hum" which means "I am." As I spoke the words and synchronized them with my breath, the spiraling in my mind slowed and my body settled. I listened. Eventually, I heard, *Trust yourself. Listen to your heart. You have it all. You know the way. You know the truth. You are the light. Just be light.*

Following this meditation, I journaled briefly: *What are you really hungry for?* I reflected on my inner stirrings sparked by Deepak's insightful words of . . . "fulfillment, not filling my stomach" . . . "I am lightness itself" . . . "shedding the weight of the past" . . . "when you are emotionally and spiritually nourished, the physical cravings stop" . . . "unmet internal and energetic needs cause the body to ask for more" . . . "sit and feast on your life." I reflected on my incessant starvation for knowledge, always convinced that more analysis would fill me with greater clarity and decisiveness while actually causing me analysis paralysis. This practice affirmed that the sounds emanating from my mind were an amalgam of others' voices who thought they knew best for me, but their expertise was misguided; and yet I was carrying the weight of their beliefs and opinions. I was understanding now that until I shed that mental weight and start listening to the voice of my intuition, I would always feel stymied and starving.

The holidays had passed and we were in February, a season that was typically a lull for me as I awaited the new birth of spring. This particular snow day, I was relieved to not have anywhere to race off to. The kids and I played together for a while; I chopped carrots and celery for chicken soup, washed and folded laundry, mopped the floors, cleaned out the pantry, and did homework with the boys. As the daylight faded into night, the snow began to taper as predicted, and Dominick and the boys went outside to shovel.

As I stirred the soup, embracing its aromas and warmth, the simple peace enveloping me was shattered by screams.

"KRIS! KRIS! I NEED YOU! HURRY! IT'S AN EMERGENCY!"

I dropped the spoon and ran to the basement steps that led to the garage door. I look down to see Dominick's hand and arm drenched in blood.

"Mommy, I think Daddy cut his hand off in the snowblower!" Antonio shouted.

"My fingers. Help! Kris, it's bad. Ya gotta get me to the hospital!!" Standing there in shock as Dominick tried to tape his fingers with electrical tape, I called 911 then ran down to him. He was quickly losing blood and losing consciousness.

The roads were so awful that the ambulance had difficulty getting to our house. Luckily, we lived right around the corner from the volunteer fire station, so they arrived quickly. One fireman tended to Dominick, and another worked to retrieve a finger from the snowblower. I watched in a state of paralysis as Antonio went outside to help by collecting snow to pack the finger in to keep it viable.

Dominick was now conscious and stable and inside the ambulance on his way to the hospital. I felt guilty for not going with him, but I knew the boys needed me. As the ambulance left, I went into the house to find the boys huddled together, arm in arm, on the couch. Antonio looked calm, though concerned. And Gianni looked like a deer in headlights. I grabbed them both and held them tightly.

"Mommy, is Daddy going to the same hospital where Grandma Marie died?" Gianni cried. "Is he going to die there too?"

My heart sank and I wanted to take their pain away. As I held them, I remembered that I had food on the stove.

"The soup!" I jumped up to make my way to the kitchen.

"I turned it off, Mom," Antonio said.

"The stove?

"Yea. I turned it off."

I was blown away by how he could have thought to do that amidst all the craziness. Once again, I was a parent experiencing my child as my teacher. Calm amidst the chaos.

Invitation

My spiritual practice was teaching me that there are no coincidences. So how could I reconcile Dominick's accident? At the time it happened, I was still in shock from the recent events leading up to it that I didn't have time to reflect on its deeper meaning. His recuperation from surgery and recovery time meant more responsibilities for me at home. As I tended to my husband and sons, my physical symptoms worsened to the point where I began experiencing persistent heart palpitations, stomach pain, and pain radiating through my muscles and joints that made walking a challenge. Emotionally numb, I knew I was drowning.

One day, I reached out to Natalie for a life preserver. Before I could even finish lamenting about the brokenness that I believed was my life, Natalie interrupted my pity party:

"Kristy, this IS the journey! Going through the shit…living this human life while carrying wounds…These are the experiences vital for your soul! You have a choice—allow life to organically unfold or try to control it.

Guess what? When you try to control it, spirit steps in and reroutes you and resistance is why things get messy and painful. Surrender, Kristy! Let go of the life you think you *should* have and make space for the one that has been waiting for you to step in. You say this is hard, and it is, of course, but this calling that is your birthright, it comes with 'stuff.' Whatever you are called to heal, that's what you will experience, including fear. Your wounds are your greatest assets and the tools of your healing work. The wounds hurt, yes, but they have a purpose. There is nothing here that is broken, absolutely nothing that needs fixing. You just have to remove all that's in the way of you seeing that."

I walked out of Natalie's office drying my eyes and snotty nose with my coat sleeve and walked to a neighboring shoppe to decompress. Two books on the counter captured my attention: *The Pregnant Virgin: A Process of Psychological Transformation* and *Leaving My Father's House* both by Marion Woodman. As I thumbed through them, I read a paragraph that felt as though it were written for me.

"... A life that is truly lived is constantly burning away the veils of illusion, gradually revealing the essence of the individual... the healing of ourselves as healers has to take place first... without an understanding of the relationship between destruction and creation, death and rebirth, the individual suffers the mysteries of life as meaningless mayhem alone..."

As I held the book, a small paper slipped out and fell to the ground. As I reached for it, my eyes began to decode the scripted gel-penned note:

"The Good Woman looks in the mirror. She changes into the Wise Woman Witch in the mirror... she resists... if she becomes this powerful woman, what will happen to her life? This powerful wise woman is her destiny, but if she steps into this power, her entire life as she has always known it, will completely shatter. She has to hold it together. Does she stay the Good Woman so as not

to cause upheaval? Or does she reveal herself, step into her predetermined power that will not make others happy? Will she be "exiled," or will she really be set free?"

This passage foretold what was to come for me.

As the cold days of winter gave way to spring, I continued to become unhinged. Abandoning my newfound magic, I defaulted to using food as a way of comforting myself, numbing the painful feelings and filling the voids that I felt deeply within. At night my vice was wine; during the day, it was doughnuts. I recall a late spring morning when I dropped my kids off at school after having yelled at them horribly prior to leaving the house. I felt so much guilt and shame. I drove to Dunkin Donuts, purchased a dozen, and sat in my car at the farthest corner of the parking lot to hide, while I binged and cried my eyes out.

By early June, I found myself sitting alone each night on the floor of my kitchen pantry with the door shut tight. Exhausted, angry, overwhelmed, and lonely; hating myself as a mother, resenting my kids who by this time were six and almost nine, hating my husband. As I lay on the floor drowning in my tears while licking every last drop out of a bottle of Cabernet, I felt broken beyond repair. My physical ailments were progressively worsening and increasingly more intolerable. I was having severe stomach pain after eating anything—whether it was kale, or grilled chicken, or a fat, juicy McDonald's Big Mac. Regardless of what it was, I felt sick afterwards and my stomach would distend like I was six months pregnant. Other times, I was afraid to eat, so I skipped most meals, and as long as I kept myself busy, I could manage the hunger pangs by chewing some Orbit peppermint gum or drinking hazelnut flavored coffee.

But it wasn't only my body that was hungry. Something deep in my soul felt uneasy and agitated. I'd be washing the dishes in my kitchen while staring out the window and hearing voices ask, *Is this it? Is this what my life was meant for—dirty dishes, half-eaten meals, and packing school lunches?* My rational brain would reply, *Well, yes, you're a mom, this is what you signed up for.* To which my heart/soul replied, *But is it? Did I really sign up for this? Is this really my purpose on this planet?* I didn't recognize the face staring back at me in the mirror, and I certainly didn't recognize the body. As the question *How did I end up here?* blared from the megaphone in my brain, my heart reminded me that I'd been asking that question my entire life.

I grew increasingly depressed and lifeless, feeling as though some inner void was expanding by the minute like a black hole and that I could actually disappear into oblivion. Loud and intrusive thoughts plagued me: *Why bother living? Nobody would miss me if I were gone. The boys would be better off without me. What happened to the girl who always had her shit together? Why don't the tasks of mothering feel like enough to satisfy me?*

My eyes opened the next morning and the harsh sunlight peeking through the blinds of my bedroom window made me realize that I had somehow gotten out of the pantry closet and made it up to my bed. Laying there even in stillness was painful, and the noise from downstairs was like an abrupt smack in the face. I attempted to close my eyes to forget about the day, but I had to pee. Moving seemed impossible. I can vividly recall crawling from my bed to the bathroom because my entire body ached. I was nauseous and exhausted. I cried yet no tears flowed as I crawled to the bathroom and when I eventually arrived, I pulled myself up to the vanity to look in the mirror. Looking at the harsh physical evidence of what I had become, I decided I didn't want to live anymore or suffer any longer. I was barely surviving anyway.

That day, determined to end it all, I ruminated on how I would do it. And then I caught a glimpse of a yellow sticky note that Antonio had attached to the corner of the vanity mirror.

"I love you Mommy. You are the best mom in the world."

I melted to the floor. With my finger I traced the hearts drawn in pencil and suddenly became aware of the enormous pain in my heart. Crying turned to sobs and moans and suddenly I was shedding tears for everything that had happened in the months prior—Gianni's illness, Ma's death, Dominick's accident, and the years prior from my childhood up until that moment. The dam had broken, and the floodgates opened.

With that forward rush of energetic momentum, something critical shifted. I decided that Antonio's note, my physical paralysis, and the memories of the trauma, all represented an invitation to live—to actually come to life. *To feel in order to heal.* I started to pray the same way I did when I was a frightened child, and something or someone took over to help revive me. I eventually crawled to the phone and scheduled an appointment with an integrative wellness center that had a team of professionals that I trusted. It was time to dive deeper "under the hood" to reveal my core wounds.

The Invitation

I met with Dr. Blum, an integrative physician and functional medicine specialist, a few weeks later. The initial stages of treatment were rough. I felt like I lived at the doctor's office, constantly getting poked with needles for bloodwork, IV/infusion therapy, having meetings with specialists and nutritionists and reviewing test results. Already tired of micromanaging food intake, I was placed on restrictive diets in which I tracked every morsel. I was 35 pounds overweight and grossly inflamed throughout my body. I couldn't poop, sleep, have sex, walk or eat; none of the basics. I would later recognize that like wild animals who become domesticated, strange consequences happen the further away we are from our natural state.

I cried constantly. In contrast to the intense anxiety that I experienced for most of my life in which symptoms took over like a powerful storm that launched fierce attacks, depression felt like a huge dark immovable boulder lying on top of me that suffocated me and squeezed out every last tear that could be shed. It was on those days that I struggled to breathe, speak, leave the house, see anyone, make decisions, or be alive. And once completely smoldered, the numbness ensued. The pain of feeling nothing hurt more than the pain of feeling anything.

The core physical issue seemed to be Leaky Gut, also known as intestinal permeability; a condition in which the lining of the gut becomes unhealthy and full of holes and cracks thereby allowing for particles, toxins, and bacteria to permeate and infiltrate the tissues and cells underneath. It then progressed to Small Intestinal Bacterial Overgrowth (SIBO), in which excessive bacteria in the small intestine releases hydrogen and methane in the intestine. And what followed: Irritable Bowel Disease, systemic Candida overgrowth, thyroid and autoimmune issues, Epstein Barr infection, histamine intolerance, Mast Cell Activation Syndrome, constipation and diarrhea. I had tremendous back and joint pain, somedays I was not able to move at all. Leading up to this, acupuncturists, chiropractors, craniosacral therapists, and massage therapists all "diagnosed" me with pain secondary to my central nervous system being stuck in flight/flight mode. I was caught up in monitoring and managing symptoms and how my body felt. Every sensation triggered more fear and perpetuated the vicious cycle.

Having worked with so many clients managing a variety of chronic health conditions, I had always witnessed the psychological effects of the illnesses being more difficult to manage than the physical. When I was in graduate school working on my doctoral dissertation, I conducted research on adolescents and young adults with Type 2 Diabetes at a prominent hospital in Bronx, New York. Though the physicians were concerned with helping the patients adhere to their medication regimens, and checking and interpreting their blood sugar levels, the patients were challenged most by feeling depressed and anxious about managing their illness.

Like those teens, I blamed myself, thinking that I wasn't doing enough. I was already consumed with guilt and shame for the years I spent running my body into the ground creating illness. Now I wondered if I could heal the damage I had done. My healing journey became yet another pressure-cooker, as I turned up the heat by making even more demands on my body. I was losing touch with my identity. *Was I a chronically sick person? Was I healing and in recovery?* Making this worse was the fact that my illnesses were for the most part invisible to anyone else. I was too healthy to look sick, yet too sick to be healthy.

One day, Dr. Blum asked the pivotal question: "Kristy, can you tell me about your childhood?"

I was not prepared for that direct of a question. Tears poured out of me faster than my fistful of tissues could manage. But something changed in that moment, like I had been given a much-needed snap-out-of-it slap in the face.

It's been said that *trauma isn't what happened to us; it's what happened inside of us as a result of what happened to us.* Trauma is residual energy stuck in the connective tissues of the body. The energy blockages wreak havoc on the brain and body, suffocating cells and obstructing life flow, creating fertile ground for illnesses to breed with lasting and oftentimes deadly consequences. In his book, *The Body Keeps the Score,* Bessel van der Kolk refers to trauma as "one of the West's most urgent public health issues."

In those years of transitioning from a traditional therapist to a holistic healer, I had begun offering my clients an innovative approach that focused on healing instead of curing. I began teaching them that illness of any kind represents an invitation to see beyond the illusion of their physical symptoms to excavate the rich stories about their lives, not just a snapshot of what may be happening with a particular organ in the body. The mind-body-spirit exists as an interconnected energy system, so simply focusing on physical symptoms creates a separation in this system. The physical body is just an outward expression of an internal system of energy. Seeing all physical symptoms as manifestations of energetic needs, desires, or conflicts reveals a deeper underlying story that the body is trying to communicate about where we have gotten lost and disconnected from our true selves. I know now that this radically transformative approach to health and wellness gets to the root of illness and transmutes the pain and suffering into a beautiful self-healing journey.

Yet here I was living day after day lost in the vortex of physical symptoms and running on empty trying to make them go away. I wasn't walking the walk. Dr. Blum was right. I was having a spiritual healing crisis, not a physical one.

The Body Tells the Story

Understanding my symptoms as energetic trauma responses in my body was a game changer; discovering this immediately began to elucidate other experiences in my life.

When I was a bright, ambitious 19-year-old in my junior year of college, I had planned to spend the summer interning in Rochester where Dominick was attending school. I had gotten a car, and since it was an older vehicle, my parents and I figured it best to bring it to a mechanic for a check-up. Knowing I was living on a budget, Dominick's father suggested a "good guy who won't charge you an arm and a leg." Something really didn't feel right to me about this situation, but he insisted, and I was grateful for the help. So, I stayed quiet.

From the very first phone call to Mike, I got that *feeling* again, but I chose to say nothing. I dropped off the car on Wednesday morning, had knots in my stomach as I dropped off money to him for parts on Thursday morning, and by Friday (which happened to be Friday the 13th!), I anxiously awaited his call alerting me that my car was ready for pickup as he promised, but it never came. As my best friend Patty and I finished work for the day at a busy internist's office, she drove me home and when we approached my street, we noticed police cars surrounding my house and policemen on my front porch. I thought something must have happened to my parents and they were looking to inform me. I pushed open the car door and jumped out. One of the officers approached me, took me by the arms, and ushered me inside while they searched my house, lifting couch cushions, rummaging through drawers and through my bedroom.

"Ma'am, your car was involved in three separate accidents today, severely injuring 13 people including Michael Sancino. All 13 people are in the hospital. In the glove compartment we found drug paraphernalia—heroin, cocaine, marijuana, pipes, straps, needles, all over the car. Do you know anything about this?"

I felt the blood drain from my face. The officers continued to fire questions about how I knew Mike, if I allowed him to borrow my car, and whether I gave him money for drugs. It was all surreal.

"He told us that you lent him your car as a friend, that you have been friends for years, and that the drugs in the car are yours."

I shouted that it was all a lie. "I don't even know this person! I don't know him at all!"

"Well then why would you give him your car? How'd you find him?"

I paused. If I told them that he was a friend of Dominick's father, then he would be incriminated. I knew I had to lie to protect him.

"I needed a cheap mechanic and I was referred to him. This is the Bronx. Everybody knows everybody, you know how it is."

The interrogation started. "So, Kristy, you just left your car with this man, trusted him, kept bringing him more money without getting receipts? You assumed he was fixing your car, but he didn't. He bought drugs, drove around high as a kite, and nearly killed 13 people, and some may end up dying, including children. None of this seemed strange to you?"

I was filled with shame for not heeding my intuition. "Are the people okay?" I asked through tears. I was ignored by the police who instead wanted to talk about my "drug problem."

"WHAT DRUGS, I DON'T DO DRUGS!"

"Well, they were all over your car, front seat, back seat, glove compartment, center console, all over."

That day turned into a decade-long series of legal proceedings in which I would sit on the witness bench giving my testimony. Screens were set up in the court room so that the jury could see the horrific details of the crash scenes and the victim's injuries. Each story was more traumatizing than the next.

This memory surfaced while on my yoga mat one bright, sweltering July morning, just four weeks after having begun my healing work with Dr. Blum. And as the memories of that traumatic decade of time enveloped me as I lay on my mat, I was struck by the awareness that when I finally arrived in Rochester that summer, I got very sick; first with mononucleosis, then chicken pox; and my symptoms of anxiety and panic escalated. I now realized that these symptoms arose from the residual energy from the traumatic experiences that had not been released from my body. The energy remained trapped, wreaking havoc on my system. As I learned, trauma reveals itself as bodily reactions, not as memories. My body was telling the story of a traumatized child who had yet again betrayed her gut instincts to make everyone else happy.

As the class prepared for savasana, I reflected on past classes in which laying down like a corpse terrified me and while the other students covered up with colorful crocheted blankets and lavender-infused eye pillows, I would quietly sneak out the back door. By this time, though, I was considered "chronically ill"; and armed with the knowledge and awareness of the deeply buried wounds creating my physical and energetic paralysis, I knew that running from discomfort was no longer an option. Yet my mind raced at lightning speed as I lay immobile: *I can't see the clock. What time is it? I'm freezing! How did that skinny chick in the front row do that headstand? What a showoff. I'm starving. Why is it so dark in here? I should leave, this was a mistake.* But my escape was sabotaged by these lyrics:

> *You're not running out*
> *You're really running in*
> *Confusion clouds the heart*
> *but it also points the way*
> *Quiet down the mind*
> *The more the song will play.*
> *You can't rush your healing*
> *Darkness has its teachings*

Immediately, as if I had been infused with a sedative, my mind was silent, my heart was still, and my body was glued to the mat by the moisture of my tears.

In that moment, I was painfully aware that I had embarked on this healing journey towards recovery in the same way that I had always done everything in my life—hard and fast, all in, giving 200 percent out of fear and desperation to "get better;" fiercely and incessantly searching for the "cure" in courses, workshops, online challenges, and expert practitioners. Yet all the fancy mantras, journaling prompts, mindset training courses, and supplements just created more noise and distraction. I remembered the messages I had received years ago in my journeys with Natalie . . . that the only way my true self could emerge was in calm stillness so that I could feel safe enough to hear my own voice. It was time to slow down and listen to my body with intention. I couldn't heal in the same chaotic conditions that made me sick. I couldn't rush this journey. Unlearning three decades of programming that disconnected me from my essence would take time. This was a quest to recover my truth, my wild, and I had to trust in the timeline of my soul.

The wisdom of this message felt like an invitation to take a deeper dive into my body in yoga sessions with Pam Golden, a yogi and energy healer in my professional circle. Pam initially taught me extensively about the opening and balancing of the chakra system for health and wellness. From my first session, Pam showed me how my root chakra was completely blocked such that I was ungrounded and felt unsafe. *How could my organs work properly if my body felt unsafe?*

"Sure, you have been taking flight and taking risks, and that's wonderful; but you also need to land. Grounding is the only way to bring you to consciousness. It's the only way for you to feel steady, centered, and calm so that you can heal. Healing is only possible in a parasympathetic state."

I knew Pam was right. I had to admit with radical honesty what my body was clearly communicating that I was still locked and loaded, waiting for the other shoe to drop. Persistently hypervigilant, scanning my life for possible danger just like I had as a scared child who sat at the top of the stairs and listened to every conversation and noticed every nuanced facial expression. I had to admit where I was still stuck in my head, analyzing everything, preparing 10 steps ahead. Retreating to my mind felt safer than being in my body. I was avoiding feeling, and in doing so, avoiding myself.

As Pam guided me to lay down on the mat in child's pose, she asked my body: "What's the story that you hold inside of you that you are dying to tell?" As words immediately fired like a machine gun from my mouth, Pam interjected, "Kristy I'm not asking your brain. I'm asking your body."

I consciously shifted my awareness to my body which was in an obvious state of tension. I felt a surge of energy in my chest and throat. Sensing my contraction, Pam gently spoke, "Kristy you have this unbelievable gift of sensing and feeling so deeply! Your intuition is sharp, and you use it to help others. Yet you're afraid of your own feelings and what you might discover about yourself. Can you imagine how amazing your life would be if you allowed yourself to feel and express your truth?"

Moving into an inversion pose, I sensed immediate discomfort as my neck stretched, punctuating the cysts and nodules on my thyroid gland. As Pam gently assisted, I closed my eyes, found my breath, and felt a release in my throat chakra. And just then memories came racing into my consciousness. I heard the story my body was trying to tell about all the times in my life that I stayed quiet so that I wouldn't upset anyone. I reflected on a childhood in which being unheard and misunderstood shaped my beliefs that nobody cared or viewed my thoughts or feelings as important, that I should say only what was expected of me, and that I might as well just stay quiet since nobody is listening to me, anyway! It's no wonder my throat chakra was blocked, thereby limiting communication, vibration, creation, and manifestation.

As I leaned my head back on a bolster, tears flowed, and I thought of myself as a muted child forced to keep secrets; considered too sensitive and too dramatic; walking on eggshells to keep the peace; unable to take sides without conflicting loyalties; the conscientious student who was called a nerd when she raised her hand to participate in class; the painfully shy child who received I's (Improvement Needed) on her report card for conduct when she tried to socialize; the mortified student whose desk was moved into the hallway alone so that she would be silenced. She was taught to be agreeable even when it didn't feel right, and to be nice to people who hurt her. And when she became a teen who was taken advantage of and she tried to assert herself by saying NO, her voice was ignored and she got hurt.

The good little girl who was told to apologize when she wasn't sorry matured into a woman incapable of setting boundaries in her personal and professional lives. She couldn't handle confrontation of any kind; was terrified of disappointing family, friends, or clients; obsessively mentally rehearsed her words before speaking them; often rambling so fast when she did speak hoping that nobody would actually hear her so her words wouldn't disappoint anyone; or she tried to dominate conversations by raising her voice and talking over people so that there was little opportunity to be questioned or criticized, allowing her to have the last word. And when she thought she found safety in a spouse and let down her guard, she was told her feelings were complaints.

When speaking professionally, she hid behind the truths of the thinkers who came before her and regurgitated their theories and research. And with matters of the heart, opening herself and communicating freely and coherently was daunting. She struggled to be direct, and instead gave every detail of an event without actually saying anything meaningful about it to keep it devoid of feeling. Other times, she overshared out of desperation to be listened to, and to feel some relief for all that was bottled up inside of her. She was simply talking to discharge energy. But eventually she got quieter, making herself invisible, losing connection with her truth.

Afraid to be open, expressive, and free to be herself out of fear of consequence created a chronic state of living in fear, which closed her throat chakra. She literally became "choked up." In recent years, that had manifested as an itchy irritated throat that was constantly infiltrated with strep bacteria, as well as thyroid disease. Her body was desperate for the flow of breath to release the unspoken words that fear entrapped for so long.

The awareness that, in stifling my truth, I had abandoned myself hit me like a ton of bricks. Tears overflowed onto my mat. As my body began to soften, I felt a surge of anger rise from my hips up through my throat; and before I knew it, I was screaming at the top of my lungs:

"I've been so scared! I've been terrified of being abandoned. I have desperately clung to Dominick because I feel no roots, so I cling to *his*. I have been ungrounded. I have abandoned myself. You want to know about my childhood? My childhood was a joke. I wasn't a child! I was too scared. I worried all the time, torn between two parents who couldn't get their own shit together, desperate to be loved and seen worthy, terrified to be abandoned, eager to please and placate, concerned with taking care of their needs. And me ... what about me? Nobody ever asked if I was okay. Nobody! Nobody even knew anything that was going on with me. I wasn't seen or heard. I have all the secrets in here. That's my childhood, Pam. That's my story."

As the impact of those words vibrated within the acoustics of that small yoga studio, I could finally breathe for the first time in forever. As Pam guided the process, I reflected on what expressing truth had meant to me, considering all the times I was lied to in my life. I had been shown the message that honesty wasn't the best policy. My mother had good intentions, as she thought she was protecting me and didn't want to overwhelm me with anything that she decided I couldn't handle or wasn't ready for. But her deceptions made it difficult to trust her. And when things happened that were so obvious, yet their existence or importance was denied, I wasn't allowed to ask questions. So much was off limits to discussion. Things were never what they seemed, and I couldn't trust that anyone was telling me the whole story. So, I became hypervigilant, always looking for clues in every detail that was spoken like a detective. I got good at concocting stories to satisfy my curious mind and restless heart that was aching to understand things like my father saying "I love you and I will always be here for you" but never showing up for me; being told "I care about you, you're my best friend" by a friend who gossiped about me and mistreated me; being told, "You're so special to me" by a boy who attacked me. So many mixed messages.

And I never saw anyone in my life stand up for themselves. My mother was great at setting professional boundaries but didn't assert herself at home. I learned to swallow everything. I would suppress until I couldn't take it anymore and the dam burst, and the raging waters caused eruptions of yelling and violence. And sadly, I was just behaving the way I had been taught. Whenever I begged for the yelling, arguing, screaming, berating, scolding, hitting, slamming, punching, kicking to stop, I was told to stop being disrespectful, to never challenge authority, and to "keep your mouth shut." Sadly, this continued into my adult relationships.

I felt enormous relief in that yin yoga session as the slow and deeply held postures in the presence of a warm, loving guide offered my body the opportunity for safety in which to release and express my stories in a healthy way. It reminded me of my very first craniosacral session with Annie, when the first layer of the shock and trauma that were living in my tissues was released. Cultivating the practice of calm abiding on that mat allowed the turbulence of my mind to simmer as my body settled. Through this, I was able to read those stories and extrapolate their teachings with an open mind and heart, with love and compassion for myself, and for the first time, trust in my truth. I was reparenting my inner child.

Just Breathe

Pam also introduced me to the practice of Pranayama; *Prana* means life force or breath sustaining the body, and *ayama* means "to extend or draw out." Together, this is the process of extending and controlling the breath. Interestingly in Latin, the word *inspirare*—inspire—-actually means breathing in. Breathing in intentionally is inspirational for the soul. Inhaling and exhaling, while two seemingly separate phenomena, when done properly are actually one flow —the inhale and exhale should blend so that the difference between them is almost indistinguishable. Breathing, then, becomes a constant life- giving flow that allows for physical health as well as higher and healthier states of mental clarity.

Pam taught me that to breathe is to be conscious; the breath is the vehicle that drives awareness and connects awareness to movement. On the yoga mat our breath is linked to each movement of an asana, and breath is the force that gives life to actions that we take off the mat. Breathing is an opportunity to connect with the moment in stillness to counterbalance all the motion in life. By flowing with the rhythms of the breath, I could calm my mind, ground my body, and move energy in my body, thereby achieving a focused, connected, and energized state. Using my breath and body in this way was in striking contrast to the years in which hyperventilating was a daily occurrence. Productivity had been my drug of choice for decades; and just like any drug, it felt amazing when riding a high, until the crash. Connecting with the breath was the only way

I learned how to break free from the grips of addictive behaviors that were fueled by a web of tangled limiting beliefs and fears. Breathing allowed me the opportunity for intimacy with myself.

It hit me that day on my mat while listening to Pam's teachings that in years and months prior, I had been using my yoga and meditation practice to bypass feeling. It had become glorified avoidance. I was now learning that in stillness, with my breath as my guide, when sensation of any kind was detected, I could stay with the inherently neutral energy and allow it to move through me, interrupting the brain's tendency to hijack the situation with its interpretations. I understood now that sensation isn't the problem, interpretation is!

It was possible for me to cultivate a non-reactive state of being in pure and loving awareness and acceptance of myself, with openness and curiosity, without needing to *do* or *achieve* anything. As Matilde taught me all those years ago: meditation is a state of being that has no purpose, aim, focus, goal, or timeline. It's a noun, not a verb. Our mind and body become trained in calm abiding which then allows for clarity, insights, and understanding. Calmness leads to insight, and insight leads to calmness.

Now I was beginning to understand that practicing asana and pranayama in this way was a metaphor for life. I could stay with a challenging posture when my brain was telling me to run, and I could explore where there might be moments of joy and bliss amidst discomfort. Instead of either/or, it could be both/and: *I am uncomfortable in Eagle pose AND I am amazed by the wondrous ways that my body is learning how to move.* There's no denial of the discomfort, but there is an acknowledgment of an alternative. Discomfort may be an inevitable part of our lives at times but resisting it and suffering through it is only one possible choice. As Natalie had taught me, every dark space one finds themselves in represents an initiation. The shamans say that the one who feels it, and chooses to use it, actually gets out and is the wise medicine person. The person who chooses to avoid, resist, or suffer through it while feeling sorry for themselves stays stuck and sick.

Through the next six months, as I continued to work with Pam consistently, I realized that my healing quest for truth was going to be anything but linear; it was circuitous with high peaks and low valleys that continuously circled me back to uncover more. Revisiting these stories brings us back repeatedly to previously discovered truths so that we can see through new lenses, make new discoveries, and integrate those breakthroughs into the whole. We may come back around again and again to the same memories, but with each go round, the pain lessens, the wisdom is augmented, the heart is opened, and the soul is advanced. Life is a journey of ongoing awakenings, and so our practice becomes getting curious, gracefully opening our minds and hearts so that we can see the magic in discovering what every experience has to offer. It was an interesting landscape to navigate, and it wasn't always pretty.

Sometimes the sessions looked like sitting on the floor for 10 minutes, hugging my knees into my chest, rocking my hips gently from side to side, using my five senses to shift from thinking mode to sensing mode. Pam taught me to ask myself questions such as, "Where do you feel this in your body;" and "When I'm scared, what does my body do; does this behavior settle me or activate me; what is the truth of my body right now?" all focusing on the neutrality of sensation to prevent the fearful mind from hijacking me. Pam taught me invaluable somatic practices for healing trauma that not only supported my own journey, but also inspired my continued training in somatic healing therapies that I could offer to my clients.

In other sessions, Pam watched me wince as my hip flexors were engaging. She gently asked, "Kristy, do you allow yourself to experience pleasure; what is your story of pleasure?" Suddenly, another story revealed itself. As a kid, Mommy was adamant about empowering me to be a strong independent woman. Lessons about hard work, not having to rely on anyone for money, and sacrificing to provide for the family were drilled into me. Mommy worked multiple jobs running a laundry mat, selling houses as a real estate agent, and creating and selling silk flower arrangements at flea markets. When I wasn't in school, I went to work with her every day, seven days a week. There were no off days or holidays. Every day, we hustled to survive. And I saw all that Mommy sacrificed for me to attend Catholic school and to put food on the table. I learned that working *hard* was the only way to work. And working hard in school also earned me the love and attention of Daddy.

Pleasure was not even on the radar. In fact, I always felt guilty about doing anything that made me happy as a kid. So, I cut myself off from things that made me feel good. Pleasure invoked immense guilt in all areas of my life. Ironically, I believed that feeling guilty was what made me a good person! There's nothing like Catholic school and Italian grandmother conditioning!

Anodea Judith, an expert on somatic therapies and the chakra systems who I studied extensively, refers to guilt as the "demon of the sacral chakra." Guilt is so toxic to the energetic and physical body because it literally halts all movement of life force. It takes any pleasure out of movement. Any step you take, any choice you make, is instead marred by shame. As Pam continued to guide my asana practice, I realized how everything in my life either became good or bad; either completely enjoyable, or horrible. And I realized that the more guilt I carried, the more I tried to compensate with radical perfectionism. Fastidiousness, combined with a belief that working hard was the only way to survive and be loved, became the perfect storm for my neurotic overachieving Type A personality to develop.

My private sessions with Pam were instrumental in reacquainting me with the inherent wisdom of my body such that I could see where I was still penetrating the world with brute force. Once convincing myself that I was in control, I could see that I was actually in anxiety! And my healing journey up until that point was akin to a research project in which I dutifully analyzed all the details objectively and distantly. Healing was about taking control by going all in, embodying the story, lovingly encouraging its expression, and gratefully letting go in order to surrender and flow. Now I realized what Dr. Blum meant when she told me I had to stop working. I didn't need to learn how to *stop*; I needed to learn how to *move*, but differently. I had to learn how to relate to and use my life force energy in different ways guided by the calm ebb and flow of my breath. Stillness was actually a dynamic state that could allow me to move with life, not against it, so I could calmly strategize when to take action and when to rest and recover. I was discovering that calm emotions come when I can trust that what I feel is actually my own choice . . . and I could make the choice to feel good!

But *calm* didn't immediately feel good; and it was through my somatic work that I realized just how strongly wired I was to find comfort in intense and volatile emotions. I felt everything dramatically-- either feeling immense joy or heavy distress with little in between. Experiencing either polarity was ironically what made me feel most alive, but now I was ready to release the drama. I was ready to choose peace.

I was learning now that spiritual growth was about an emotional maturity that came from learning how to bring energy into balance; an ability that is innate to all humans. Pam was teaching me that gaining mastery over my feelings and emotions to cultivate inner harmony wasn't about numbing myself with food or alcohol or disassociating from my body or talking myself out of feeling; rather it was about thoroughly experiencing the energy in my body as it was happening. I had to drop into my body, identify the sensations and remain connected to the sensations so that my brain had no shot at getting involved with its intrusive and oftentimes inaccurate interpretations. Instead of thinking about *why* I felt the way I did, I only had to focus on the sensation itself. As I learned to calm my emotions and release the tendency to make assumptions and interpretations, I could raise my energetic frequency, remain aligned with my true self, and experience peace and calm even in the most turbulent of times. And that's when it started to become clear that my evolution would require the opposite behaviors of what had always kept me safe.

Rooted

Moving my body consciously was showing me the necessity of working with trauma at the energetic level, as the issues live in our tissues. Around that time, I did a journey in which I asked my guides to help me uncover and release what was still blocking my access to my true self. In the journey, my animals guided me to an open field for a fire ceremony where we burned hundreds of books. An eagle flew overhead and dropped a scroll that read, *Burn the books.* A charoite sphere appeared in my hands and as it seemed to magically "charge" me, children, adults, and families multiplied before my eyes, forming a circle around me. I sang while drumming and an eagle landed on my head and communicated to me, *Your vibration is rising; you're moving on to the next level. You are now an elder for the next generations. Trust your inner wisdom.*

In another journey, I discovered my plant ally, which appeared as a twisted oak tree with ivy wrapped around it. I was inside the tree cooking leafy green vegetables and giving out the food to people who came to eat. As I observed, the phrase *rooted connections* was heard; and I trusted in that moment that I was being called to create collective healing experiences.

I have always been considered by people to be a connector. I deeply value relationships and the interconnectedness of all beings. And I somehow sensed that for optimal health and wellness, women belonged together in sisterhood, and men in brotherhood. I began to seek out empowering group healing experiences at local retreat centers and yoga studios. I participated in spiritual and philosophical book study clubs, group meditations and more. I also offered collective healing experiences for clients at my center which I started referring to as a community healing and wellness center. I witnessed something absolutely beautiful happening in all of these experiences. Individuals came together to hold space for one another to process wounds and express long-repressed pain in the context of ceremony. Together, we found our personal and collective voices. The content of our experiences was different, but the processes and themes are all the same. And because we are energetic beings, each of us is impacted by the experiences of others around us. Our wounds do not form in private, so neither should our healing.

I also knew I needed to immerse myself in the natural world again, as I was starved for the nourishment that nature always seemed ready and waiting to provide. Nature became a portal through which I could access spirit. In times of stress and chaos, I knew to look to the trees, the plants, the animals, the sun, the moon, the water, the air, and crystal specimen to receive guidance that would lead me to myself and my own inner wisdom. Instead of searching books for answers and gurus for guidance, I was learning to find meaning and truth in every life experience and encounter. Opening my eyes to witness the magic all around me, and reverently celebrating my reciprocal relationship with all beings of Earth was pure alchemy for me. Those moments solidified the truth that was now so clear: the wild and magical world that my innocent, untamed little girl-self believed in—the one that got buried under years of civilized domestication, and the one I had been searching for—was actually real. Little by little, I was reclaiming my place in it.

Ancient Medicine

hen did you stop dancing? In my studies of Shamanism, I learned that in shamanic societies, if an individual is ill in mind and/or body and approached a medicine person for healing, he or she would be asked that, and other questions: *When did you stop singing? When did you stop finding the magic and enchantment in stories? When did you stop finding comfort and peace in silence?* It was believed that to heal meant to reignite and reconnect with the soul through revitalizing life force, purifying one's being, and restoring natural cycles through reconnection with ancestral lineage and the natural world through ceremony and ritual. Though I was still taking boatloads of supplements, receiving weekly vitamin infusions, giving vials of blood for testing with naturopathic and integrative physicians, it was the wisdom of ancient medicine that would ultimately transform me.

Looking back, my first lessons in ceremony were learned in my Grammie's kitchen while making Italian meatballs. Every Sunday around noon, in her third-floor apartment in the Bronx, I would excitedly help

Grammie get out the ingredients for our Sunday dinner. It was a tradition around coming together as a family to celebrate life, and of course, food. At that time, Sunday dinner was a delicacy as the ingredients were quite expensive for less-well-off families like mine. Mixed beef, veal, and pork meat from the butcher, extra virgin olive oil, grated pecorino Romano cheese, eggs, fresh parsley, salt, and pepper.

I would stand on a chair so I could reach the counter and crumble up the stale bread to make the breadcrumbs. When it came time to add the ingredients into the bowl, Grammie took over as I watched in awe as she somehow knew just how much of every ingredient to put in the bowl. She always said, very matter-of-factly, "You just know. It's a feeling. You use your eye, your heart, and your gut." When it was time to mix the ingredients bare-handed, Grammie would say, "You gotta dive in, mash it up between your fingers. Don't be afraid to feel it. That's the only way to know if its mixed."

The aroma was intoxicating, and staring at the meat sizzle as the hot oil seeped into every crevice of these circular bits of heaven induced a meditative trance-like state. Once taken out of the pan, Grammie swatted my hand as I tried to steal one to eat.

"Wait, just watch them. They are resting. They are becoming."

When it was time to eat them, Grammie observed the meatball between her fingers, then closed her eyes and inhaled the aroma inducing a smile on her face, and finally took a small bite. And each time said, "There is nothing better than this. It's like a little miracle." It was a true sensory experience and a masterful artistic expression.

Growing up as a child in an Italian-American family meant that every Sunday was dedicated to one thing: *la famiglia*. The day began with dressing in our best clothes and going to Mass. After filing out of the wooden Church doors, we all congregated outside in community—the adults talked while the kids ran around and cheerfully played. After a while, it was time to head over to the bakery to get fresh muffins, pastry, crumb buns, and a couple loaves of seeded Italian bread. Our Sunday dinner menu was always the same—macaroni, meatballs, sausage, bracciole, and any other meat bones that Grammie had left over from the week.

The adults talked and laughed while sipping their red wine and the kids drank too much soda—the one day I could have soda. The grandparents would add in a splash of red wine to the soda, as they wanted the kids to be a part of the ceremony. No matter how full we were from all the food, there was always room for dessert--fruit, nuts, "Finucci" (Anise), and of course —cannoli, sfoiglatella, and cookies. The older generations would tell stories of their youth and glory days. Nothing was ever somber. Even if there was anger expressed, it was done with love. You made peace over the meal. These Sunday dinners truly brought out the best in everyone and it was my favorite time of the week.

For most first and second-generation Italian families, this traditional ceremony of the Sunday dinner has been going on for generations, since coming to this country. When the Italians came to this country from Italy, they initially faced discrimination. Not speaking the language and being in a new place was terrifying for many, and assimilation was tough. Family members moved into the same apartment building so they could be close together for security and to raise their kids together. Connection with the family was all they had and all they believed they needed. The Sunday dinner ceremony was a time to celebrate and rejuvenate. When the Italians arrived in this country most became laborers as they were used to doing and building with their hands back in their country. As stonemasons, carpenters, and brick layers, they worked long days without breaks and often without meals. By having enough food to fill the Sunday table they experienced pride and deep gratitude, as it represented their blood, sweat, and tears. Every morsel was honored and savored. Wasting food was considered a great sign of disrespect and leaving any food uneaten on the plate wasn't an option. Nothing made the grandmothers and mothers happier than empty plates. To this day I still love to feed people and I feel so fulfilled when I have company and they leave with full bellies and hearts.

Those Sunday ceremonies were what I lived for. After my parents divorced, things changed a bit, though initially we still had our Sunday dinners with Daddy's family. As I got older, and certainly after Daddy died, I felt like I lost my connection to my roots. When I would talk to my mother about it, she would chalk it up to times changing and flippantly brushed it off. But it was a profound loss for me.

When I got married, I promised myself that I would recreate the Sunday dinners of old with my family and Dominick's family. I had made meatballs and "Sunday gravy" ceremoniously every Sunday since I moved out into my own apartment in 1999, and that lasted for a while. But things have since changed. Many of the older generations have now passed on. Kids have so many activities that pull families away from the home, and family members live farther apart from each other. As time passed, the once sacred and intentional ceremony became a rushed to-do list item that happened on auto-pilot, and eventually it became only a distant memory.

Orienting

Looking back now, I realized just how much the loss of ceremony and connection with my ancestral lineages affected me. I felt incomplete, detached, and unrooted without these traditions, especially when everything else was changing around me. All these years later, I found myself mourning the loss and spending so much time searching for ways to fill the void that only ceremony, ritual, and tradition can fill.

Being forced by the universe to slow down to heal my body afforded me the time to focus on my meditation and journeying practices. The intuitive hints about New Mexico continued until it became a joyful obsession, something that I could not stop feeling. I was drawn to Native American culture and read whatever I could get my hands on about it, like *The Way We Lived, Black Elk Speaks, What the Eagle Sees: Indigenous Stories of Rebellion and Renewal* and *Ceremonies of the Living Spirit.* I took online classes and watched videos of shamanic practices in Peru and Siberia, animal communication, plant medicine, and sacred ceremony. All of it touched me deeply. Suddenly, images, visions and "feelings" from earlier in my life had a place to land: my connections and communications with nature and the Earth, my felt sense of being certain animals, my obsession with my long hair and feeling that it had magical powers, my sense that everything in the world could be understood by counterclockwise circles.

Through this new lens, I saw how critical our point of view is in orienting us in life. Orientation—in original Native American culture—is represented by the direction East, which also signifies new beginnings and pure potential. As humans, we oftentimes lose our way and become disoriented. When that happens, we feel as though we don't know which way to turn or where to go. Nothing looks familiar or makes sense. I was learning from the indigenous cultures that in order to truly reorient ourselves, we need to do so in both the outer and inner worlds.

This concept of orientation is the basis behind the medicine wheel, which has been utilized for millions of years by countless generations of Native tribes for healing and wellness. This "circle of life" becomes a compass that helps us to reorient ourselves when we are floundering and have lost our sense of purpose, as well as live in harmony within ourselves and the external world around us; only then can we experience true peace and joy. I was particularly interested in the application of the medicine wheel to trauma, as so much of my work with clients involves trauma healing. At that time, I was still experiencing PTSD since giving birth to Antonio, as well. I was surprised to discover that the teachings were remarkably similar to the psychology and philosophy I had studied for years. After we experience trauma of any kind and our nervous systems have been jarred out of balance, our relationship to the external world changes and it is incredibly difficult to find peace inside our hearts. What we feel instead is unrest, imbalance, intense fear and anxiety; and this influences everything from our physical and mental health to our relationships and careers.

Given my love of story, I was delighted to learn that using the wisdom of the medicine wheel gives pain and suffering a place in our story; and when we see that the pain has a purpose, we can use it as it was intended for transformation, transmutation and evolution. Traditional treatments for anxiety and PTSD are attempts to undo the damage or obliterate it from memory; to numb it with medication, or talk around it. The healthy doctor treats the ill patient—a pathologized clinical model that can disempower the individual and reduces them to symptom checklists, diagnostic codes, and drug-cocktail prescriptions. I believe now that this is one of the reasons why so many do not seek help. Medication and talk therapy have their place, but the medicine wheel reminds us that humans are multidimensional beings.

Immersing myself in the wisdom of the medicine wheel offered me a new lens through which to understand birth, loss, pain and life's challenges. As I began to compassionately and admirably reflect on my wounds,

124

I started to see glimpses of light radiating from within them. I returned to Natalie's guidance to go deeper, and in the first session she sensed a blockage—a spiritual intrusion, as she called it—in my solar plexus that was causing my chronic stomach problems. Clearing this enabled me to tap into my psychic gifts and intuition even more. We all have these abilities; we just need to learn how to access them.

Over time, journeying became an active form of meditation that allowed me to support my creative mind and fiery imagination instead of muting it. And like manifesting anything in life, journeying begins with an intention. Natalie taught me to focus on what I want to tune in to, rather than tune out. We can ask our spirit guides specific questions or requests, such as, "What do I need to let go of?" or "Show me the way when I can't see one." In one of my journeys, I was guided by Panda to climb a high tree, but was frightened and doubted my abilities. A massive condor came from behind and hooked his bright yellow-orange talons into my shoulders and lifted me up, flying faster and higher. Eventually ending up in a vast abyss of white light, a guide tossed me a large purple marbled crystal sphere with words *Be hope for others* etched into it. I later identified that stone as a charoite, a rare and complex illuminating stone with healing properties that is particularly important for healers.

With consistency in my practice, I began to see signs with increasing regularity that reflected the meaning and messages I was receiving in my journeys. Gradually, every aspect of life became a metaphor and even the most mundane moments became magical. In turn, my journeys became richer as I was able to go deeper with greater intention.

In one journey, I entered with the intention of discovering my true nature and how I could use it to serve. I saw myself as an older woman with silver hair down touching the earth and wearing an ivory cloak. She held a wooden staff in her left hand and a large spherical charoite crystal in her right. I watched her gracefully walk to an open space and draw three large circles in the sand. Groups of people of all ages started walking towards her, organizing themselves around the circumference in a healing circle. The woman outstretched her arms and wrapped them around everyone who had convened. She then crouched down in the middle of each circle and scooped a handful of earth to form clay bowls. She presented each person with one, along with a blessing. I was given the message that my role is that of a wise elder who creates from the earth.

I was intrigued by this vision and pondered it while on the drive home from Natalie's office. Just then, I saw a placard sitting in the entrance to a parking lot of a restored factory: "Introduction to Pottery Class. Call to register." Whoa. Chills. I pulled into the parking lot to register.

Clay and Consciousness

On the day of my first class, I was excited and nervous as I walked into the century-old iconic building that housed the pottery studio. The students were mostly women sitting at a long cement workbench wearing smocks and aprons. Wood and wiry tools were strewn about along with a few notebooks and pens. Armed with only a few years of Play-Doh experience under my belt, I followed the instructions to press and smush a lump of clay into a "pinch pot." As I massaged the clay, my mind quieted, allowing me to connect with it. It reminded me of the wise woman ceremony in my journey and I could feel my long-stifled creative forces loosening up.

During those first few classes, as I worked to perfect bowls and coasters and trivets, all my inner egoic shit came up—perfectionism, not being good enough, overthinking, comparing. I decided to meditate for a few minutes before touching the clay. This allowed me to access my creative unconscious in much the same way that I was getting other downloads in other areas of my life.

One evening while meditating at my workbench, I saw her, a stunning majestic goddess who dances with infectious joy as her long flowing coils are in rhapsody with the breeze. As she graciously moves, her natural curves mirror the gorgeous mountainous landscapes that surround her, as her feet reverently grace the Earth honoring its sanctity. The sun reflects off the turquoise jewel on her headdress creating a radiant aura of light around her. The feathers in her hair blend with those of the large winged one perched on her shoulder. She commands the respect and admiration of all beings--the four legged, two legged's one-legged's, for her alluringly captivating green eyes are a portal to spirit. Her poetic speech summons circles of beings in an ecstatic yet prayerful chant, creating a circle of seekers eager to receive and embody the wisdom of the elders that channels through her vessel. She is a conduit of dynamic energy and a keeper of sacred stories. She heals all who know her.

I was blown away by this vision, as it had been almost three decades since Allegra Topanga came to me when I was an anxious and quirky 13-year-old questioning the religion I was being indoctrinated with yet feeling inextricably connected to the entirety of the universe. And this connection was reaffirmed every time I stepped foot into nature and could hear the voices of the trees, rocks, and water; and fairies emerged who spoke to me in native tongues. At the time, I was equally as mesmerized as I was confused by this vision that appeared so familiar and so real as if I could touch her. She felt like me . . . from another lifetime, yet the conditioning of my childhood called the validity of that belief into question.

And now, sitting at this workbench in an introductory pottery class all these years later, while in the throes of a spiritual healing quest to find my true self, she came to me again. I recognized her immediately—the sparkling green eyes, tousled wavy hair, whimsical feathers in her headdress, and the luminous turquoise on her forehead. I felt as though I had teleported to a time and place that I longed for, a place for which I didn't even realize I had been homesick. Tears flowed as I felt Allegra's energy move through me as buffalo held me and roamed about. I realized in that moment that Allegra Topanga was the activation of my soul's past, my connection with lineages that had been forgotten but were always with me. And instantly I watched myself in amazement as I sketched her image on a crisp white sheet of paper, even though I could barely draw a straight line up until that day. Even more astonishing was the confidence that beamed from within me knowing that I would hand sculpt her into existence just as magically as I had drawn her.

Feeling my hands in the clay felt as old as time; and with every intricately carved detail using only my fingertips as tools, I felt invigorated and imbued with life. It would take nine months of dedicated work to create a piece of art that I could only have imagined in dreams. I was proud of myself for creating this woman who had an energy, a purpose, a resonance, a song to sing, and a dance to dance. Allegra Topanga: Goddess of Transformation, Sacred Storyteller, Wisdom Weaver, and Medicine Woman came to life by my own two hands.

My reunion with Allegra Topanga catalyzed my homecoming; and from that moment on I heard the voices and songs and stories again, just as I had as a child; I saw the glorious lands upon which my feet roamed alongside the wild buffalo; and I remembered the medicine that lie dormant within me. I felt empowered, my heart activated, and my soul nourished by the land as I ventured out each day to connect with nature in the same way that I used to as a child. My life became a continuous shamanic journey as my guides accompanied me as unwavering beacons of light creating a bridge between spirit and matter as I journeyed through the quest of my soul's remembrance.

Each day I prayed: *Mother Earth grant me the ability to find appreciation, fascination, and awe with the little things within the larger works of beauty you have created. Help me to align with the elements of earth, to live in accordance with the seasons, and to trust in the natural order of things. In doing so, Mother Earth, I will live in communion with nature, with my ancestors, and light the way for future generations. And help me to shine light into my shadows to reveal all parts of me so that I can feel whole again. Help me remember my way home.*

In one shamanic journey, a panda and a black panther guided me to an opening in the brush where drums were scattered around the landscape like rock formations with trees growing out of them. "The answers you seek are in the drums," they said. "Let them heal you. Let yourself heal them. Return to ceremony. Don't abandon the old. Go back to your roots."

I listened. Getting my hands on a drum was as familiar as riding a bike. It felt like an innate skill, and each time I played I remembered pastimes of sacred ceremony around a fire, dancing, singing, storytelling. I reminisced about days of walking through desert villages in the blazing sun while talking and harvesting plants to create bundles of medicinal herbs.

And with every beat of the drums, I saw signs everywhere. I had learned that signs are about seeing the extraordinary in the ordinary when we are open and ready to receive. I was beginning to understand spiritual growth as the process of becoming our higher selves, the very essence of who we are. This loving and compassionate self holds the accumulated wisdom from all our lifetimes. I began to reframe my journey of personal development and healing as a quest of spiritual inquiry and evolution. Doing so amplified my growth and the more I strengthened this higher connection, the more it communicated to me through synchronicities, insights, and revelations. Seeing the "signs" meant I was listening. And I finally understood what I had spent my life searching for. I was remembering my roots.

Dancing Trees

The further into my shamanic work and the more time I spent in nature, the more parts of myself were revealed. I started to understand what concepts like spirit, soul, and Source meant; not from books but from an experiential practice that revealed a much deeper sense of knowing and feeling. When in nature, surrounded by trees, plants, lakes, ponds, streams, and rocks, I felt true companionship. As my senses were heightened and joy expanded, I felt a primitive version of myself being resuscitated. She rolled in the dirt, made love to the trees, charged herself in the sun, walked on all fours barefoot as she climbed boulders and mountains, and talked to spirit in the same way that she had as a child.

I was becoming part of nature, and I felt so connected to every tree in the forest and could communicate with them. It was humbling to stand at the feet of these majestic elders who offered so much wisdom. Each had its own essence and way of relating with itself and the other trees around it. I was enamored with how each tree moved, with its limbs reaching out like arms, dancing their dance as the air moved through their leaves.

Watching this one afternoon, I heard the story emerge from within as my body shook and shimmied ecstatically, and as I was enveloped in a haze of oneness and bliss:

She has beautiful, graceful legs that move as though she is floating, her toes grazing the earth like lips salivating for a kiss.

He has strong, steady groundedness from which he roots to rise.
They lock eyes, and the abundance of love between them creates the dance.
He rejoices, and his arms reach the sky as the energy of spirit flows through
him.
Feeling his joy penetrate her entire being she smiles,
Creating a portal from which rivers flow and waterfalls cascade, in a
cleansing ritual that offers renewal.
And all the while, the sacred landscape that is their dancefloor—the huge
boulders and rocks, majestic mountains, jagged cliffs, lofty fields of green,
crunchy leaves, blue sky, beaming sun, gentle breezes, trickling streams—
transforms.
And every creature –the winged ones, four legged, insects, are drawn to the
dancefloor, front and center, in celebration.
And the vibration of their collective dance becomes the musical spheres of
harmony around which the universe moves.
And just like that, there is life.

From that moment on, words of poetry and stories flowed from me just as they had when I was a child. It was as though I remembered fluently a language that had become extinct just by immersing myself in the wild. And now I longed for any opportunity possible to speak in my native tongue.

I began to offer clients sessions in the woods in which I guided them to return to their roots to see, hear, and feel in new ways. I sought out opportunities to liberate my mind while using my hands in conjunction with my heart to learn ancient skills like foraging and basket weaving. In pottery class, I sculpted trees and experimented with color and movement, and felt called to infuse the sculptures with reiki energy. I learned the "wheel", as I saw the process of throwing clay to be a teaching metaphor for life. "Centering," for instance, is the process of getting the clay to be perfectly aligned before morphing it into a desired shape. It requires a careful balance of applying pressure and force, while finding the correct amount of water to keep it moist but not flooded. Above all, this process requires patience. If you force the clay, it moves and throws your hands and itself around the bat, leading to a crumpled and contorted mess. It's a delicate balance between clay and potter. I recognized the lesson that in navigating the chaos of modern life, calmness is actually mastery.

The more I creatively danced with clay inside the studio, the more I craved moments to be outside, barefoot, dancing through the grass and leaves, moving on the ground, placing my hands on trees. Yearning to learn even more ways of accessing this earth energy, I decided to pursue my Reiki level II certification. Practicing Reiki meant that I was attuned to become a conduit, a hallow reed, for universal life energy to pass through me and be received by another. The level II training deepened the energy, allowing me to channel it to others from a distance. I was learning that this energy is universal and is available to everyone; however, in modern times, life moves us away from both the natural world and the natural essence of our being. The attunement process allows the practitioner access to that energy once again on behalf of another.

Essentially, Reiki is a process of waking up. The more I studied it, the more I noticed parallels to Shamanism. Much like a Reiki healer, shamans call upon the universal forces of energy in nature—the animals, plants, trees, rocks, water, wind, fire, minerals, earth for healing, as well as the energy of ancestors and spirits. Going forward, I wanted my healing space to have this vibration. I got instructions for how to do so in my next journey.

In this journey, Panda greets me and takes me through a wooden door into a dark area with a small body of water. An eagle lands on my head. I carve three circles in the ground with a wooden staff. I sit down by the circles and look around to see crystals and rock formations everywhere. It looks like a cave with stalactites and stalagmites. Smoke billows from a campfire as I mix ingredients into a black bowl over the fire. My arms are adorned in bracelets; feathers attach to my hair and are flying in the breeze. A tiny green plant appears next to the circles. Through the firelight, I see the elements needed to set up my healing space.

I knew the journey was an invitation to prepare an altar for my own sanctuary, and instinctively knew to create it on a gorgeous, hand-carved bench gifted to me by Jorge, 16, a client who had a profound impact on me during my second year of graduate school. I had been selected to be a Pre-Doctoral Fellow at a prestigious program at the Rose F. Kennedy Children's Evaluation and Rehabilitation Center. It was a unique program in that as a therapist for predominately inner-city kids, I provided both academic remediation and intervention, as well as psychotherapy and counseling. Jorge had been diagnosed with dyslexia and anxiety and had failed out of traditional school. He struggled to read at a third-grade level, though he was relentlessly determined. Jorge arrived for his session one day carrying a stunning wooden bench with ornate details and unique carvings.

"It's for you. I've been working on it for few months in my woodshop class." Seeing my tears, Jorge continued. "Miss Kristy, nobody believes in me, not even my mother. To everyone else, I'm just messed up; but you make me feel like a real person who might actually get somewhere someday. Thank you for showing me it's possible."

Neither of us knew at the time that we were helping each other, and now his sacred gift would become my altar. I placed on it the elements I was shown in my journey: a clay bowl filled with water (water), a candle (fire), essential oils and herbs (ingredients of the earth), and a small rock (earth) that I found during a labyrinth walk. I also knew this altar was the perfect place for the spherical chrysocolla that seemed to find me as I sifted through crystal specimens while at Natalie's office the previous week. Natalie had commented, "I actually think you picked exactly what you need. It's a stone that emanates grace and connects the throat, heart, and root chakras to help you to trust your innate wisdom and to communicate it in a healthy way. It also helps to regulate the thyroid, adrenal glands, and illnesses of the throat."

Ceremony and Ritual

Excited for more opportunities for ceremony and ritual in my life and driven by the visions and dreams that continued to present themselves in my consciousness, I dove into studying and practicing Native American elements of ceremony and ritual. The practices felt like home to me, like my Grammie's Sunday dinners. The elders teach us that the simple acts of giving in a selfless manner, being humble, and living a prayerful life are core elements of every tribe. Nothing is rushed in these ceremonies. Everyone takes their time and every action and word spoken, and song sang, and dance danced is sacred. And ceremonies aren't reserved for special occasions; even commonplace activities such as preparing a meal is done with reverence—again, something that was part of my DNA.

One of the key elements of sacred Native American ceremony that resonates deeply with me is storytelling. The elders would share colorful tales with animals as main characters in order to make them relatable to even the youngest members of the tribe. These fables and tales were meant to teach, guide, and mentor. And storytellers considered their stories to be gifts—their offerings for each member of the tribe for celebration and healing. As I have always loved stories, I saw how valuable and healing writing had become for me. It was cathartic. Stories were a vital component of healing ceremonies as they tap into the universal connections between us all. It's been documented that stories, particularly those that were sung repeatedly, contribute to changes in neural pathways and activate mirror neurons responsible for empathy. For instance, indigenous cultures included a variety of storytelling rituals to help returning veterans reintegrate into society. The ceremonies were essentially medicine to help the veterans rewire their central nervous systems to process their traumatic experiences so they could acclimate into civilian culture.

I craved more experiential moments in which I could connect with ceremony. I attended healing circles, Shamanic retreats, and Native American festivals; and in every ceremonious gathering, I felt an intense desire to remember and retrieve the threads of a past that had since been forgotten. And with each piece remembered, I felt a sense of belonging to lands, to people, and to myself. I took time to visit the home of the 17th Century Wampanoag tribe on a plantation in southeastern Massachusetts. They were a group of hunters, fishermen, and farmers who held deep respect for the earth and all living things. They led minimalistic lives focused on ceremonies to honor Mother Earth for all her gifts through feasting, games, playing musical instruments, praying, and dancing. They cared for their souls, and of one another, by doing things that made them feel joyful and connected to the land. With that, they had everything they needed.

During a warrior goddess ceremony facilitated by an incredible shamanic healer by the name of Donna Brickwood, who I immediately recognized as a soul sister from another lifetime, I reconnected with the wild warrior parts of myself in nature. Through dancing and dueling with sacred sticks as swords in the forest, practicing wilderness scouting, archery, and shamanic journeying, a part of my soul was revived. Donna taught us to practice *wide angle vision*, rekindling our ability to sense the energies of the land and broadening our perspective on life inside and outside of the forest. Connecting with forgotten human survival skills that were at one time essential like tracking animals, locating water, and using land clues to find your way, was invigorating. As I rooted into the energy of the forest and of myself, and confidently aimed my bow and arrow as if I was born to hunt, I was transported to a time and place that I had been before and longed to return. The words I continuously heard were, *you belong* and *home.*

I felt that day what a sword means to a warrior: it's a tool to cut away all the things that we don't need anymore. Donna taught that we must battle the opponents inside of us, but those opponents aren't bad; they can be our allies as they teach us about the depths of ourselves. *Meet the attack, but don't be so quick to push it away.* As Donna's prophetic words infiltrated my consciousness as we sparred, I saw my own internal sparing happening as I was learning to excavate the false parts of myself, to hold them lovingly and deliberately and with gratitude seeing what they have taught me; and then patiently waiting for the moment to intentionally strike and release them. Our closing ceremony was a shamanic journey in which my guides placed a sword on my body and said, *You have been chosen. Accept the invitation. Heal yourself, and you heal all.* I then shapeshifted into a horse and spoke, *Give me back my power!*

These incredible experiences of immersing myself in ancestral wisdom taught me that each ordinary moment of each ordinary day is an opportunity for enlightenment in and of itself. My responsibility to truly show up in this world meant that every opportunity to sit and reverently observe my life with moment-to-moment awareness of the here and now was a powerful experience in cultivating a connection to this earth and my own innate wisdom. I learned how to read the energy all around me in any situation and trust my instincts to make decisions when navigating day-to-day life. Intentionally engaging with the world with presence and an open heart allowed me to discover the magic, peace, and wonder of life. The mundane tasks of daily living were rich with opportunity for ceremony: watching the leaves fall off the trees, cooking dinner, folding laundry, cleaning the house, watching my boys while they sleep. Some days, all I could see were the moments of darkness, the clouds, the ugliness. Those moments, too, had to be honored. This is what it meant to be fully and authentically alive.

Following these ceremonies, I reflected on how far I had come. Just a short decade prior, rituals meant compulsive habits of hand-washing, counting steps and sidewalk cracks, checking the stove and locks, lining up my pencils and pens, check-in phone calls every 10 minutes, and focusing on the number patterns on the clocks. Those habits were created and motivated by fear, and at one time in my life, they helped me to feel safe. I was now establishing healthy rituals motivated by love and trust and what was in alignment with my growth.

And I wanted to pass these practices and rituals on to my boys. By that time, Gianni who was now around six or seven, was having difficulty sleeping, as anxiety and fears were consuming him, particularly about death. As I celebrated my birthday that year, he crawled into my arms, and whimpered, "Mommy, I don't want you to get old and die and leave me alone without you." Another day while in the car driving home from school, amidst sniffles from the backseat I heard, "Mommy, one day I'll be an older man and you won't be alive anymore and what will I do? I don't want to be without you!"

I would have done anything to take Gianni's pain away, but I knew that this was all a part of his journey. By now I was learning firsthand that feeling emotions and sitting with discomfort is the only way to grow and evolve our souls. Our kids have the same need. Rather than distract him from his feelings, or try to take a positive spin on it, I leaned into him, hugged and kissed him, told him I loved him, and invited him to participate in ceremony with me. We sang, danced, drummed, walked mindfully in the woods, watched birds, and laid down on the bedding of grassy earth. Gianni called upon a wolf to help him with his pain. He said the wolf reminded him that he won't ever be alone; that the spirit of his pack is always with him in his heart if he can get quiet enough to find it. Ceremony helped Gianni to feel connected to something larger than himself, and to have faith in the universal order of things.

I continued to witness the profound benefits of consistent ceremonial practices in myself, my clients, and my children, including calmness and inner peace, less anxiety and fear, more experiences of joy and happiness, greater feelings of love for all beings and for self, more mindful and focused moments, greater introspection and self-awareness, feelings of belonging and community, and deeper gratitude. And most importantly, I was giving my children the greatest gift, which is that of my own growth and expansion of consciousness. In doing so, I offer them an invitation for their own evolution. In remembering my own roots, I was helping my children connect with theirs.

Spirituality was really as simple as falling in love with each moment, with one hand on your heart, and the other on the earth. Inspired by the primitive, unfettered, and minimalistic ways of the native peoples, I realized that the outer landscape of my life no longer matched what was on the inside. I had been living in a way that wasn't authentic, and yet I wasn't sure what to do to change it. I didn't know where I belonged— feeling as though I fit in more with those primal, earth-loving natives, than the cultured and conditioned woman who stared back at me in the mirror. My eyes had been opened to a different way of living that was both graceful and grateful, and incredibly familiar. Yet most people closest to me at the time were (same as I had been) so deeply entrenched in and seduced by the fast-paced, pressure-cooker, materialistic, race-to-nowhere lifestyle that they navigated using the roadmap of inherited and imprinted wounding and absorbed indoctrination. *How could they understand any of my experiences? Would there be anyone besides my teachers who I could share my insights with?* I felt more like a stranger in a foreign land. I was beginning to feel somewhat alienated by friends who balked at what they considered to be my "woo-woo beliefs" and "earthy-crunchy-granola" practices.

Even Dominick, who had always supported my ideas, was now making sarcastic comments, or rolling an eye when I attempted to share stories, which I did in an effort to create a bridge between our increasingly separate worlds. Ironically, whereas Dominick was once attracted to me for my creativity and compassionate ways, he now seemed to only notice or care about my housekeeping skills that kept me tethered to him. And yet no matter how hard I tried, I could no longer find fulfillment in scrubbing toilet bowls, packing school lunches, and sitting in front of computer screens. And despite having all the material possessions I could want, and more, the feelings of unrest inside of me were growing. Like wild animals who are captured and caged, I was depressed, afraid, angry, irritable, agitated, sick, and now completely preoccupied with planning my escape.

I wanted to run free, reclaiming my true nature—the wild woman inside of me who is curious, not fearful; awake, alert, and aware, not distracted; adventurous, passionate, and vibrant, not dull; open, graceful, and calm, not stressed or frenetic. Whereas life inside the cage had programmed me to believe that I was flawed and fractionated, I was now beginning to see glimpses of an alternate reality in which I was physically, mentally, and spiritually complete.

But how could I accomplish this in a culture determined to keep me enslaved?

As I meditated through this wave of fear and insecurity, I heard a voice say, *Go inside.* So I journeyed. A black panther and an older woman greeted me and brought me back to a place out West that I had been seeing in some journeys for quite a while. When we arrived, I climbed to the top of a mountain. I felt the sun baking my skin as I sat at the top looking out at the horizon. I sang, chanted, danced, and then sat in stillness. I repeated words that initially I couldn't make out. The woman told me to say the words louder, so I could hear them. The panther began to recite them along with me:

"Mother Earth grant me the ability to find appreciation, fascination, and awe with the little things within the larger works of beauty you have created. Help me to align with the elements of earth, to live in accordance with the seasons, and to trust in the natural order of things. In doing so, Mother Earth, I will live in communion with nature, with my ancestors, and light the way for future generations. I will remember my way home."

Part Two

Rekindling My Instincts

The Heroine horse, who once led an illusory life propelled by her mind, runs out of the gate on a soul-searching quest guided only by her heart.

Though she grieves the loss of the life she left behind, she is determined to reclaim the lost parts of herself in order to be whole again. As she enters unknown realms and confronts adversaries and challenges, she meets guides who mentor her through the many trials that will test her skills, threaten her resolve, and try to jeopardize her freedom.

Will she succumb to domestication, or will she engender the courage to blaze her own trail and inspire others to do the same?

Labor Pains

*I*t was time to answer the howling cries of my imprisoned soul that was dying for release and rebirth into the wild world of which it had only seen glimpses. It was time to bust through the gates to explore the life that was once known but had since been forgotten. What I was seeking was rebellion; and ironically, it was my own children who helped me to give my soul's craving a name.

One late fall morning, after dropping my kids at school following a chaotic exchange in which Antonio and I argued over his decision to "forget" to attend his tutoring class at school the day prior, while Gianni forcefully asserted that he would not be wearing a jacket to school, I exploded like a powder keg as we frantically rushed to get out the door. I burst into tears and a tirade of self-deprecation for behaving in ways which, by now, well into my journey, seemed to be inexcusable. Unable to see through tears, I pulled over at a quaint corner marketplace with a big country star on the exterior of the rustic brown shack, with stunningly vibrant foliage and sprawling horse farms in the background. It was a bucolic spot for my pity party.

After finally exhaling, I spotted the worn chalkboard sign staked into the ground that read: *What stirs us up, wakes us up.* As I stared at the sketch of a steaming hot cup of coffee with a stirrer sticking out of the top, this message was loud and clear, and it had nothing to do with caffeine.

I was now painfully aware that what stirred me up in parenting my children was actually a critical part of my own awakening. When my boys' behaviors triggered a reaction in me, it was showing me where there was still inner work to do—wounds to heal, patterns to erase, and truths to unveil. I feared my boys' intense emotional expressions because I had never learned how to feel safe with my own. They were seeking autonomy; and the truth is that I was, too.

In my mindful parenting workshops, I had been teaching parents that if we pay attention with nonjudgmental awareness to every moment, not only can we cultivate deep appreciation for and understanding of our children, but we will see that our children reveal the depths of our wounds, our greatest fears, our unspoken truths, the limits of our patience, and our most venomous angers—all of the patterns that shape who we are as parents. That country store sign was a reminder that my own rebirth was not only a gift to myself, but it was a gift for my children!

Despite what society tells us, and what we read in the *What to Expect When You're Expecting* books, pregnancy and childbirth are not just about the baby. There is a parallel processing happening. For the first time, I now understood why birthing my babies into this world turned my life upside down. As a woman, a creatrix, my body is a book that holds the sacred stories of all the resiliency and trauma that came before me. Every inherited and personal physical, energetic, and spiritual interaction with the vast universe shaped my being and created the habitual patterns by which I learned to navigate my life. And If I wasn't conscious—awake, alert, aware enough to confront them, I would inevitably pass all this conditioning on to my babies.

Women are reborn through the birthing and parenting experiences. These are times of renewal and transformation during which there are profound changes in all dimensions of life. Physiological changes of pregnancy and childbirth literally alter the molecular structure of the mother's cells and DNA. Psychological changes of pregnancy and childbirth bring with it an array of emotional and psychological processes. It's a spiritual change as one's higher self is communicating the need to heal and grow. I now realized that the day that each of my babies came into the world, another incarnation of myself was born, too.

Both mother and baby are fledglings in what is essentially a whole new world; and the same way that a baby must learn how to crawl before he can walk, mothers must do the same. Both baby and mamma are pushed out of that comfortable and secure womb and expelled into a world of unknowns; a process that can be painful and terrifying. Both baby and mamma cry. Both baby and mamma open their eyes for the first time and see a new world before them; a world that is filled with possibilities and hope, and also potential threat and dangers, and each new step must be learned. They fall, they get back up, they fall again, through life. As difficult as this new world can be at times, there is no going back to the safety of the womb. Both will have to learn how to stand on their own by trusting that they have everything they need right within themselves.

Parenting the souls who chose to come into this life through us, is actually about resolving our own issues while actively raising our child and mentoring this other human being in life. It's not about getting it right and being the perfect parent. It's about personal evolution. How healthy and evolved we are as women, is what gets engendered to our children. It's not what you say to your children, rather it's what you model for them and the values you demonstrate. We can only take our kids as far as we have gone, or are willing to go, ourselves.

It has been said that our children are our greatest teachers. With childbirth, a woman is ushering her greatest teacher into the world—a teacher who chose you as his student for the purpose of giving your soul experiences that it needed to evolve.

What if we have been thinking about the post-partum period all wrong? It lasts and persists because it's when the mother begins her growth process. What if instead of *post-partum depression*, it's really *post-partum transformation*?

Reflecting on the experiences of birthing both of my children into the world, I never could have been prepared for the profound changes that were to take place in my life. Stretch marks, cellulite, and sagging boobs were simply physical manifestations of a much deeper change that was percolating under the surface that no amount of belly butter can reach.

Parenting opens us up, exposes every facet of who we are, who we once were, and who we will be. Alexandra Sacks, a reproductive psychiatrist coined the phrase "*matrescence*" as the period of time after a woman births a baby into the world that is similar hormonally and developmentally to adolescence, a time we all remember to be marked by dramatic emotional, physical, and psychological changes that carry great transformational capacity. This is a natural process for all women, and yet it is often silenced by shame or misdiagnosed as postpartum depression. Postnatal physical and psychological care for moms remains one of the most underdiscussed and understudied issues in medicine.

Like so many women who I had spoken with inside and outside of my office walls, I didn't feel happy or whole like I had expected that I would or should, and it consumed me with guilt. And getting condescendingly slapped in the face with a diagnosis of post-partum blues only confirms the belief that something is wrong with us. Like all the women who I met, and all the women who Sacks studied, I spent a long time stuck in a fantasy about what motherhood was supposed to be; and when we compared ourselves to the fantasy, we fell short, and instead felt broken, inadequate, shameful, and sometimes even suicidal.

Ambivalence is a natural part of the transformation from woman to mother. To believe that birthing a human into the world wouldn't profoundly change the inner as well as outer landscape of a woman's life is absurd! Yet popular culture made me, like millions of other women, believe I was crazy. I can remember when the boys were babies, standing in puddles of vomit with week-old dirty hair, wearing the same moo-moo for days, nursing on demand, trying to cook dinner, keep up with laundry, provide adequate amounts of tummy time with Baby Mozart tunes playing on repeat, not knowing the day of the week or my own address. Not to mention that I was doing all of this while still trying to grow my first "baby" which was my business. Like any other mother of multiples, we always feel guilty if we are giving one kid more attention than the others. Sometimes my business became the classic "middle child." Antonio was the first born and so he was special because he wore the crown, and Gianni was the baby so I had to fuss over him, and the middle child, well, it was always just there, dependable and loyal, the peacekeeper, but sometimes invisible and forgotten about. Now, it's not that I ever forgot to go to work or neglected my business per se, but I couldn't always give it the attention that I wanted to, that it deserved, because my time had to be divided. And I felt incredibly guilty about that. And then if I spent time focused on the business, I felt like I was neglecting my other kids. I felt like a failure, constantly.

Mothers—whether stay-at-home moms or moms who also work outside of the home, are always barraged with mixed messages about their responsibilities. *Stay home with your baby as long as you can, but get back to work immediately; wake up early to get the house clean before work, but sleep when the baby sleeps; breastfeed for as long as you can, pump at work, but don't let "them" think you need any special treatment; be present for your kids and never miss a school event, but don't ask for too much time off from work; be the work hustler, the home manager, the kids' chauffer, the Easter Bunny and Santa Claus and the Tooth Fairy, the Pinterest crafter, the PTA president, the soccer mom, oh and don't forget the sexy wife.*

And all this pressure makes it almost impossible to derive any joy and satisfaction from parenting! What's more is that in today's society, women are parenting alone. Long gone are the days of women mothering with the collective wisdom of generations before them or with the close support of other women friends, family, and communities. Our ancestors birthed and raised babies surrounded by other tribeswomen. Biologically, we are not programmed to do it alone; yet we are so estranged from our roots that we try to function as isolated beings, and all this creates is frustration, hopelessness, and helplessness. We are disenfranchised by our own two hands.

Here I was, in my mid- to late-thirties, incessantly striving to prove myself in all the roles in my life, with the chatter of a starving soul in the backdrop, and dreams and visions of a time and place that felt like home, and now realizing that I had embarked on a vision quest to rediscover my roots and rekindle the essence of my being. I was beginning to stretch beyond my comfort zone to try new things, to become autonomous, independent, and create my own identity. Sounds like adolescence to me! I wanted to dress up more; at the very least, trading my maternity and post-partum nursing bras and girdle c-section panties, to matching bras and underwear. And not cotton. I wanted lace! I didn't want to wear the "soccer mom uniform." I wanted to look . . . dare I say it . . . sexy!

Having always been the good girl and playing by the rules and playing it safe, I never dared to explore the limits of myself. I never pushed the edge or took risks. And yet now I wanted to do all those things, like a teenager who was kept under tight lock and key for far too long. I wanted to go to concerts, dance with my friends, go out for drinks, and have spa weekends with my girlfriends. I wanted to sit and talk under the stars with new friends and have my soul set on fire by these new interactions. I wanted to have fun! Much like an adolescent, I wanted to connect with others who were unabashedly dealing with their own awkward becoming.

And I was done making small talk with people. I could no longer handle the fake niceties that we perform for the sake of politeness. I wanted to connect with people who had depth; individuals who were real and capable of being raw and vulnerable in my presence. I wanted the conversations to be real and raw, like the ones I used to have with Missy, my diary.

And I wanted to balance those times with time alone, in silence, to hear my own thoughts and connect with my own heart now that I had reclaimed its voice. I didn't want to spend as much time with Dominick. I had spent so much of my life giving to him and to the relationship; now I wanted this to be my time. Dominick didn't understand the changes. "Kristy, I don't know who you are anymore." Damn right I'm different! I don't want to be that same girl anymore! It was an ironic parallel process between me and my kids; they were trying out different versions of themselves, feeling their oats, and I was too. Much like my boys resisting the force to do homework, clean their rooms, and wear a bowtie to Easter dinner, I didn't want to hear about the mortgage payments and home repairs. I didn't want to feel bogged down by responsibility. I didn't want to be told what to do or how to think or what to say or how to feel. After years of being the responsible one who held it all together, I wanted to be light and free. Spontaneous. Unpredictable. Unexpected. WILD!

So many similar-aged women who I've talked with, both inside the walls of my office and elsewhere, all share a similar story. They were tired of "just" being moms and wives and felt that their lives had a larger purpose. They were receiving signs and hearing whispers from within, but they didn't understand what it was. And oddly enough, although most of us complained about the trials and tribulations of parenting, as our kids advanced in age there came with it more sadness knowing that we were finished having children. There was a mourning process that I felt strongly in my heart, a pain that would often stop me dead in my tracks when I least expected it. I would never again feel the sensation of a baby growing inside of me. I would never again experience nursing a baby. I would never again get to hold and protect my boys so tightly.

Every now and again, I'd hear a client or friend mention the words *midlife crisis,* and it got me thinking. I remembered the words of Brene Brown who said that midlife is not a *crisis,* it's an *unraveling.* It's a time in which we start to feel the pull towards the life we want to live, the life we were meant to live, while letting go of the life that we thought we were expected to live. It's a time to discover and embrace who we truly are.

Examining the process of raising my own children shed light on the way in which I was parented, and on parenting in general; and watching their development elucidated my own journey. Right out of the gate, our parents domesticate us as their parents did, and the parents before them did. We are taught to suppress the very things that have made us most human—primal instincts, innate wisdom and intuition, presence and moment to moment awareness, and unbounded joy and curiosity. Our natural essence is tamed, or worse, shut down. Like a wild animal who is captured and civilized, the soul will always long to be free.

Now I was the one unraveling, going from tightly wound and terrorized, to free and courageous. My midlife rebirth was a rewilding. The more I connected with my intuition, the more I could hear her guidance like an internal compass telling me which way to go. I was finally learning to listen at all costs, even if it meant making choices that nobody else understood. It wasn't my job to translate my life into a meaningful story for anyone else's benefit; my job was just to live fearlessly and unapologetically.

I reflected on the advice I had given to clients for so long, the idea of taking the leap and having faith that the parachute would appear; guiding people towards pulling themselves out of the "not this" situations without knowing with certainty if there was a better alternative in sight. Like my client Claudia, a mom of a teenaged son about to go off to college, a high-profile Wall Street banker who kept hearing the call of "not this" for years about her seven-figure job. She felt awful at her job; she knew it was causing her tremendous stress that took a toll on her health. She was working crazy hours and never saw her son or her husband, and she was miserable. And yet she went to work, day in and day out, arriving in her huge corner office with window views of the Manhattan skyline and her secretary handing her hot coffee. Yet she heard loud and clear from within, *Not this.*

Ironically, around the same time, I, too, was working round the clock, 80 hours per week conducting neuropsychological evaluations for children, seeing clients for therapy and coaching, all while trying to be a present mother. I began noticing intense feelings of anxiety with every new testing referral, paired with same inner shouting of *Not this.* Yet aside from testing being the most lucrative part of my business, it was also an aspect of my work that earned me a stellar reputation in my field. I knew it was time to let it go, but like Claudia, I didn't feel *ready*.

By this point, I knew that not feeling *ready* almost always happens in response to considering doing something that brings us closer and closer to our most authentic selves. It feels insanely risky to contemplate radical changes, as our nervous systems cajole us into seeking sameness to protect us from the potential dangers of uncertainty. Rewilded animals are always frightened initially until the conditioning wears off. But the time comes when we must get honest with ourselves when the risk of staying stuck where we no longer belong far exceeds the risk of changing. As I listened to myself advise Claudia, against the backdrop of Dr. Blum's words in my head, *You can do what you love, but you have to do it differently,* I knew I had to pivot.

Abraham Hicks once explained pivoting as shifting our focus to thinking about what we *do want,* and not what we *don't want.* Sounds pretty simple, almost to the point of it being silly, but science demonstrates that it's actually quite efficacious. Just as Claudia took the leap, quit her job, and pursued her dream of being an artist, I surrendered to the voice of my own intuitive heart by letting one aspect of my business die so a new one could be born.

In the words of Osho, "One birth has been given to you by your parents, the other birth is waiting. It has to be given to you by yourself." Understanding and embracing the midlife experience as a rebirth was liberating; but I knew that much like thriving children, there would certainly be growing pains. I had to be ready to have my life turned upside down, to have everything that I thought I knew be questioned. To strip away the crutches that I relied upon to keep me detached, dissociated, and disillusioned. To let the old version of me die in order to breathe life into my true self. I knew now that what was lost was my wild, fiery, untamed spirit and that it was fear that stole her dancing shoes.

Until now.

Having been entrapped in lifelong conditioning that equated strenuous, effortful work to worth, I had traded all my creative childhood passions— playing guitar and piano, singing, painting, writing, dancing, and being with animals—for more serious academic endeavors that checked all the boxes on society's goals. Yet I had been burnt out and unfulfilled for far too long. Once guided by the notion that my life was only as successful as it appeared to others, I now recognized that true success was an inside job. It was about creating a life that felt so real and so true, motivated only by the desires of my own soul and the unwavering belief that I deserved to live a life that brought me joy. Now I was inspired to explore again; to courageously leave my comfort zone and start over at the bottom, stripped of habituation, humbled by limited knowledge, and often challenged by failure. Yet my newly recovering primitive state was authentic, rooted in something bigger than me, and it reignited my essence as a woman.

And now my radical rebellion was energized by the profound epiphany that reconnecting with the essence of womanhood is vital for motherhood. Rebirthing ourselves as wild women is how we can parent our children from a place of true unconditional love. When I am aligned with my truth, connected to my intuition, and empowered in my inherent sovereignty, I am imbued with instinctual and ancestral wisdom necessary to allow my children to be themselves, completely. I love them, heal them, support them from a place of love and trust in who I am as their mother, and who they are as the children who chose to come through me.

When my boys see my natural, messy, magical, creative, witchy, and genuine humanness, they recognize that they too have permission to be themselves. Now more than ever, I want my boys to challenge what is fed to them, to ask questions with an open mind and heart, and to rebel against anything that threatens to control and stifle their life force. I want my children to experience the uninhibited joy and ecstasy that comes with the fullness of their souls' expression. And I cannot teach this to my boys with words alone. I must embody this each and every day. They must witness my rewilding in order to feel confident in theirs. My healing journey is my greatest act of rebellion, and my greatest gift to my children.

First Steps

"Kristy, come to my Nia class."

I was confused by these words spoken by a colleague and friend Eve who I happened to run into at the gas station after a yoga session one day. During conversation after hearing about my healing journey thus far, Eve took my hand in hers, looked into my eyes, and said, "There is a class this Friday morning at 9:30am. Please come."

Although I knew nothing about this thing called Nia, her words carried so much resonance and I felt them deeply in my heart. Friday morning arrived and I threw on whatever yoga pants still fit my inflamed body. I was skeptical as I hesitatingly opened the door of the small strip-mall studio. As Eve offered me an introductory speech, I was so nervous that I could only make sense of a word or two here and there: "integrating mind, body, and spirit," "listen to your body to find its way," "exploration and fun," "Yoga, Martial Arts, Feldenkrais, dance." Then I heard the words, "Let's step in." Beautiful melodies flooded the room and I drifted away, and the rest of the world disappeared.

My body glided, moved, danced, punched, kicked, swayed, pulsed. My heart expanded. My mind vacillated between relaxed and focused. Then suddenly I was sobbing as I soared through the room like a bird. The class ended. I was sitting in the middle of everyone on the floor. Everyone congratulated me on my first class. I felt exhilarated, cracked open, high, confident, and light. I felt seen.

Following that life-changing class, I found myself dancing around the house every chance I got, the same way that I used to when I was a free-spirited little girl. As the weeks progressed, I couldn't believe how much joy I felt in my body, and in life! Dancing felt like the answer to the howling of my soul in desperation for release from captivity. Movement was setting me free.

The glossy, golden wooden floors of the Fred Astaire Dance Studio will forever be remembered as the place where Allegra Topanga took her first steps. Nia taught me that healing is living. Allegra showed me that fear isn't the enemy; paralysis is.

Dancing was opening me up to parts of myself that had been hidden for so long. Relating to my body and all that it housed changed my relationship with myself, and with others especially my children. I recognized that in relating to my body differently, I was disrupting the transmission of imprinted patterns of trauma to make space for the birth of a legacy of resiliency that I would pass on to all those who came after me.

As I danced, I visualized myself as Allegra Topanga twirling, spiraling, flying, and gliding through the room. Other times I became a primitive animal—stealthily crawling, unruly undulating, and wildly thrashing. I was ushered back to the purest time that I recall in this lifetime; a time when my unbridled spirit wisped through life as frivolously as my strawberry blonde locks waved in the wind as I spun around while singing songs or strumming my Mickey Mouse guitar. It was pure soul, magical connection, and uninhibited freedom each and every time. This bliss was contagious and meant to be shared with the world, so I knew it was time for me to become a practitioner.

The joy and release that I experienced from dancing was nothing short of life-changing, and I knew I needed to bring this practice to others. My heart told me it was time to pursue professional training to become a certified Nia practitioner. The training involves five levels organized according to the model of Martial arts, with an advancing journey of self-exploration from White Belt to Second Degree Black Belt to develop skills in teaching holistic movement practices

Nia (which stands for Neuromuscular Integrative Action) is a unique fusion of Yoga, Martial Arts (including Tai Chi, Tae Kwon Do, Karate, Aikido), Healing Arts (Alexander Technique and Feldenkrais Method), modern and jazz dance, and spiritual self-healing. Through beautiful rhythmic moves to a variety of music, vocalizations and visualizations, and interpersonal support and connections, Nia is an exhilarating journey of following the body's innate wisdom. Each dance was a process of working out and working in—physically and emotionally harmonizing and synchronizing the mind and body. Nia was teaching me how to witness all sensation with beginner's mind, and instead of reacting in preconceived ways, I pause, notice, reflect, and then respond with curiosity, openness, and unconditional love. I was becoming physically fit, mentally strong, and spiritually aware.

For two years prior to finding Nia, my relationship to movement involved flipping monster truck tires, burpees, 20 laps around the CrossFit gym parking lot, and dropping F-bombs as fast as I was dropping squats. It was the classic "no pain, no gain" mentality driven by a desire to achieve the type of body that I thought I was supposed to have. When I got tired and slowed down, the coach motivated me by calling me "slacker" and "a loser." I left the gym sore, exhausted, palpitating heart, puking in the parking lot, and drained for days. I berated my body for its fatigue, consumed workout accelerators and recovery drinks, and repeated mantras such as "Keep your goals high and your squats low." Sounds badass, but the only thing that happened was my ass hurt bad!

I was now learning to move with minimal effort and maximal efficiency. Like a black panther who elegantly and skillfully saunters around showing her prowess, when the body is given permission to move in the absence of struggle and strain, strength and ease are the natural consequences. I also became aware of how the body always aims for balance. A healthy body is balanced in yin and yang energies. Yin energy is the feminine, "soft" inward receiving energy reflected in smooth, graceful, melodic and slower movements. Yang energy is the male "harder" energy that is outward directed and penetrating. It's an energy that is always moving, giving, striving, doing; it is intense, explosive, fast-paced, aggressive, and larger in quality.

I was learning how to relate to my body as an intricate holistic portal infused with energy from my mind, spirit, and emotions; a vessel that housed so much more than organs, flesh, and blood. Nia was teaching me how to use every muscle, joint and tissue in the body for feedback and how to tap in to the energetic bodies. Practicing Nia was helping me to cultivate the ability to find safety in exploring the inherent neutrality of moment-to-moment sensation with openness and curiosity, instead of fear, so that I could be present and responsive instead of reactive in any situation. I was learning how to stay in my body when things got uncomfortable. And the practice emboldened me with its stance on personal choice such that I could decide the intensity, the duration, and the quality of my movements and actions. This was profoundly empowering and healing because of the many times in my life when I didn't have a choice.

That White Belt training also offered me an invitation to consider what I was trying to digest that my body and spirit did not trust. As I danced with these questions, I uncovered so much stuck energy that had been hiding out for years in my solar plexus—the energy center associated with self-confidence and personal power. My belly, that for so long literally looked like I was eight months pregnant was distended, round, full, swollen, and hard. It was full of so much energy that wasn't mine. More memories flooded me and suddenly it became clear to why I couldn't digest the food that I ate. When I created space to ask my heart what it needed to feel love, I heard *forgiveness*.

On day two of White Belt training, standing in stillness in the dark studio and the sounds of 47th Street echoing through the walls, I closed my eyes to access a communication channel with my pelvis. The dance floor became our laboratory to practice somatic skills for connecting to the physical sensations in the body and listening to the body with openness, curiosity and focused awareness absent of judgement. As we were guided to visualize the pelvis as a bowl, a sacred container of energy, I had a realization that although I thought I had always moved this area of my body when I danced, or walked, or had sex, I was really just going through the motions. It was all surface level movement. I had shut down that part of my body. The outside world faded away as I remained with my eyes closed envisioning my pelvic bone structure. Instead of an expansive pelvic bowl, mine looked closed and small and tucked away, like a petrified wooden box.

As my hands traced my pelvic area, I could feel the ossification. Suddenly, memories consumed me:

The *petrified* child who in first grade clung to her mother's leg at school drop-off.

The *petrified* child who was forced to be touched against her will.

The *petrified* child who stood outside of a crack den and watched her father be attacked.

The *petrified* teenager who just wanted to fit in.

The *petrified* mamma who almost lost her baby.

The *petrified* pelvis that tilted and curved, blocking my baby from entering the birth canal.

I melted into the floor, rotating my pelvis in circular motions, sobbing uncontrollably. I flashed back to the delivery room years earlier. Not dilating, Antonio pushing down and me not allowing him to descend. The realization hit me so hard that it took my breath away: the reason my body couldn't deliver my baby naturally was because it was just trying to protect me. Now I understood Dr. Shaw's words. My body saw the pregnancy as yet another threat, so my pelvis put up a wall. It would not create space. My body was not the enemy. It didn't fail me at all. It had only been trying to save me! As the beautiful women in my training group held space for me, I experienced a huge release, my pelvic bowl opening, the ossification cracking.

The next day, I felt lighter, free, open, safe; and full of love, gratitude and appreciation for my body. The trapped energy that had been stuck in my body was brought to the surface and eradicated. That is truly what is meant by "processing" and "releasing" a traumatic event. Regulating our autonomic nervous systems in this way through such practices as dance, gets us out of survival mode so that we can thrive.

In my studies of somatic healing for trauma, I recalled Bessel van der Kolk saying that people remember trauma not as a language-based story but as a collection of sensations. He emphasized that science has proven that bodywork such as dance therapy is more effective for PTSD and all the associated emotional and physical consequences of trauma than any other therapy or pharmaceutical drug ever investigated. And now I knew why!

The more I danced, I was so intrigued by the many ways I could connect with my body thereby tuning in not only to my own memories, but also to the rich ancestral threads that connected me with the generations before me. Our bodies hold onto every experience because they are first felt as a sensation. Epigenetics shows us that nerve impulses are messengers between cells that have been encoded with ancestral patterning. Our bodies are merely storage vessels for energetic frequencies corresponding to every experience, emotion, thought, ancestral history; as well as the stories of other souls with whom we make connections. Everyone is a teacher for us, so their story influences ours, and ours influences theirs. And when we make space for our bodies to move with these stories, we allow memories to emerge from deep within our cells. In this way, our bodies are our greatest sources of history, and our bodies have the capacity to heal themselves.

Moving to Heal

As I shifted my focus from feeling *better* to just feeling *everything*, my body finally had permission to dance the story that it had been carrying for so long, but this was overwhelming at times. Feeling good doesn't always immediately *feel good*. Nevertheless, I had fallen so deeply in love with Nia that I continued to immerse myself in these practices that were instrumental in uncovering my truth and recovering my instincts. Through movement, I was discovering the audacity to take risks and trust myself. Like making the decision to travel to a Nia training that was four hours away from my home. To anyone else, a road trip such as this wouldn't seem like a big deal. But for me, it represented a huge developmental milestone. At the age of 40, I would be traveling somewhere alone for the first time in my life. Yes, you read correctly. Prior to that point I had only ever traveled anywhere with someone else, almost always being Dominick. I was ready to break this pattern.

Taking that risk led to so many beautiful epiphanies about my life that I never before recognized. For example, I had never before contemplated my personal philosophy on healing. It was an interesting question for me, having been consumed with sickness for so long. In order for me to contemplate health, I had to consider what it meant for me to be "not sick." I inhaled and exhaled, conscious of my breath, my life force, and visualized with ease a healthy version of me. What I saw was a woman who lives with intention and grace; has an intimate connection with mind, body, spirit; creates her own life guided by the unshakable knowing of her instincts and intuition; is aligned with the elements and nature; is excited by change; dances ecstatically accessing otherworldly realms of existence; makes time for rest and recovery; and accepts herself lovingly while freely speaking her truth at all costs. I saw Allegra Topanga.

As I lay on the bamboo floors of that Syracuse studio envisioning myself as a healthy self-healing woman, it occurred to me that I had spent the last decade "wound shopping." Searching for the right symptoms and diagnosis and something more to work on and fix became yet another addiction. There is a fine line between introspection and creating problems that don't really exist or need to exist, and for me, that lined blurred really quickly. Identifying with problems and choosing to be a suffering victim was ironically a pattern that made me feel safe. I held on so tightly to pain because it was the remaining link tethering me to all that I was afraid to lose. So, my choices involved continuously putting myself in situations where I would over-give to the point of burnout, while feeling extorted in the process, causing me to feel sick which only caused me to try to do more, creating a cataclysmic cycle of pain, misery, and martyrdom. Yet I still held on tightly. But I realized now that white knuckling this ride was getting me nowhere fast.

I thought about the "backwards law" that philosopher Alan Watts spoke of. It states that the more you desperately and incessantly seek feeling "better," the sicker you will feel, as pursuing anything only reinforces the belief that you lack it in the first place. Wanting positive experiences is a negative experience, while acceptance of negative experiences is actually a positive experience. It seems twisted but I was discovering the truth of this.

I also reflected on how I had spent years as a master complainer. Complaining is draining energetically; and created a negative cesspool that toxically infiltrated everyone around me. Dominick felt it and always said, "All you do is complain." Complaining was like incessantly picking at a scab and then wondering why the wound wasn't healing. I had also become an incredibly self-absorbed martyr, investing all of my energy and efforts on my illness, my trauma, my pain, crying the "poor me" story. And with each tantrum I was sucking the life out of the people I loved. And what I received from them wasn't love; it was placation intended to shut down my tantrums. But external validation became a drug that I couldn't live without.

In those contemplative moments I also reflected on the stories that I held about pleasure. I had to be honest and admit that in most areas of my life, being bogged down with obligations, I was tolerating a great deal and not actually deriving any pleasure from the experiences. Just "tolerating" life depletes our energy sources because it creates an internal conflict between what we desire and what we want to reject. On the dance floor that weekend I asked myself: *What if I chose pleasure instead of pain?* And I was seeing now that I had the power to create the conditions of my life.

Another aha moment emerged. I realized I had still been dealing with addiction; except now it wasn't to alcohol, sugar, or people-pleasing. I was addicted to my personal and spiritual development, and to healing. I had become so immersed in my rebirth, in healing trauma, breaking patterns, rewiring my brain and body, unlearning and unbecoming, rebelling against dependency, fiercely erecting boundaries; and while all of this was necessary on my journey back home to myself, it was exhausting. Taking blame for things that weren't my fault, under the glory of "See, I am doing my work. I can call myself out on my shit, this is evolution." Seeking new things within me to work on, seeking new patterns to break. Seeking new problems to fix. Seeking something else to make wrong about myself that I could attribute to trauma, and then get high off of trying to heal it. And all that did was take me out of living in the moment. *What's the point of all the work?*

On an energetic level, as a seeker, I was only manifesting the power of destruction. Consumed with knocking down the old paradigms left me with no energy to build anything new. Scrutinizing every action, feeling, belief, and behavior as if on trial for over two decades of time left me stuck within the confines of my mind, imprisoned by a web of overthinking and overanalyzing, devoid of all feeling other than immense exhaustion and burn out. It had become grueling. When I was so busy seeking, I was sending energy out, leaving no space to receive. The constant motion of doing created so much noise that I couldn't allow spirit to come through me. I knew now that as a healer I needed to be a hallow bone through which spirit could freely be channeled at any given moment. Yet my incessant striving created resistance to the present moment. I was forgetting that I am already calm, peaceful, and love. I had been wasting time seeking that which I already was. I was so done doing the work and I had to face the music—my suffering was all self-created. I just need to let myself out of the cage so that I could live!

On the final day of training, we had a "test" of sorts in which we were to take one of the 52 moves of Nia and create a routine with it to teach to a partner with whom we were paired. Still feeling insecure in my Nia teaching skills, and in my body, I was nervous and intimidated, and it didn't help that I was paired with Casey Bernstein, one of the Nia Technique's master trainers.

Casey is a vivacious and vibrant woman whose smile was as bright as her orange and yellow bellbottoms. She exuded confidence, playfulness, sensuality, and grace. *What in the world was she doing partnered with the likes of me?* When it came time to begin, she taught me a move and we had to volley back and forth between us teaching each other a move. When it was my turn, I immediately froze. I felt my face flushed and every sweat gland in my body firing. I laughed nervously, tried to make a joke to distract from the situation, and ended up tripping over my own two feet! I picked myself back up and tried my best to compose myself. As I began again, I started asking questions about the moves and about theories about why they worked, and I laughed nervously and made jokes in between. Casey, who had been facing me, leaned in, took my hands in hers, looked into my eyes, and said, "Kristy, shhh, stop talking! Just listen. Close your eyes, take a breath. Feel into your body. Feel into your heart. Feel the vibration of the music and let your heart and your feet take the reins. All you have to do is listen."

I closed my eyes, and as I inhaled and exhaled, I put my left hand on my heart and my right hand on my belly. I shifted my focus of awareness to my feet, then to my legs, to my arms, my hands, my back, my chest, my neck, my head. As I became embodied, something shifted and although my critical brain was still calling me a clumsy fuck, the volume became lower and lower until eventually all I was able to hear was the voice of my intuition, and all I could feel was the intense rhythmic connection between the pulse of my heart, the beat of the music, and the rawness of my instincts that moved through my body joyfully and wildly. In that moment of surrendering the heavy armor that had muted and drained my energy for decades, I found a peaceful pleasurable flow and an unextinguishable fire that would ignite my heart and soul.

Where the Wild Things Are

Moving my body primally and instinctually as an animal inspired me to consider how I might rewild other aspects of my life. Years ago, our ancestors spent their days rising with the sun, hunting under the light of the sun, eating their harvest, then fasting, and retiring to sleep with the sunset. They didn't rely on clocks, calendars, or to-do lists. They listened to their intuition and the voice of nature. Our human bodies have been created and designed to live in a harmonious relationship with nature's cycles. For instance, women's menstrual cycles are in sync with the moon cycles every 28 days. We also have a circadian rhythm—a 24-hour cycle that corresponds to light and dark, and the closer that we align our daily life with the rising and setting of the sun, the healthier we will be.

Today, humans are the only beings on this planet that do not live according to the natural cycles. We are experiencing "evolutionary mismatch"— meaning that the demands of our modern lifestyle are at odds with our inherent genetic programming. This is precisely why so many of us feel completely disoriented, disconnected, and devoid of a purpose.

During the day when we should be outdoors getting physical exercise in sunlight, we are indoors sitting at a desk for eight to 10 hours per day. We stay up late at night staring at computer screens in brightly artificially lit rooms. We sleep erratically, eat high carbohydrate foods that are processed in factories and carry a shelf life of 20 years, are exposed to a variety of air pollutants, use hormone-disrupting products containing known carcinogens, and use birth control to shut down our natural menstrual cycles.

All of these cultivated practices create fertile ground for illness, including viruses and bacterial infections, imbalanced hormones, thyroid and metabolic issues, adrenal fatigue, gut dysbiosis, depression, anxiety, obesity, early-onset dementia, infertility, and more. It is estimated that 88% of people are metabolically unhealthy!

I was learning firsthand that one of the most profound changes that we can make to influence our health is to live according to the natural cycles and flow of the seasons. Winter, the element of water, is a time to slow down, bunker down, hibernate, to be in stillness. Spring, the element of wood, is a time of new beginnings—we manifest the seeds that were planted during the winter hibernation. This is the time to start new things and manifest the intentions. Summer is a time of fire. Now in full bloom, it's the time to stand out and express your gifts. Fall, the element of metal, is the time of letting go, releasing some of the fire, preparing for hibernation of winter.

To continue reconnecting with my roots and sharpening my instincts, I knew I had to restore my natural rhythms. I began to prioritize aligning myself with the natural order of things, which really meant considering my most basic needs. I adjusted my sleep/wake cycle to be more in sync with the sunrise and sunset, I made a point to get outside in the middle of the day for natural vitamin D infusions from the sun and electromagnetic field, which is the source of our cells' mitochondrial coding, and I shifted my nutritional lifestyle to include more protein and healthy fats as they are the building blocks of our brains. The more I purified my being by removing processed foods and sugar and carbohydrate-heavy meals, and adding in fasting to allow my cells to clean themselves, I noticed that my mind became sharper and my instincts keener. I seemed to have almost instantaneous energetic communication with the universe. I was witnessing what science has proven, that a clear body is a clear channel for connection with Source.

I also learned about how the five elements—earth, water, wood, metal, fire—influenced my life. For instance, knowing earth to be my dominant element offered clarity around some of my behaviors. Earth-dominant types are the nurturers, the caretakers, grounded people who are dependable and reliable. When this element is in balance, these types derive great joy from nourishing others, and are usually empathic and compassionate people. We are often referred to as the archetypal "Earth Mother." We enjoy preparing food and feeding others. Earth-type people like to feel connected to other beings, and crave peace and harmony between all beings, and with the earth. We are the peacemakers.

However, when this element is not in balance, us earth-types can become filled with anxiety, worry, and fear. As a root chakra imbalance, there is an absence of feelings of safety which can lead to obsessive overthinking tendencies. When out of balance, we can feel lack and scarcity (instead of abundance), and over-give and over-work to the point of depletion, exhaustion, and illness. Earth types who are out of balance tend to suffer with digestive issues, food allergies, constipation or diarrhea, gas and bloating, weight gain and difficulty losing weight, and excessive mucus in the body, and heavy periods. Knowing this gave me insight into what I needed when I felt out of balance—namely, practices such as meditation and grounding, eating soups and nourishing warming foods, connection with the sun, setting strong boundaries, and moving in conjunction with my breath. Harmonizing with the Earth in these ways cultivates an inner balance that empowers me not only in my Earth Mother role as a peacemaker, but also to experience peace within myself.

Ahimsa

"Let's start on our backs with eyes closed. Check in with yourself. What brought you to your mat this morning? What brought you to your practice today?"

Invigorated and euphoric from my movement experiences, as well as syncing with my natural rhythms, I craved more movement and a deeper understanding of the roots of Yogic history and philosophy. I committed to the Ahimsa Yoga & Music Festival, where renowned teacher Seane Corn, the queen of yoga, was giving a workshop. On the first day of the festival, she walks into the room in all her goddess glory and begins to talk about …hmm…our responsibility to the planet? How we are all activists? *Is this going to be some political agenda? When are we actually going to do yoga?*

"Yoga is a call to action," Seane announces. "We each have a role and a responsibility in creating a climate of equity, inclusion and social justice. Our personal transformation through our hearts and off the mat will change the world."

I felt myself becoming bored and annoyed, and I had to pee so I quietly rose, and tiptoed my way between mats to exit the room. At the bathroom sink, another workshop attendee made eye contact with me in the mirror and whispered, "Isn't Seane's message so beautiful? Ah! It makes my heart so full to know that it's possible for all of us."

"Umm… what is possible?"

"To change the suffering in the world. When the world suffers, I suffer. Where I suffer, the world suffers. Yoga is union. Every choice I make directly impacts the larger world. That's the mystery of the Anahata, the heart chakra!"

I tried to hide my eye roll as I walked out of the bathroom. *More of this social justice nonsense.*

In the days leading up to this event, I had envisioned meeting Seane, and was eager to have her personally assist me in postures and hopefully establish a professional friendship. I imagined practicing in a gorgeous bamboo-floored yoga studio with the sound of water trickling from fountains. It would be magical. But arriving that day after navigating narrow country roads through several upstate New York towns in torrential rain, zipping through the registration line, running through a smoky bar in the old ski lodge with my gear, and finally entering a dining hall transformed by a sea of 250 yoga mats, only to hear a lecture on social reform, felt anything but magical.

By the second night of the festival, I was in my groove as I attended a Kirtan, a night of sacred devotional singing and chanting. There is a call-and-response element to it: the Kirtan leader chants one verse then the participants chant the same verse. The instruments used include accordions, flutes, drums, banjo, and more. There was something so mysterious and intoxicating about the frequency created in the room that allowed me to surrender and let go in a deeper way than ever before. Every song spoke so deeply to my soul, as if playing just for me. My body had been moving, my tears flowing, my mouth singing in a language that I had never spoken before.

Suddenly, a memory came forth of when I was a little girl, and those songs would appear in my head. I would hum the melody and sing the lyrics, but I could barely make them out—they weren't in English. I could speak them, somehow, and doing so comforted me. Throughout my younger life, I would hear that same song when feeling alone and frightened—but then I stopped hearing it. Until now.

As my body glided instinctually, and my breath fueled the sacred vibrations echoing from my throat and my mouth, I felt the flow of energy channeling through my entire system like gentle harmonizing waves that were simultaneously tranquilizing and revitalizing. Sinking in deeper, enchanted by the dance between my internal rhythms and the external melodies, I envisioned rays of light beaming from within. And that's when it all made sense. That was the defining moment when Sean's words finally found a place inside of me to land. Inner peace is necessary before we can try to move society towards peace. It starts within. From the time I was a small child humming to that mystical melody in my head, I knew I was called to change the world, and it seemed to be within the realm of possibility. So, I embarked on a career in the helping professions to achieve that goal. I wanted to touch as many lives as possible and crusade for social reform for mental health, spirituality, education and nutrition. I went onto spread my mission by bringing my work into schools, hospitals and community mental health centers. Yet the real work was totally an inside job, "reforming" myself.

Seane said something else that weekend that struck me so profoundly: When we think we can save anybody it means that we assume we are better than them, and that kind of thinking automatically creates separation between us. Trying to save the world as if I was some expert onlooker separated me from everyone else. It removed me from the social order and abdicated me from meaningful responsibilities to the betterment of the world. It was the opposite of my mission. I was blown away, as I had never thought about it from this perspective. Seane inspired me to look deep inside and find the ways, sometimes subtle, that I create separation and division. That is *Himsa*, the opposite of Ahimsa. That is what perpetuates violence.

Seane's words taught me that true service to others was only possible when I was in recognition of our equality—when I was open and able to see the divinity in both of us; and in doing so I could work towards empowering others, rather than helping, healing, or fixing. When I was in alignment with my true self, and connect with another's true self, we empower each other's growth and expansion in consciousness. In that way, we are teachers for one another. I wanted to empower individuals to help themselves, to guide them back home to themselves so they could rely on their own inner wisdom to become autonomous and self-sufficient. And in that moment, I realized that empowering people was about unconditionally loving them, whereas fixing others was about trying to control and save them.

Following the teachings of Ahimsa allows us to create a yogic "lifestyle" off the mat by responding lovingly and compassionately to ourselves and others, honoring and holding space for all feelings and emotions, releasing toxic expectations and limiting belief systems, respecting the boundaries of our bodies while also challenging ourselves to reach past our comfort zones for optimal growth and evolution. Considering how my process serves others, and the ways in which my own integrity and values can influence others, shined an even brighter light on my responsibility to the world. Empowering others was only possible by continuing to do my own work. If I wanted to shift the consciousness of others such that they could take greater responsibility for themselves, I had to do the same for myself. I had to consider how I could best serve others with my words and actions. And I realized that I could only reach the deepest and truest parts of others when I was connected to those same parts of myself. Working with people in that way, taking action from the heart and expressing myself with love, honors their divinity and in turn expands their consciousness so they can recognize their own divinity. That is true empowerment from an enlightened place.

I also realized that spiritual growth can only emerge from a place of complete love and acceptance of myself for where I am right now in each moment. For years, I believed that my life would be better when I met some arbitrary benchmark of perfection. I criticized myself constantly, treated myself punitively, and beat myself into submission when I failed to evolve according to expectation. But I realized now that growing spiritually isn't something to work at. It's simply a state of being in my process, aligning with my truth, and loving myself and seeing myself as perfect right now. When I can do that for myself, I can offer that same unconditional acceptance for others. When I can see the good in myself, I will see the good in others and empower them from that place.

Now Matilde's prophetic words from years ago had a place to land: "When you finally stop punishing yourself with your actions, and scolding yourself with your words, you will feel the beautiful peace that awaits you from within, and then you will create it in your life. That's how you will be the change that you wish to see in the world. Kristy, not only is it your essence, and your calling, but it is your responsibility."

My spiritual evolution could be the inspiration for the world's evolution. Every person has the innate ability to serve others in the world. As their consciousness expands, and they connect with their true self, they can shine their light in the world to elevate humanity. Serving the world's highest good isn't a fancy occupation or special calling. It's a responsibility that we all carry; it's a gift that has been bestowed upon us all. You don't need advanced degrees or superhuman abilities to change the world. You just need to be your true self and live your life fully as if every moment is an opportunity to evolve and awaken.

That weekend I felt like my eyes were completely opened to a new way of seeing myself, others, my work, my yoga, meditation and dance practices, and all of my life experiences up until that point. Managing my own humanness responsibly becomes a template for how I will help to guide others in their humanness. Sitting in that hotel room in the freezing Catskill Mountains, I had the profound realization of the extraordinary responsibility that I have each day to everyone with whom I meet; a responsibility to continue to dive into my own shadows, to treat myself with Ahimsa, to offer love and compassion to myself. I am no different than any other person who walks in my office door. The anxious, distractible six-year-old is me. The terrified, panic-stricken 16-year-old is me. The depressed, overworked 20-year-old is me. The exhausted, stressed mother who feels her identity slipping away is me. When they suffer, I suffer. When I suffer, they suffer. Underneath it all we are all just wounded humans having a spiritual experience.

Even what I had been searching for—the golden panacea of health and healing—was also part of the illusion. My efforts to heal myself and others up until that point had been so outer focused. Healing required connection to my true self, and only then could I offer anything of value for anybody else. As Seane said, "You have to start a personal evolution before you can participate in a revolution." I guess I did learn the great mystery of the Anahata chakra, after all.

With eyes wide open, I reentered my daily life after that transformative weekend festival.

That night in a shamanic journey, my body shapeshifted into open and outstretched hands beaming with bright white light, and I heard the words "hands-on healing." This vision was a premonition of the next signpost on my journey.

Inner Compass

*I*mmersing myself in more ancient wisdom continued to inspire memories of who I was before the civilized world got its grips on me; a time when, much like our four-legged relatives, I was naturally wired with instincts and the ability to sense and read the energy of my environment. I was beginning to remember what *they* wanted me to forget.

In one retrieved memory from when I was around 10 years old, I pedaled faster and faster towards home with a heaviness of a truth inside of me that hadn't made sense logically when I first sensed it; but now the screams of the sirens heading in my direction verified what I already knew. *Dear God, please let this feeling I have inside of me be wrong. Please let her be okay. Please save her. Please!*

My bike fell to the ground as I pushed through the crowd that had gathered outside of the deli in the neighboring building adjacent to mine on that Saturday morning, so I could get a closer look at the doorway that led up to the tiny apartment where the elusive Vera and Jose resided. My attention was immediately captured by the shiny gold necklace that adorned her broken neck as she lay lifeless at the bottom of the stairs. Loose strands of her dark hair framed her lips that had only moments before shouted her final fearful screams. And her hands, though limp, rested together, cupped, as if she was keeping the fragile contents of her soul alive.

My heart ached; I had been too late. Somehow, I knew that would be the day. As the officers handcuffed the man who she called her lover, and the paramedics checked one final time for her pulse, I closed my eyes, found that place in my heart and in my belly and imagined light shining from within me to her. She wasn't ready to go, I heard that. She was scared, I felt that. She needed my help, I knew that. And before they could cover her corpse, I looked into her eyes, deeply, strongly, until she wasn't afraid, and I knew that I had helped her soul in the only way that I knew how.

This is one of my earliest memories of knowing and understanding something immediately without the need for conscious reasoning— otherwise known as: Intuition. All of my teachers and experiences up until this point in my journey had shown me the necessity of getting out of my head, where my incessant intellectual pursuits only disconnected me from the most important fund of knowledge that I have: my intuition, without which I would always feel lost no matter how much I studied or learned. *Hands-on healing* in the form of craniosacral balancing was about to reconnect me with my inner compass so I could find my way back home.

Craniosacral balancing is a gentle, non-invasive, hands-on healing modality that focuses on the wave-like rhythmic pulse that goes through the entire body. The goal of craniosacral therapy is to help get rid of restrictions in this system to improve the functioning of the central nervous system. Craniosacral balancing is rooted in the philosophy that our prenatal and perinatal experiences leave energetic imprints which become containers of stuck energy in the body that create blockages in the flow of fluid and breath in the body leading to disease.

Chills electrified my body when I first saw the flyer for the year-long immersion program in craniosacral balancing just a few days after my return from Ahimsa festival and that prophetic shamanic journey. Seeing Annie and Natalie's names as the instructors made this an obvious pursuit. As the initial training weekend progressed, and we were taught various points of the body and hand positions, I found myself getting caught up in whether I was doing the practice correctly.

"Kristy, stop intellectualizing this. Put the book down." Annie pointed to my head. "Forget what you know here and listen to the wisdom that is here. Just trust what you know."

As Annie placed my hand on my heart and stared deeply into my eyes, I had a flashback of the day that Vera's life tragically ended. I don't know how I knew that would be the day that my neighbor would die. I don't know how I knew that her volatile relationship would end with her violent death. I don't know how I sensed that he had thrown her down the steps that day. I don't know how I heard her spirit communicating with me. I had no idea how I knew how to help her spirit transition on safely.

I never understood how I knew things, I just did. I learned a few years earlier on my quest that this inner knowing actually had a name; a psychic gift called "claircognizance," the ability to just know things without logic or reason, and beyond what can be perceived with the five senses. It's an intuitive sense of clarity about things that have yet to happen, and you have no idea how you know this information; you just do. I was always told by everyone from healers to friends that I had great psychic abilities and I never knew what that meant. As a kid I would have gut feelings, but as I got older, and became more disconnected from myself, the only inner voice I could decipher was the one of the fearful ego. As my journey advanced, and meditation, writing, dance, yoga, and craniosacral healing became part of my lifestyle and personal practice, I felt the same hunches and intuitive hits that I did as a kid. The more I trusted myself, these intuitions were never ever wrong.

As I stood over the massage table, Vera's spirit felt like it was communicating with me through Annie's words. Suddenly, I found the courage to release the course manual that I had been gripping like a life preserver. I shook out my arms, my hands, my legs. I ripped off my socks and rooted my feet deep into the earth. I closed my eyes and took a few deep breaths and listened. Just listened . . . and waited. Then there it was—the "intuitive hit"—and I knew exactly where to put my hands.

That's when I really started to understand this gift of intuition to be our "sixth sense" that transcends the physical senses of sight, hearing, tasting, touching, and smelling, and connects us with our highest form of truth—our higher selves. These intuitive nudges that came to me sometimes in the form of full body chills, the hairs on my arms standing at attention, vivid dreams, or just a sense of knowing that transcends logical reasoning, represented direction from my higher self. Our higher selves connect us with all of humanity, so each time I was tuning in their communications, I was tapping into a collective energy from other realms.

We all have this powerful ability. It was given to our souls at our births. It's just who we are. We don't have to do anything to become more intuitive because it is just our innate ability. What we can do is remove everything that is in the way of intuition. I realized that trauma disconnected me from that innate gift. Trauma is what dismantled my core and resulted in a personality that was terrified to trust her instincts, unable to hear or trust her inner voice, riddled with anxiety, paralyzed in indecision, brainwashed to believe that power resided outside of myself, and dependent on others' opinions, needs, and choices.

Doing my trauma work meant removing the blocks to accessing my inner voice. The "work" was in training my body and mind to resiliently manage the angst that arose from even contemplating listening to my intuition. In the past, when the fear presented itself like a fierce bodyguard, I backed down, and ran away to hide behind the walls that my ego erected to protect me. But now I knew I needed a different approach. It was time for my rebellion. It was time to stare fear in the eye, hold still in my quivering, and march forward right into its epicenter as a fierce animal would. It was time to allow myself to be more courageous than I ever had. It was time to start trusting myself, my voice. It was time to be the authority of my own life.

And just two short months later, life presented me with another opportunity to try it again. I ventured to Baltimore, Maryland for the Green Belt NIA certification offered at one of the most coveted studios in the Northeast owned by the jubilant and incredibly inspirational Lola Manekin. Considered the "teaching certification" belt, the goal of the week-long intensive was to learn and teach a new routine artfully and aptly named "Wild."

Long days at the studio were followed by long nights of training videos and practicing executing every move with precision. In the midst of my panic in class that day while trying to follow the instructor's choreography, I heard, *Don't forget who you are.* Those words, spoken by Kara, a woman in my class with whom I had an instant connection, penetrated my core like a sound bowl, and instantly I was reminded of Annie's wisdom, *Trust what you know in here.* As Kara looked into my eyes much the same way Annie did, I realized that they both saw the medicine woman in me. All I had to do now was see it and trust it for myself. Much like releasing the cranio books, I released the Nia videos and instruction manuals; and on the final days of training when it was my turn to teach, I dropped into my body and confidently stepped into my power in front of the massive floor-to-ceiling mirrors in that downtown Baltimore studio.

With my eyes closed, the echo of Kara and Annie's words created space for me to hear my own voice as I remembered that the highest form of truth comes from within me, not outside of me. I became a clear channel for spirit to course through me, giving my body permission to freely move intuitively, authentically, lovingly, and magically. What I offered to the world was my own instinctually driven rendition of Wild, a flawless routine choreographed from my own truth, beauty, and love. Afterwards, Kara and I embraced.

"Welcome home," she whispered.

These pivotal experiences in somatic healing did bring me home to myself. I was finally able to hear my own voice and sense and act from my own instincts. I was finally reclaiming the freedom to cultivate my own belief systems, and the strength and tenacity to express my truths unapologetically.

For years, I had been indoctrinated with dogmatic belief systems that I allowed to govern my life. Whether it was Catholic religion or lessons from parents and teachers, I was told what to believe and how to live without questioning anything; to just be the "good girl" even when my intuition told me otherwise. Even my professional belief systems weren't my own early on in my career when I was trained to buy into a medical model of illness and disease. I had also had beliefs about illness indoctrinated in me that influenced my own inability to heal. I was taught to not trust my own body which created a dependency on doctors, pills, and external sources for cures, in the same way that I was taught not to trust myself and had become dependent on my husband in my marriage. The cost of domestication is just so high.

My revitalized vibrancy was infectious and every move of my body was an effervescent sensory awakening, making the dancefloor a natural laboratory or playground. I could connect with my body in a shared exchange of sensations and feelings that moved me out of my head and into all of the realms of my physical, energetic, and spiritual existence.

What had once been the default state of my body—constriction and restriction; prolonged disconnecting and disembodying tension; bound by shackles of defense, coping, and survival tactics; a bland and numbing existence—was now being replaced with radical pleasure, joy, confidence, and voracious vitality with every turn, kick, flow, and cha cha. Each opportunity to dance was a surrender as I allowed my body to move in its own authentic time and rhythm, removing all barriers to accessing my inner light and power, my magic, my medicine. Each movement was an invitation to confront myself, releasing more of what no longer served my highest good, so that I could be the clearest conduit for spirit to move through me. The deeper dive into my own soma reassured me that the light I found within my own wounds would offer healing for others. I was now certain that movement was an essential healing elixir for the soul. Movement is indeed a process of excavating and expressing one's story. As a guide, I was helping clients translate their stories through an understanding of the language of the body that spoke through sensations, such as pain and tension, into information that could be used to help the person feel better in mind, body, and spirit. Every movement is a captivating word of a sacred book.

In allowing my own body to tell my story, I was posturing myself differently in life. I was learning about GRACE—an acronym used in Nia for Grounded, Relaxed, Aware, Centered, Energized. This is a term from the Aikido Martial Arts which teaches that true power comes from stillness and calm, not forceful aggression or striving; being relaxed, grounded, and aware leads us to discover the truths of ourselves and our opponents in life. Only from that place of grace can we take focused action towards solving problems and living our lives. Grace allows us to find our flow and freedom. I now could easily recognize when I was not aligned with grace and out of flow.

While dancing one day, I was guided to notice my body's impulses without judgement. As I witnessed my laughs, cries, and shouts, I realized that I spent years stifling my tears—building a dam so high and so strong to restrict their flow that I felt pain from burning in my throat and constriction in my chest. I spent years clamping my mouth shut denying myself laughter, especially in the presence of others' despondent moods. I spent my childhood squeezing myself with the urge to pee or defecate because I was embarrassed to go to the bathroom in school. I spent years shamefully throttling sexual urges that I believed contradicted my images of being the "good girl." And whenever my body let me know that rest and relaxation were needed, I spent a lifetime pushing through the fatigue and overriding my body's alarm warning that sickness was imminent.

As I laughed, cried, sang, and shouted on that dance floor that day, another memory from childhood appeared in my consciousness. Anytime I cried or expressed anger, my grandmother would say, "Stop making that face! God is gonna punish you by keeping your face stuck in ugliness like that." Expressing the truth of feelings was ugly and intolerable for others, so I repressed it all to appease their needs.

As we moved through class that day, I also reflected on the penetrable orb that seemed to be around me since childhood that allowed other's feelings and emotions—whether it was happiness, or misery, despondency, and anger, to enter my being, completely obliterating any sense of self. In fact, I realized on the dance floor that day that I had completely neglected myself. I only existed through the reactions of other people, and I was motivated by fear to do whatever it took to get others to meet my needs. I believed I was responsible for everyone's feelings. I thought that boundaries were only for strangers, and that the way to show love was to fuse with another so much so that their pain became my own so that we experienced the dark cloud together. I didn't know at the time this enmeshment was not love; and it was only fairly recently through my clinical work with clients that I learned that this pattern had a name: co-dependent personality—and it had been siphoning my life force for far too long.

In that moment on the dancefloor, as I focused my eyes, sunk my legs into a sumo stance, and delivered punches with my arms, I realized that erecting boundaries and fiercely protecting my holy grail of inner peace and joy was a priority. This healing journey was a quest for me to recover and reconnect with myself as that is the foundation for all other relationships. Others can feel their own feelings, but they don't get to have the privilege of access to mine. Discerning between my own sensation and experience, and what belongs to others is what allows me to hold space for someone—witnessing them lovingly and unconditionally, but with a clear boundary between their experiences and my own.

Truth is the only way out. I listened to my beautiful teacher Irene's words at the end of Nia class one day as we prepared for a *savasana*. As I lay in stillness reflecting on this disease of co-dependency that I was now healing, I also considered the years spent ruminating and analyzing. Being deeply entrenched in the depths of my mind, incessantly swirling in chaotic ramblings and questionings, only fueled more confusion, more distorted thoughts, more shame and guilt, and more disconnection with my body. I am a natural scholar and seeker of knowledge, but without dropping into the body, knowledge is nothing more than loose strands of generic information that tether us to the mind and disconnect us from our bodies, each other, and our experiences. A true sense of knowing is only possible by translating the intellectual knowing and conceptual understanding into a tangible sense of truth in the body. Embodiment is the only way to truly experience life; my rekindled instincts and intuition were showing me the way home.

I could intellectually identify chakra imbalances, prescribe myself some hip-opening yoga poses, listen to sound healing music at a frequency of 303hz, breathe and meditate while placing a carnelian or orange calcite crystal on my pelvis, but all of that would simply be conceptual in nature and shallow in action, actually quite meaningless unless this information was sensed, felt, and honored within my actual body. Embodying truth meant going much deeper to honor the sensed experiences in my body. It would mean sitting with myself, connecting with my body, actually feeling the chards of shame that pierced my being and veiled my life force energy. To lovingly hold myself even at the pinnacle of discomfort as I open myself to the truth of what I actually sense and feel inside of me. Pulling myself out of the safehouse of the mind which does nothing more than cause me to bypass. But this journey was about staying the path, bypassing nothing, feeling everything, unbecoming what isn't me, and opening to the truth of all that is.

This aha moment also created quite a shift in my healing work with clients, as I realized where I was working with others' energies in disembodied ways. I can teach people about the physical, mental, energetic, and spiritual aspects of being, opening up their minds to accept this as new knowledge and new ways of thinking about themselves and the world, but none of that will translate into meaningful healing for them if I don't guide them in embodying the information and teaching them how to reconnect with their roots to sense, feel, know, and trust the innate wisdom within their bodies that would guide them along their journeys as a compass.

Conceptual knowing is the necessary first step; it's what creates the idea that something else exists. But without taking the next steps to enter that newly discovered portal into alternative realms of possibility, nothing will change. After all, knowledge can only become wisdom through felt experiences. Allowing ourselves to feel and get honest about our experiences is uncomfortable, as we have been conditioned to avoid anything that could bruise our ego or make it squirm. Bypassing what is unpleasant may feel good in the moment, but the long-term consequences of living a disembodied life masked by a false persona is choosing to suffer a long, slow, insidious and painful death . . . the death of the soul.

Instead of choosing to be a helpless, sacrificial, and defenseless bystander who was nothing more than a casualty of life's circumstances, and a receptacle for the incessant energetic intrusions of others, I could choose to be a fervent participant; taking action to make things happen *for* me, because there is a *ME*. I always had a choice: I could escape when things got uncomfortable as I had always done; retreating into a mystical fantasyland in which I could cowardly hide behind the superficial knowledge from books and courses, running around searching for "truth" outside of myself, burning all the sage, lighting all the candles, cleansing all the crystals, posing in all the asanas, taking all the supplements and receiving all the treatments to numb the pain, stifle my feelings and smother my voice for the sake of being polite; smile for the camera, post the pictures on social media with the hashtag "#evolved AF", and lay my head on the pillow of fluffy love and light each night, hiding behind it all and calling that all a spiritual awakening. Or I could choose, once and for all, to remove the mask, to go to the places that scared me in my body and allow the truth to surface; to sense it, to feel it, to breathe in to it, to sit with it like an unexpected visit from a long-lost friend; to get curious about the sensations, knowing that curiosity and fear cannot co-exist in the body, to learn how to speak and move when urged to do so from within, to lean in to the discomfort and feel it in every cell and tissue of my body; to show the world with daring humility the authenticity of my messy and muddled complicated existence, thereby exposing my truths in the light for all to see, to courageously show up in the honesty of raw feeling and being, and allow myself to flourish with unbridled passion coursing through my veins.

The only sensible choice is pretty clear. The concepts of spirituality that I had been learning can only be true, purposeful, and meaningful for awakening, enlightenment, and freedom for evolution of my soul when they are embodied. And right in that moment, as this awareness bathed my entire being, cleansing me of yet another layer of the veil of illusion, I realized a truth that all of my teachers had been trying to show me all along but I couldn't see until right now: I didn't need to acquire more knowledge and theory to evolve and grow; I just needed to allow myself to feel more of my own truth.

The experiences on my vision quest represented a personal paradigm shift in that I was abandoning the conditioning and imprinting to reorient to myself and the world. I was now making my own discoveries, solidifying my own truths, and seeing the world though my own lenses. It really didn't matter what I did; what mattered was *how* I did it. Living authentically would be my greatest gift to others. I now believed what my teachers had been telling me for years: *Your presence alone is what heals people.*

My reflections reminded me of Gabriella, 8, who I met while doing an externship at the children's inpatient unit at Four Winds Hospital. Gabriella was a gorgeous child with long, thick, dark-brown curly hair, and huge chestnut-colored eyes that were sadly absent of typical child-like innocence. Not a first timer on an inpatient unit, Gabriella was savvy about how life worked "on the inside." She knew the rules, and how to break them. Gabriella introduced herself to me with the words: "Wanna see something?" She excitedly lifted her shirt and pulled down her pants to reveal a knife wound by the hands of her father that traveled from her throat down to her pubic bone. Gabriella reveled in my obvious shock. She was precocious; knowing just what to say to get a reaction or to manipulate to get what she wanted—behaviors that I recognized as trauma responses. But it was always shocking to see such behavior in children. It always felt so heartbreaking to think that such young kids had been so jaded by the world when they barely had any substantial time in it.

My initial sessions with Gabriella involved her pushing me away—sometimes physically, other times she wouldn't speak, or she lied and manipulated me to avoid our sessions. On the unit, she had meltdowns all day long during which she needed to be restrained. She would become enraged to the point where she would slam her head into the floors and walls. Blood would gush out of her head and sometimes she would wipe the blood with her hands then lick it. The doctors and nurses increased her medicine and kept her in the padded isolation rooms much of the time. I was intimidated by her, and I felt completely inept to help her. She wouldn't even make eye contact with me. Day after day, I just sat in the room as close to her as she would tolerate. It killed me to watch her outbursts, especially the ones in which she hurt herself. But I remained with her, just holding her hand through it all, praying she would be okay. Sometimes she talked or screamed, other times she threatened to kill herself right in front of me, or she'd spit, kick, punch, or smack me. I stayed.

Months passed (at that time, they would actually keep patients there longer than 48 hours) and eventually she started to open us to me. We colored together, ate lunch together, and walked around on the grounds. She shared her favorite doll and told me her dream of being a dancer. I would bring out a portable radio from the unit and we would dance together on the playground or inside of the unit. We laughed as we did silly dances and made silly faces, while my supervisors would lambaste me in private about how I wasn't doing enough CBT and DBT skills with Gabriella. I may have been defying the indoctrinated Hippocratic views of my formal training about fixing symptoms, but the truth in my heart told me there was no evidenced-based protocol in the world that would help Gabriella. She only needed two things: a stable presence and unconditional love. That's all I wanted to give her.

Over time, Gabriella's meltdowns lessened and she was doing so well. When the decision was made to discharge her, although I was happy for her, I was admittedly devastated because I didn't want to see her go. I had such strong feelings of connection with her, and I wanted to make sure she was going to be taken care of "on the outside." Before she left the unit on that final day, she climbed onto my lap and handed me an unevenly folded piece of construction paper with a hand-drawn picture of a girl dancing. The girl wore a purple dress, had long blonde hair, and was twirling around under a rainbow surrounded by flowers and animals. Inside the card was Gabriella's crooked yet carefully executed handwriting.

"Dear Miss Kristy, my favorite therapist ever. Thank you for helping me. You are the only one who stayed with me. You never left me. Everyone left me, but you stayed with me. You held my hand and loved me. I am gonna miss you so much. Maybe you can visit me one day. I will always love you. Love, Gabriella."

As tears released down my cheeks, Gabriella said, "That's you, Miss Kristy. You bring the rainbows and make all the flowers grow and make all the animals come out of hiding. I will always remember how you danced with me when nobody else even wanted to talk to me. Thank you for showing me how to dance."

The Fruitful Darkness

rriving at the 10-year mark of my initial vision quest—which, over the decade, looked more at times like a precarious minefield than a windswept field of wildflowers—I had definitely begun to reclaim my role as a warrior. Yet true warriors know that regardless of the quantity of battles fought, they never reach mastery. Each opponent presents as a respected teacher from whom they will humbly and graciously learn, if they have the courage to face their fears. The humble warrior must also admit when she has brandished her sword irresponsibly, and seek advice from those who went into battle before her.

As the seasons shifted to shorter days and longer nights, I continued to deconstruct more layers of the illusory veil of conditioning that had enslaved me, and shed more outworn armor that encaged me. This process involved decimating the very foundation upon which I had built my life, causing me to cycle through periods of grief, mourning, and despair. The more I self-discovered on my journey, the more I distanced myself from the life that I had been inauthentically living. Some of my decisions were incomprehensible to others, often leaving me feeling alone and lonely.

Reaching out to Alex was what I knew I needed to navigate yet another cycle of death, that was undoubtedly bringing me closer to birthing my truth. Alex was first introduced to me by Natalie during the thick of my physical health issues several years prior. In addition to being an incredibly attuned acupuncturist, certified Traditional Chinese Medicine practitioner, and skilled Martial Arts expert, Alex was a gifted Taoist Shaman who Natalie described as "magical." When I met Alex for the first time, I knew why.

Like so many times in the past, I knew now that what I was experiencing wasn't a depressive episode or monumental existential crisis. Instead, it is what's referred to as the Dark Night of the Soul—a concept that has its root in almost every religion, spiritual practice, and belief system known to mankind. It's a developmental period in which a person's sense of themselves and the world changes radically, such that they question and contemplate all of the beliefs, actions, identities and relationships that once gave their life meaning, purpose, and direction. The shamans call this a soul loss or descent into the underworld.

With each needle that pierced my skin as I lay on Alex's acupuncture table one late autumn day, he reminded me, "If you keep running from the darkness you will never see the light." I thought about how harrowing the darkness was for me. Memories flooded my consciousness of the many nights as a child when I would awaken in the middle of the night to discover my mother on the couch sipping hot water to settle her "nervous stomach" while waiting for my stepfather to return home. The way she sat, facing the window, and the shadow of the moon cast over our living room walls always felt so eerie and dreadful. He was "out there" somewhere in the depths of the night where danger was lurking, and she was afraid, so I was afraid.

Trying to settle in as I felt the prick of a needle penetrate my forehead, I felt emotions rising to the surface and knew that tears were imminent. Rather than allow them to fall, I took a breath, composed myself, and then smiled, announcing proudly that I was using my breath to stay calm.

"Trying to *stay calm* or trying to *stay numb*?"

Alex's words landed on me like a ton of bricks. I was short on words, but not on tears; while staring out the window, mournfully watching the last of the leaves make their final descent to Earth, my tears fell as freely as the cold, late-November rain tapping on the windowpanes. I felt as dismal and dreary as the day.

"Kristy, don't *fear* it; *feel* it!"

"I thought I was more evolved than this by now. How am I still fucking this up?"

"Oh Kristy, you're not! You're human and this human life is a circle. You know this. Look how far you have come. Look how much you have allowed yourself to feel. But there is more. You're on the precipice of something big. There is more because you're ready for it. It's time to peel away another layer to go deeper. That's why it's so painful. Don't choose fear. Stay open. You are supposed to feel this, Kristy. This is your calling. You can't step into your power without getting to know intimately all parts of you, all feelings. So sure, keep breathing and moving and bathing and smudging and journeying, but surrender as feelings and emotions arise. Be with it. Don't dance around it, dance *with* it! Own your medicine!"

Alex introduced me to a Shamanic practice of meditating in a dark room, completely devoid of light; the longer you sit, fear naturally emerges. When you want to run, you stay, and over time this is how you learn to sit with discomfort. Alex explained that this inward retreat without distraction or stimulation is the essence of all alchemical work, as it would allow me to go beyond the chaos of the external world and the noise of the mind, so I could meet the depths of myself and all of existence. Over time, this practice would allow me to see myself and the world for what they really are, as opposed to what I had been programmed to believe about them.

Though my initial attempts at the dark room meditation practice felt like epic failures, as the darkness seemed to suffocate me and I bolted seeking light, I eventually learned to stay even when it was uncomfortable. Like going to war, sometimes it felt like death bringing harrowing sorrow, raging anger, and mortifying shame. Other times, it was like a birth bringing magnanimous joy and harmonious peace. Sometimes, it brought both simultaneously. If I had learned anything by now, it was that healing was anything but linear, and that growth often resembles utter destruction, creating emotional debris that takes time and patience to clear.

One evening while immersed in darkness, I had the startling realization that Daddy's feelings and behaviors had nothing to do with me. He had his own wounded and unhealed inner child. His behaviors weren't actually conscious acts of abandonment. He wasn't actually doing anything *to me*, he was doing things *for him*. What a revelation! Then another one: The fate of my parents' marriage was not my responsibility. They were two wounded people dealing with their own issues, and I was caught in the crossfire—a bystander, not an accomplice. I had to release them from my belief that they failed me; and I needed to absolve myself of the guilt and shame that came from my belief that I failed them.

My perceptions were shifting as I leaned into the dark places that once scared me. Seeing my childhood and my loved ones through clearer lenses illuminated the truth of their contributions to my soul's evolution and my mission of service in the world.

For instance, I now realized that my belief that I was invisible as a child and then again during much of my marriage, was actually inaccurate. I was seen; but others only saw me as deeply as they could see themselves. While the belief that I was unrecognized caused me to feel chronically lonely, and had caused me to chase and cling to others, and overextend myself to others so I would be recognized, I realize now that this was providing me with the foundation necessary to learn how to believe in myself and love all parts of myself—not just those that I believed to be acceptable— without needing external validation. Ironically, those co-dependent moments offered me the lessons necessary for my own independence, as well as for empowering others to become autonomous. I was again reminded of Natalie's teaching that whatever we are called to heal in others is what we will first experience ourselves.

I was seeing an abundance of light from the darkness, but perhaps the most discomforting revelation from this fruitful darkness was acknowledging the distance that had grown between Dominick and me. The more I extricated myself from the tangled web of co-dependency, the more uncertain we were about whether it was possible to create parallel webs. Energetically, we were holding onto any fibers that might remain; yet I knew they were blocking Allegra Topanga's further unveiling. Admitting this truth was excruciatingly painful, but it would hurt much more to deny it. We can only evade the truth for so long. I felt guilty, of course, that my self-development was causing this divide in our relationship. I didn't want to grow apart, but my view of the world had changed so dramatically. I could no longer deny that Dominick and I were clearly on different energetic planes. As I continued to evolve, it was scary for him to make the choice to also shift and evolve. It was often at my prodding, but deep down he knew that it was impossible to stay static when the current of change was spiraling so rapidly around him. He had become a *part* of my life, whereas he had always been my *whole*. And that didn't feel so good for either of us.

All of my efforts to rush his healing journey were attempts to open his consciousness to the parts of his heart that he kept hidden—the parts that he didn't even know existed and the very parts I desperately wanted to connect with now that I could show my own vulnerability. I incessantly schooled him on spiritual concepts, dragged him to meditation retreats, texted him phone numbers for colleagues, suggested books and articles to read. The more I pushed, however, the more I robbed him of the opportunity to discover on his own. It was disempowering when I expressed doubt that he was doing his own inner work, and it created even more of a chasm between us. Honestly, carrying him in this way was burdensome to me, as it left me energetically drained and physically sick.

I admit that it was challenging for me to accept Dominick just as he was, right at that moment, when I could feel the enormity of his innate potential through my empathic and energetic gifts. I realize now that I had been waiting each day for him to become all that I knew he could be, and I was increasingly frustrated when it wasn't happening according to my agenda. I wasn't loving him unconditionally for who he was right at the moment. I criticized and judged him, rather than compassionately acknowledging his process.

Being on a reform crusade for the people in my life was not only a huge expense of my energy and effort, but it was also creating separation and division between us. It reminded me of Seane's message. I couldn't make others hear a message they weren't yet ready for. All that was needed was care without control—unconditional love. That meant I had to stop worrying about what my husband and children thought of me, hiding and denying parts of myself just to appease them. I just had to be myself. All anyone needs from me is my authenticity. To ignite others, I just had to allow my own light to shine brightly and radiate the same qualities that I wanted to inspire in others.

Looking back, I could appreciate the fact that Dominick and I have been each other's greatest teachers. Through the intensity of our union—with all of its beautiful moments of passion, as well as volatile moments of conflict—I have unearthed so many parts of myself and discovered so many truths of my existence. Letting Dominick in, lowering my guard, opening myself up, created a ripple effect that started by skimming the surface of the water, only to create rumblings down deep that awakened all that had seemingly been asleep. When all of that got shaken up, I had no choice but to look at all the moving parts. I had to find the courage to allow all the truths that were waiting to be discovered to be revealed.

Truths change as we change; so continuous conscious introspection is necessary in order to live a life that's real instead of one that's just "nice." I loved Dominick immensely, but being on the same life path just wasn't our *truth* anymore. We were no longer in alignment, and that terrified me. I didn't know if I could live without him.

I no longer believed in the myth of romantic love in which I needed Dominick (or anyone else for that matter) to actualize my destiny. I knew now that genuine love is about non-attachment. I had always loved Dominick in the way I did everything else—hard, strong, fierce. The way in which we do anything is the way we do everything, even in matters of the heart. But love is actually who we are—it's our natural state, our essence, and relationships are one way in which we share love with someone else.

The sharing of love is about lightness; a gentleness and tenderness that communicates commitment without confinement, and concern without clinging. Sharing love is about recognizing our own completeness and about freedom—with each person feeling enough air space in which to breathe and be themselves.

Dominick and I came together in personality—two fearful egos struggling to find their way. He had always seen me at my lowest points—the panic and intense fear, the insecurity, the incessant worrying, the obsessions and compulsions, the continuous text messages, complaining and lamenting, the constant comparisons, the inability to leave the house or to be alone, anger and rage. I saw him at his lowest points, too. We confused intensity with love, and unconsciously created more and more drama just to feel the "highs."

The truth: we connected wound to wound, not soul to soul.

The amount of courage required to be truthful is extraordinary. When we live from a place of truthfulness, we show up completely, vulnerably raw, but refreshingly authentic. Words have the power to shatter or drive a dream, break or heal a heart, shame or empower a soul, cage or free a spirit. Every utterance is a brave and heroic act, as we just never know how those words will land or be received. It's always risk. Do we take the risk and grow, expanding our soul; or suppress the words, stay comfortable, dull our shine, and watch our soul die a little more each day?

For years I had suppressed my words and clung to falsities out of fear. I know now that the fearful, clinging little child wasn't actually me in the first place. It was the mask of personality, and that is what Dominick fell in love with. All of our dysfunctional and unhealthy patterns of ego became enmeshed, co-conspiring to keep us tethered through fear and control. The result was an unhealthy co-dependent relationship. As much as we have always deeply loved each other, had an amazing ability to communicate, were great at co-parenting, and made a fantastic team, we were bound by fear at the core of our union. We had a symbiotic need for survival. Me needing him to feel safe; him needing to protect me to feel a sense of purpose. The parts of our union that worked became Band-Aids for the parts that did not.

And this worked for decades! But it wasn't working for me any longer, and I'm not sure it was for him either. Lying on that floor, I realized the irony in that it was our relationship that brought me to this place. Dominick helped me to discover my strength and courage, and I helped him learn how to open himself so that he could feel. And for all of this, I am immensely grateful. We both needed to spread our wings and fly; but that freedom carried the hefty price of sorrow for both of us. As I contemplated our marriage, the cost of my inner knowing seemed so high. I either sacrifice myself for the marriage or lose the relationship that had defined me since the age of 16.

Tears flowed as I realized that Dominick and I were left with only two options: evolve or repeat.

Baptism

I slid my Wayfarers over my eyes, rolled up the sleeves on my camo shirtdress, turned up the volume on my favorite playlist, and pressed the gas pedal, ready to satisfy my cravings for sisterhood, ocean waves, starry nights, and magical forests. My next adventure: Maine.

I was feeling much more confident taking this road trip alone. How far I'd come in just a few short years! A few hours into the drive, I made a pit stop to gas, pee, and grab a snack. While waiting to pay for my hazelnut decaf and bag of shelled pistachios, the intensity of staring eyes on my back prompted me to turn around.

"Hey! Where ya headed?" I noticed that this dark-haired man with a mysterious, yet warm smile, had a huge eagle tattoo on his arm. I had been working with eagle medicine for over a year, and frequently shapeshifted into an eagle in my shamanic journeys. I took that as a little nod from the universe that I was on the right path.

Roughly four hours later, I caught sight of the sign upon crossing the Maine state line: "Welcome home. The way life should be."

I laughed and snapped pictures as I drove past signs for moose crossings. For weeks prior, I had been working with moose medicine and had even ordered a new drum made from moose hide. Now as I made my way through back roads, the massive mammal revealed itself to me in person. As I slowed down to witness him, I realized that whether I was taking flight with expansive wings like an eagle, rooting, grounding, and dancing with a fairy knotted mane like a horse, or bellowing jubilantly and confidently like a moose, the wisdom of these prey animals guided my rewilding and continued the birthing of the potent medicine that was gestating within me.

Continuing my venture through dirt roads in town, I saw a tree with a painted sign that read "Ubuntu" ("I am because we are"). Struck by the magnificent beauty all around me, I felt homesick for a place I didn't even know existed. In each direction were gardens, lush trees and plantings, and in the not too far distance, mountains and water. Hundreds of butterflies hovered over a garden at the bottom of the hill not too far from the car path. They looked too perfect to be real, as their vibrant orange and black wings fluttered through the air landing on the bright pink leaves of the plants and flower bushes. The smell of the flowers was incredible. My senses were completely ignited.

I was here for a Heroine's Journey Retreat. Mythologist Joseph Campbell defines a hero as "someone who has given his or her life to something bigger than oneself." Anyone has the capacity to be a hero, but the hallmark of the event is that it will take great pain to precede greatness. Maureen Murdock proposed a model of the Heroine's Journey—a cyclical model beginning with the archetypical heroine separating from feminine values, seeking achievement and acknowledgement in a patriarchal climate, experiencing an initiation through a spiritual "death," and eventually turning inward to reclaim her sacred feminine power and harmonize it with her masculine energy in order to better the world.

Just as the iconic stories unfolded, my journey had been no different. As I am recounting in these chapters thus far, the journey commenced over a decade ago when my ordinary existence was shattered by crisis, and the coping defenses and perfected skills that once worked now no longer did. Suddenly the accumulated beliefs that I previously maintained about the world were destroyed and I had no choice but to surrender and contemplate how to act differently by discovering new skills and strategies, and forming new belief systems and boundaries. Though armed with the guidance of allies who walked before me and whom I've included throughout these pages, there were many moments of insecurity and doubt in my newly found skills, identity, and actions. Some shame crept in as I started to listen to and honor my intuition telling me to let go of some relationships that were inhibiting my growth and were no longer in alignment with my truth. Others didn't always understand the journey and became threatened by my newfound powers. Though fear sometimes forced my hands to reach for the old coping skills, I knew I had to completely let go of the crutches and instead rely on my inner wisdom.

I knew this trip to Maine represented the continuation of my journey in the presence of guides and mentors who, just as in the tales, would remind me to go within. I took comfort in knowing that my journey may be personal, but it isn't private, and it was never meant to be walked alone.

As I walked the grounds of the retreat center, my ear caught the sound of laughter coming from the house at the top of the hill. As I approached, the red wooden screen door flung open revealing my friend and mentor Lola with her infectious smile. After introducing me to the other women, she showed me around the farmhouse and to my guest room. It was a breathtaking rustic Maine bedroom, with the sounds of waves crashing right outside the large bay window. The room was perfectly quaint: wooden plank floors, brown shiplap walls, an antique schoolhouse desk in the corner with a bright yellow chair, and an old wooden rocker draped with a cozy blanket. In that moment, so many emotions came over me—pride for traveling all this way alone, gratitude for the opportunity to be there, and exhilarating excitement in anticipation of something epic on the horizon.

We freshened up and headed out to the main lawn for our opening ceremony. We were chatting and laughing frivolously and I almost didn't hear my name called when it was my turn to walk up the path. I turned and looked at the women behind me who nodded and bid me farewell. It felt very solemn, like I was leaving for battle . . . and I was about to find out why.

- Presence
- Grief
- Nourishment
- Sadness
- Fear
- Not enough
- Anger
- Authentic Power
- Acknowledgement
- Manifestation

We were invited to stop at each word on the sign to connect with our bodies and sense the feeling of the word, noticing how it landed internally. Standing there in that moment, courageously accepting the invitation to feel, I understood in my bones that I was about to embark on a true heroine's journey. It's why I was here, after all. At the end of the path, we were robed with a long white scarf to signify our initiation into the next part of the journey and ushered to a flat grassy area to sit in circle around a gorgeous tapestry.

I opened my eyes as I was rattled out of my quasi-meditative state by the sound of Lola drumming. I scooped up a piece of the earth, the grass, the dirt, and breathed it in. I brought my cupped hand to my heart. I felt held by Mother Earth, by my ancestors, by those guides who came before me, by all those who will come after me. I never before knew what it felt like when people said they felt their ancestors. But in that moment of sitting on the earth, with the sound of the drum and ocean waves in the distance, the birds singing, the feeling of the dirt in my hands, I felt something open, ignite, an activation of a bloodline that had been there always but was lying dormant. I heard the voices and the cries and felt the tears and the joy of my lineage. I felt a potency of their medicine inviting me to activate my own medicine. I felt their guidance to find my courage, my resiliency, my passion, my devotion, my dance, my song, my storytelling. To honor myself as an elder. To find the compassion and self-awareness to dig deeper into my shadows to remind me of who I am when I have forgotten. I felt the presence of my own wisdom. My chronological age had finally caught up to the age of my soul, and it was time to be the elder I was born to be.

Lola invited us to sing and chant with her. *I release control and surrender to the flow of love that heals me.* I felt my heart open with an explosive force that I have never felt before. I could feel every cell of my body activated as waves of energy coursed through me. I was acutely aware of the feeling of death; as I felt shedding of residual layers of all that wasn't me, so that I could experience who I had truly been all along. I felt ready to be attached to nothing yet connected to everything.

That evening after the ceremony, I walked into the kitchen of the main house and saw Maria, Lola's assistant, speaking to Lola. Though I didn't understand Spanish, I could tell she was saying that she missed her family and that she was scared and wanted to go home. I felt her fear. It was so familiar. She was a version of my personality—the version that in the past would have bailed on the trip, had never been away from my husband before, and felt weak, small, and inept to care for myself. I watched her from across the room, closed my eyes, and connected with her heart. I started to energetically send her healing, the same way I used to send my Daddy love like a Care Bear, the same way I work with clients, the same way I sent healing and love out into the universe. I felt my arms become feathered wings that swept away fear from her solar plexus, her heart, and her throat. I was breathing safety and love into her from her root up. Something magical happened in my connection with her; I felt an overwhelming sense of my own identity and purpose in the world. I remembered who I was, and who I always had been. I felt so palpably in that moment the medicine in me that I have carried in every lifetime that my soul has lived. I was here to fully reclaim this truth.

Armed with this knowledge, the signs revealed themselves almost magically. The second morning of our retreat, Lola announced that we would be driving to a "surprise" location for our Nia practice. Driving through the country roads, watching the sun cast shadows on the ground, we turned off the main road down a narrow path and when we arrived, right there before my eyes, was a big red barn. My heart exploded and my eyes welled with tears. For at last five years prior to that moment, I had visions of dancing in a barn. As I contemplated some shifts in my practice, my dream became to purchase an old, restored barn that had private rooms in the back or loft for private healing sessions, and a huge open space where I could offer collective healing experiences by forming groups, workshops, and retreats. To me, barns represent good old-fashioned values, a connection to the past, simpler times of ease and minimalism, nurturance, abundance, and community. They reminded me of my deep connection with horses from as far back to childhood. My dream was manifesting.

After dancing each morning, we headed back to the house and made breakfast together; it was true communal living. It felt so natural, comforting, and easy. There was so much love. It felt like the way it was supposed to be—the way I always longed to live: women in tribes preparing and eating meals together, taking care of one another, and sharing in the responsibilities. As we all ate together, I felt memories surface of times when I did live this way. Oh, how I missed it! Along with the joyful memories, pain shrouded my heart. I believed that we all should be living that way, and in fact I believed this was the missing link and the reason why so many people in our times were suffering and not living their truths. It reminded me of the story that Brene Brown tells of the village in which all the women washed their laundry together in the river. When the women got washing machines, there was a sudden outbreak of depression. Yet nobody could figure out why.

In these modern times, life has become so much of an individual race to the top. We are so isolated. We don't work collaboratively, share in responsibilities, or ask for help because it's all perceived as weakness. Each woman on her own "should" be able to raise her babies, cultivate a close and loving marriage, take care of a home, and have a job that contributes financially. We say we are fine. We say we have it under control. We say that with just a little more wine we can push through. How removed we all are from our natural states of being!

Gathering with this beautiful tribe of women at all ages and stages and from all corners of the world, it was so evident that magic was created. We sat around a fire, shared stories, beliefs, ideas, rituals, prayers, our histories, our gifts, our skillsets, in much the same way as women have for Millenia. Each woman contributing her own unique gifts to the group. Every voice was heard, every need met, every feeling and emotion had a safe space to land. And if one of us needed space or time to rest or cry or be alone, it was encouraged, no questions asked. There is no way that connection like this can be a luxury—it's a necessity, and it reminded me of a place I used to call home.

Insightful Waves

Being right on the beach in Maine, the ocean became the backdrop for many of our activities, as we let the natural rhythms of the ocean tides and phases of the sun guide our days and nights. Being near the ocean was always simultaneously terrifying and exhilarating. When I was six years old, I went too far out into the waves unattended. From that day on, I became terrified of water. As an adult, the summer during my pregnancy with Antonio, my step-brother was catapulted into the ocean by a rip current forceful enough to carry him away. While under the water he hit his head on a sand dune, snapping his spine, and leaving him paralyzed for life.

The ocean became a huge abyss of uncertainty, chaos, and destruction. The tide, the currents, the life invisible underneath the surface was all daunting. Yet I was always drawn to water and the polar opposite state that it invokes—a sense of calm, serenity, cleansing. Even the crash of the waves had its own beauty and allure. Yet watching it from a safe distance was all I could handle.

As Lola facilitated a discussion about the element of water, I applied her teachings to my life, recognizing immediately how the element was showing me where my masculine and feminine energies had been off balance for so much of my life. I realized that my fear of water had also been a metaphor for fear of my own feminine power and innate calmness. It was a revelation that I contained within me a flow that is deep and slow-moving, instead of strong and forceful. When in balance, feminine energy is about intuition, emotion, sensitivity, and ease through change and fluctuations. I realized where I was still struggling to soften my grip, let go, release, and flow; where I was still swept away by my own forceful and penetrating currents of fear.

I reflected on the messages impressed upon me throughout my life about hard work and hustle; and priorities of achievements, financial security, and preparedness for the future—all propelled by a dominant masculine energy. I wasn't shown women who receive, slow down, or nurture and protect from a place of softness. I saw that caring for someone was an intrusive, manipulative, and penetrating energy. I was taught that my sensitivity was weakness, that feelings were meant to be suppressed and stifled, and I accumulated and stored emotions like fat deposits all over my body. When those emotions became so overwhelming, without knowing how to handle them, I froze; and just before slipping into a hypothermic state, an inner fire ignited causing me to erupt into a destructive fiery rage. All that created was more imbalance—as ice and fire can't coexist.

In those revelatory moments on the beach, as waves of insights crashed into me, I now finally understood that my life had been lived as an expression of rejection of the feminine; denigrating intuition, creativity, spirituality, and emotional expression while extolling and exalting the masculine drive for power and control over myself and others in a forceful attempt at attaining mastery and perfection. I heard the incessant inner chanting of "I got this!"

This quest was a discovery of balancing the feminine and masculine; healing the wounds that caused me to bully myself and bulldoze through life without rest or regard, in order to reclaim my connection with my intuition while nurturing the healthy aspects of masculine energy that energize and empower my sovereignty and self-expression, and manifest the visions of my intuition and creativity. *If there was no harmony within myself, how could I bring harmony into the world?* Remembering the essence of the union between feminine and masculine was necessary for Allegra Topanga's voice to be expressed in the world.

The second day of the retreat, we headed to Popham Beach State Park. A magical beach with miles of beige sandy shoreline, rare geological landforms, breathtaking views of offshore islands and rivers at the borders, and crystal blue waters that pooled like gemstones. That day the sky was the most magnificent shade of blue. We were invited to sit down on the beach on a yoga mat facing a partner. We were told to look into this person's eyes and take turns saying, "I am afraid . . ." letting whatever came to the surface be released during a timed period. My partner, Aly, went first and then it was my turn. It all poured forth.

I am afraid of not being good enough
I am afraid of being seen
I am afraid of feeling
I am afraid of my children dying

I am afraid of my own death and leaving my children without a mother
I am afraid of my marriage ending
I am afraid to release my grip
I am afraid of being out of control
I am afraid of being alone.........

The list continued to pour out of me. It was the longest three minutes of my life. Tears poured down my face and pooled on the yoga mat beneath us. It was truly amazing to see what happens when we really stop to listen—to really dive deep into the ocean of unspoken longings and allow them to flow. That's when we create a safe space for our inner child to speak all that she has been dying to say. What comes to the surface, out of hiding and into the light for us to look at compassionately and lovingly, and for us to share vulnerably in the world, is our truth. It is only our truth that will set us free.

With my newfound freedom, I walked to the water's edge; and on that gorgeous day, as I hurled globs of wet muddy sand into the ocean, feeling that this mud was like all the internal sludge that had been holding me back and weighing me down for years, I shouted, "I am no longer afraid. I AM NO LONGER AFRAID ..." The blood-curdling screams burst from my throat and I kept screaming and throwing sand until I collapsed. When I had cried every last tear, my head lifted, and my eyes caught a glimpse of the vast ocean before me. All I could see for miles was water—my nemesis for over three decades. And I knew it was time. With determination and fierce tenacity, like a gladiator approaching her opponent, I walked into the ocean, looking it square in the eye. As a massive wave approached, I remained still, confronting the force of my rival. Armed only with a saber of trust and truth, I surrendered; and as the waters gushed over my body, submerging me in their flood, leveling me to my knees, and seizing my breath, I found strength. As the waves cleansed and purified my being in a sacred baptismal ritual, I rose victorious as the heroine.

It was exhilarating and petrifying. I found the parts of myself that had previously been tossed around and strewn about from the tumultuous waves of life's storms that had threatened me and tested my resolve. In diving into that ocean and rising triumphantly, I compassionately coaxed my hardened heart to soften and my traumatized inner child to trust again. The very place that scared me was the very place that saved me. Standing in the sea, surrendering to its whims, letting go of struggle, allowing, and releasing my grip; only daring to cross the ocean when I found the courage to lose sight of the shore.

Emerging from this metaphorical baptism, with even more falsities stripped away, I was inundated with the truth that as I fearlessly immerse myself in the infinite depths of womanhood, instead of fearfully hovering in its shallows, I find all that I need. Embracing my shadow and my light, my water and my fire, the essence of my natural wild woman within—with her vivacious passion, life-giving creativity, and unconditional love, is restored. As I stared at the hues of greens and blues, I saw my own crystal-green eyes as potent portals to spirit that show me that in the waves of change, I find my direction; and in the rough seas, I find my buoyancy. As I am but one drop in a vast ocean that connects us all, I was confident that my rewilding was not only for me, it's for the world.

A part of me died in that water so that I could be reborn. As Lola had taught, water is the element of the womb, the place of emptiness from which all potential is possible and to which all things return I was overcome with excitement as my life now felt full of possibility. It felt like I was starting over, a baptism that washed away all that was false so that my truth could be revealed.

With the energy of new life pulsing through my veins, I lifted myself off the sand and walked towards a huge boulder out in the water. I climbed on top feeling liberated as the wind danced with me. As I moved, I called in the four directions. I felt held and supported and protected and reaffirmed by guides and by all the elements. My truth naturally flowed from within me in a meaningful prayer:

I start with the East, the place of the rising sun, the birth of all new beginnings, the beginning of life, the beginning of understanding, clarity, and intuition; the birthplace of ideas; with air as your element, guide me to flow with the winds of change; with the majestic Eagle as your keeper, guide me as I birth on my journey, help me to soar high above challenges reaching new heights, and to see with clear vision from all angles and vantage points. Guides, please fly with me, wing to wing. Thank you.

Turning to the South, the place of rapid growth, expansion, playfulness, exuberance, and aliveness; a place of learning, discovering, and growing; the element of fire that warms with passion, grace, patience, and electricity; home of the snake, help me to stay in the moment, help me to see clearly, to shed what no longer serves me, so that I may honor my physical body, reclaim my natural rhythm, and all of my truths so that I may integrate and become one with all beings. Thank you.

Great Spirit of the West, the place of the great waters of lakes, rivers, oceans, and rain. Grandmother ocean, womb of all life, place of darkness and death, and the pure potential of new birth, pure consciousness, peace, the place of dreams, home of the Bear and the Orcas, help me with your power to cleanse, let go of what no longer serves my highest good, and to heal. Thank you.

Great Spirit of the North, the place of the mountains, home of the Owl and Buffalo, direction of our ancestors, help me to overcome what is cold and harsh in this life. Connect me with the earth element, the foundation that we always return to, and the reminder to nourish my inner landscape. Help me to slow down, journey inward, nourish myself, and rest. Thank you.

That night, as I lie in bed reflecting on the enormity of the ceremony that had taken place that day, my prayerful words continued to flow:

Dear spirit, thank you for reconnecting me with the elements of earth, fire, water, wood, metal that ground me in the physical reality; and the air and ether elements that remind me that my essence transcends the physical realm. Guides and spirit, please help me to harmonize with the elements such that I can feel myself and spirit in each twist and turn of my journey. Help me to remain in a state of graceful flow—welcoming in the tide with peaceful contentment, and bidding it farewell when it's time to go; loving without attachment and knowing when the time has come to release what no longer serves my highest good. Continue to guide me so that I may transmute force into flow as I dance through life.

Then I heard the spirit of the water respond:

I have left you thirsty for more. For cleansing, for flow, for renewal, for birth. This nourishing water that I give to you is a life-giving force, and if you drink from my springs, you will be filled with the peaceful ease and purposeful determination necessary for rivers and streams of light to flow out of you and into the world. Dive in, deep into my depths, and you will discover a trust in your own oceans of magic that flow within you.

Naked and Unafraid

The next morning, I looked at my reflection in the glass windows of the gorgeous rustic house as we prepared for our day. I was unrecognizable, covered from head to toe in a white robe, with pin-straight manicured hair coiled neatly in a bun, and makeup that I applied robotically that morning. But now, feeling as though I had awakened as a newborn being, that image no longer resonated, as that persona had dissolved in the waters. So, like all babies when they first enter the world, I got naked. I flung off the robe, ripped my hair out of the bun, and hosed the makeup from my face. All the girls cheered, and the power of their collective energy fueled me to boldly explore the world through my naked senses for the very first time. I rubbed mud on my skin, in my hair, between my legs, everywhere all while the sun warmed my skin and the breeze danced through my hair. No shame, no guilt, no hiding. I was naked and unafraid, standing unapologetically in my pure essence of love.

When it was time to shower, I watched my pale ivory skin emerge under the flow of the water as the grey mud melted off my body, dissolved, and swirled down the drain. It was yet another metaphor, washing the remnants of the womb away as I emerged. As I stepped out of the shower, I recognized the woman staring back at me in the mirror with the natural skin and untamed hair. The feral foal was reclaimed.

That evening, on the first day of the new moon, as we witnessed the stunning soft rays of warm light disperse along the landscape as the sun set over Morse Mountain at Seawall Beach, I was overcome with gratitude for this newest round of my awakening. Tree limbs outstretched like arms scooping me up to place me at the top of the tree where hawk and eagle flew overhead telling me I needed nourishment; and when I descended from the tree, snake greeted me with the message: *Remember your roots, tend to the roots, your essence lives in your roots. Remember who you are.* Vultures circled and showed me my death. Eagle arrived soon after to help me visualize my rebirth.

My rebirth and baptismal rites required one more layer of the veil of illusion to be decimated. That night after dinner, as we gathered around the grand stone fireplace, and Lola invited us to share about a time in our lives when we felt most betrayed, I knew it was time to exfoliate the residual anger and resentment that had been clogging my pores like the makeup I wiped from my face.

As I allowed the memory of Daddy not keeping his promise to show up to my high school graduation, I released my voice from the shadows:

"Daddy, how could you have chosen her over me? I am your child, your little girl. And I lived my life for you, to make you proud, to make you love me, to make you smile, DADDY, ALL I EVER WANTED TO DO WAS TO MAKE YOU FUCKING SMILE! And there I stood on that stage, staring out into the crowd searching for you so that for five seconds I could see pride and joy in your eyes. You were the only person who fucking mattered to me, and I had done this all for you. I believed you were there, daddy, I held up my diploma as an offering to you and trusted that you were watching proudly. I stood there like a fucking asshole posing for your imaginary camera! And when we gathered outside, I pretended not to see the look of sadness on Mommy's face because she fucking knew—everyone knew, everyone saw what I couldn't see, what I didn't want to see! THAT YOU WEREN'T FUCKING THERE, DADDY! That you didn't fucking love me enough to show up for me. TO JUST FUCKING SHOW UP, DADDY! And I just smiled and took it. Well, I can't shove these feelings away any longer! You lied, betrayed my trust, over and over again throughout my life, and I am angry at you! REALLY FUCKING ANGRY AND SAD, DADDY. And I'm done hiding behind excuses just to preserve your memory. You hurt me, and I'm allowed to feel that. AND NOW I RELEASE MYSELF FROM HOLDING ON TO THIS ANY LONGER!"

In finally releasing the pain of anger and resentment that kept me stuck and sick for years, I now understood so clearly that although none of us are responsible for creating the wounds of trauma, it is our responsibility to heal them.

On that final morning of the retreat, I journeyed to the upper world where all the winged ones—eagles, hawks, and condors flew around me as I approached tall, locked gates. Smaller birds flew around the larger ones, almost as protegees. The largest Eagle flew toward me asking for my offering or my question that would allow me to gain a gift from him that would be used to enter the gates. I handed him a brown leather box that was filled with thousands of questions to which I sought answers. Eagle took the box, flung it up in the air, and it disappeared. He smiled, nodded, and handed me a mirror to look into; and when I did, I saw myself as Allegra Topanga. I immediately merged with this image, spoke the words, *And so it is* . . . and the gates opened.

Just as in the iconic Heroine's Journey tales, this one ended with my courage, faith, and resilience restored, an understanding of my mission and purpose, and an unwavering trust in my medicine. I had one thing left to do: introduce Allegra Topanga to the world.

Part Three

Reclaiming My Sovereignty

The Heroine horse now expanded in consciousness and confidence, and vehemently trusting in her true nature, runs free, blazing her own trail as a spiritual warrior. She realizes that what she once considered breakdowns, were really breakthroughs.

As a priestess, she returns from her quest armed with the wisdom accumulated from her travels and her vision for a brave new world. She finally trusts that her voice is relevant. She is the muse of inspiration, the queen of materials ready to manifest her medicine for the greater good of the world.

Her fiery grace and unbridled passion inspire all horses to run free.

Her story is her legacy.

Home Again

As a sovereign queen, Allegra Topanga could confidently admit when something or someone was threatening to inhibit her growth, express compassion and gratitude for it, and then let it go. She was allowed to redefine her life and reroute her course when necessary. She gracefully said "no thank you" or "goodbye" in relationships that no longer served her highest good. And she was allowed to leave the house, city and state that no longer felt like home.

As the newly appointed authority of my own life, deciding to sell our beloved home of 15 years was a natural pivot towards obtaining the fresh start that I desired to earmark this part of my journey. It was time to downsize and purge the house that had become a storage unit filled with superfluous "stuff" that was mistaken for necessities. The further along I was on my rewilding journey, the less seduced I was by material things.

When our house sold and it was time to say the final goodbyes to it, I observed lovingly the enormous sadness that swelled to the surface and let it have its moment in the light. The hardest part of leaving anything or anyone is actually doing it—leaving the people you once thought you could never live without, or the places that you once thought you would always stay. But sometimes leaving is exactly what we need for our growth and expansion. Leaving creates opportunity, space, beginnings, freedom, and liberation. Though this loss felt uncomfortable, I knew that the pain of staying in a place I no longer belonged would be excruciating. Something had to die in order to make space for something new to be born. I couldn't reach for something new if my hands were tied up holding on to the old. That was a truth that I surely trusted in by this point in my journey.

When the last box was loaded on to the truck, I stood in the kitchen and looked at the empty rooms, much the same way I had 15 years earlier on the day we moved in. Except now I was a dramatically different person. Memories flooded my consciousness: hearing Antonio running through the rooms shouting, "Fire! Fire!" with his fireman trench coat on when he was three years old. The day we brought Gianni home from the hospital. Boisterous laughter from the dining room on Thanksgivings and Christmases. Seeing the boys take their first steps. The cousins arranging themselves on the stairs shooting nerf guns from the upstairs landing. Smelling the aroma of Sunday gravy in the air. The scent of the candle that burned in the living room when we told the boys that their grandma had just died. Touching the wooden banister as I held onto it while telling Dominick that I was pregnant for the first time. All of it came rushing back, and I found myself speaking a prayer of gratitude to this home for providing shelter, safety, and a sanctuary for our family.

I looked forward to a fresh start and a complete change of lifestyle. Whereas in the past I was all about hosting elaborate parties for the neighbors, decorating my house to the nines and relishing all the material things that we worked so hard for, now I longed for simplicity, privacy and time alone. I valued only the things that served my highest good and enhanced my spiritual growth. We could be part of the community for my children but being around people isn't what made me feel alive anymore— it was actually what depleted me. I felt most alive when I was alone, in nature, writing, creating, meditating, dancing, practicing yoga. I now only chose the things, people, and beliefs that empowered me and augmented joy and love in my life, and I rejected anything that was growth inhibiting.

Moving to a new locale also had me "updating" many of my decisions based on who I was now. For example, we were faced with the choice of whether to enroll our boys in religious education in our new town. I heard loud and clear what I knew to be the right decision for our children, but it was the one that would be most appalling to our family. My kids had been attending CCD classes for the past several years and hated it, and I had been forcing them to betray their own strong beliefs, causing them to resent my hypocrisy. It was time to let it go. And as much as we were confident that we were making the right decision, actually doing so was quite monumental for us. Turning away from institutionalized religion threatened the very system that was the foundation for all the rules and cultural expectations that our extended families still held onto so dearly. Here I was slaying them with my newfound sword of truth, watching them crumble to ashes, so that we could build something new for our children. It was uncomfortable, but it was aligned with my truth and with theirs, so it was necessary. I was done with giving everyone else in my life the privilege of making decisions for me.

As I settled into our new town, I experienced a newfound sense of my own inner power and sovereignty from which I could orchestrate my own life. I discovered my inner fire and its ability to move me from the safety net of the comfort zone to the expansive world of the unknown in which

I had the right and the capacity to take the risks necessary to manifest change, transformation, and a profound inner evolution. My growth was my priority, and I not only desired it, but I required it to feel alive, as if it were air. Expanding my consciousness and attaining higher levels of self-awareness and connection with my true self and all of creation, made me feel exhilaratingly alive.

I could grow gracefully, remaining steadily and calmy grounded in my truth, expressing my needs with clarity and conviction, and using my sensitivities to compassionately acknowledge imprisoning behavior patterns and antiquated belief systems, express gratitude for their teachings, and then lovingly release them when it was time. It was a softer process guided by Alex's prophetic words, "You can't meet force with force."

When the forceful sensations felt like the strongest opponent, he said, the most effective strategy is to meet the force with calmness. It was still a radical concept for me, given how I postured myself in the world since childhood. If it didn't feel hard, then it wasn't worth it. If it wasn't a struggle, then I wasn't growing. If I wasn't killing myself, then I was failing. If I wasn't bulldozing through life with the intensity of a wrecking ball than I felt dead inside. If I wasn't burning down the whole damn forest, it meant I had no flame.

But now, seeing myself as this humble warrior, exuding calm abiding in the face of life's opponents, I realized that my actions didn't have to be hard to be meaningful. With a flexible mind and an open heart, I trusted in my ability to thrive and grow through joy instead of struggle.

Learning to transmute shame and guilt into confidence was a game changer. Once driven to produce and achieve from a place of insecurity and inadequacy, I was now feeling empowered with strength, security, and trust in myself and my mission.

By then I was on track to begin teaching yoga as another offering that I wanted to add to an already full list of programs at my wellness center. I was already teaching workshops, working with clients in private healing sessions that were a combination of spiritual life coaching, ancient healing techniques such as Shamanic Reiki, and somatic-based healing such as Craniosacral balancing and conscious dance. and I was beginning to receive referrals from clients from other parts of the region. I began to envision myself opening a second center that was larger, where I could accommodate more people and give more people access to my offerings. I also developed an online program that busy people in remote locations could access. I was selling out huge auditoriums giving presentations on various topics. And my practice had a long waiting list of clients. It was simultaneously exciting and terrifying.

When I lost my way, I had to remember to trust the guidance of my higher self and not be fooled by the voice of my ego. I knew by now that the higher self speaks gently, calmly and reassuringly as it reminds me of my limitless potential to expand, create and share my gifts with the world. It's a loving, persistent whisper that is heard or sensed and lights the way, revealing the signposts of my heart. The voice of personality and the protective brain, motivated only by survival, uses fear-based tactics to forcefully and intrusively cajole our actions. I had learned that the protective ego was the first and loudest voice I heard, as it perceived danger everywhere and resorted to whatever tantrums and tirades were needed to get my attention and convince me to play it safe. When I could patiently be still in those moments, tuning into my sensations to avoid feeding the ego, eventually the ego is disarmed. Then I can get quiet and listen to hear the soft, tender voice of my wise highest self who would provide all the guidance and direction I needed.

Around the same time, I was having incredibly intense and vivid dreams and visions after which I was waking up exhausted as if I ran a marathon in my sleep. I reached out to Alex for guidance.

"Kristy, you're traveling so deep into other realms during your sleep, and you are actually healing people during your sleep!"

He and I reflected about an angelic human that came to me, and felt that he was surely a guide reminding me to trust myself; that my time of searching outside of myself was over. A wolf clawed my physical body to bring me closer to my soul; to show me that the experiences of my vision quest had been a rite of passage that garnered me with the tools of self-reliance, resiliency, and autonomy; it was time for me to think for myself, trust my own intuition, sensitivities and insights; and confidently, courageously, and gracefully venture back out into the world as a lone wolf. And the fear that creeps in from time to time, as evidenced in the dream by me begging the angelic man to stay, was simply a human need for belonging—the natural human tendency to want to feel connected to something bigger than ourselves for survival. But the shaman, like the lone wolf, Alex explained, knows that she is never alone. She has deep within her being a connection with the Earth, with spirit, with other worlds, with animals, with ancestors; and she carries all of this with her as she blazes her own trail.

I also told Alex that I heard my childhood song again; the one that appeared whenever I closed my eyes as a child when I was scared. I hummed the melody and sang the lyrics that were not in my native tongue. As a child, I never questioned how or why I could know these words or where the song came from, because it just made sense and felt right. It felt like the only thing I could trust. It felt like my truth, and it comforted me in ways that nothing else could. As I got older, and the cynicism and conditioning of life got its grips on me, I doubted, much like I questioned whether Santa Claus was real. The doubt quickly gave birth to shame and its silencing motives, and the magical song of my ancestors was never sung again.

Until now. In addition to being a source of comfort for me, I would find myself humming either silently or aloud when I was doing healing work with a client—especially when the client was on the massage table for a craniosacral session or Shamanic Reiki session. It was a song that I hummed at the start of all of the ceremonies that I led in my groups and workshops, and it was the song I hummed in all my dreams.

"Kristy, you say the song just came to you, like as if it was put in your head. But what actually happened is that at some point when you were a little girl and you were scared, your guides directed you to go into the spirit world and ask for the help of a song. It wasn't an accident or a random tune that popped into your head. It was a gift all for you. The language of it—the fact that your rational brain didn't understand the words—doesn't matter. For the song to be effective, the words themselves don't matter as much. It's the feeling, Kristy. It's the ability you had to channel that song to shift your energy from scared, terrified, alone, to comforted and safe, feeling held and loved. That song is yours; you carry it within you. It's part of your deep medicine, your alchemical magic."

Alex also helped me to make sense of another dream in which I saw the entire landscape of the outside world as a bright yellow eye of a raven.

"The raven is showing you that you have been reborn. What you saw was real! Kristy, you are a bridge between worlds. That is your medicine. You offer guidance and wisdom. You provide information from other worlds and other realms that heal people. People are transformed in your presence, and you can transform your own life in such big ways. Raven is the bird of magic. The world needs you to own and share your magic!"

I reflected on this word "magic." So many of my experiences on my vision quest had certainly been what most would call paranormal, or mystical, or supernatural; and others would likely call them crazy, but I knew now that it was science in its purest, unacculturated form.

I thought about what I often told my clients: that the more conscious you become, and the more inner wisdom you connect with, the crazier you appear to those who haven't yet had the privilege of "seeing." But whenever my own insecurities crept in, both Alex and Natalie would remind me, "You are not meant to see the world and feel the world the way others do. You were summoned by Spirit to help transmute fear to love, darkness to light. You do that! So now I ask you, do you still want to be *normal*, Kristy?"

Though the spirit world is not always easy for people to believe in because people tend to not believe what they can't see, I *did* see! The seemingly invisible spirit world and this physical material earth world both showed me meaningful content rich with metaphors. I knew that I received the "downloads" from the spirit world to bring into this earthly world to deliver needed healing. As Alex would remind me, "You can see it all— what others can't even imagine, you can see and feel and connect with. I know that you know and can feel the blood of the ancestors within you as you walk this planet with love. You can't deny this. You have all the proof you need. You know who you are, Kristy, and you know who you're not. And you know it when you see it in your clients, too. You see the beauty, wisdom, and gifts that lie within every being."

I did see the innate magic and beauty in everything, and I knew it was time to reconnect with the earth-plane guides who always reminded me of my gift and would now help me to freely share it with the world: horses.

A Feral Foal

Many little girls dream of owning a horse or pony. There is something magical about a 1,500-pound highly intuitive being who walks the earth with a shiny coat and the largest eyes of any land mammal. Horses have the ability to care and nurture, and a strong enough back to swiftly carry a human into the sunset. Little Kristy, she dreamed of uncoiling her pigtails so her golden mane could feel the natural forces of the wind. She didn't want to own a horse; she wanted to *be* a horse. Not a pretty show horse, pristinely manicured and whipped into conformity; a wild one that moved at will, raw and instinctual, leading the herd to freedom.

Little did I know, at age seven when I had my first spiritual encounter with a horse, that these regal beings would contribute to my own emancipation—a rescue mission that would offer deliverance for those who came after me. The horses that came to me in dreams and journeys were parts of myself that had been relegated to the shadows. Their tangled manes, known as "fairy knots", were teaching me more about softness and grace than the regimented ballet classes and rigorous Catholic school curriculum of my childhood ever could.

About 10 years ago, horse began to show up as a guide when working with clients, as well, giving me a sense of where to work, what to say, and how to offer support. Joanna, then 16, had been experiencing what she labeled as "a depressive numbing funk of not giving a shit that makes my parents hate me and my friends leave me." She felt vacant, devoid of purpose, absent of feeling. As I held space for Joanna to release anger towards her father and disentangle herself from the confusing web of teen girl drama, horse showed me a symbol of wings and birds flying around his head while in a scorching desert. I felt the flight to a place that housed her soul, a tie that was binding her to a past and place that her true self knew of, but her personality had shielded her from. I shared this third-eye image with Joanna.

"That's crazy, Kristy," she responded. "How did you know that I just found out that I was adopted and my biological mother and sisters live in Arizona and invited me to go there?" Two months later, Joanna ventured out on her own vision quest to Arizona to meet her mother and sisters for the first time, and her life was never the same again.

Not long after this experience with Joanna, right as Ma got sick, I connected with horse energy again in both my dreams and waking state. This horse triggered within me so many suppressed feelings that I didn't even know were hiding: shame, guilt, grief and fear. It seemed to be reflecting what was happening with Ma at that time, offering me even more insight into the energetic underpinnings of her physical illness. Horse's plight was a metaphor for Ma's life.

During that time, my "dream horse" didn't look like the spectacular, majestic beings that one might imagine. He was more of an emaciated donkey, worn down to bare bones, with open sores on his skin, barely standing tall and teetering on the verge of death. He was overworked, underloved, and horribly treated. I felt the horse looking into my eyes, peering into my soul, and communicating with me so clearly. He asked me to help him run free and to help him expose what was hiding so that he could be himself. He was longing to be rescued. Yet he never complained, until he couldn't take it anymore.

I saw vividly in my dreams and journeys that when people went near him, he became incensed. The doctors who forced their diagnoses and treatment on him; the trainers who exerted their exercises and goals; the owners who thought his distress was all in his head. They all asserted their own will and agendas without actually listening to his. They were in a battle for control. They believed him to be dangerous; but they were the ones who were most lethal. He became even more mistrustful of his environment, seeing everyone and every scenario as a threat. He preferred to go off into alternate worlds where he was safe to run free. I knew it was a sign that Ma needed help, and I knew I needed to intervene.

Whenever I saw Ma and felt horse, I felt overwhelmed with feelings of sadness and grief, anger and righteousness. I felt this urgent sense of responsibility to save her and crusade against those who inflicted cruelty upon her, like her family and the doctors.

The feelings this horse totem roused in me made it no surprise that he appeared every time I was with Ma during her rehab stay and assisted living. During my visits, when anxiety rose and I wanted to charge the gate like gangbusters to take control of her care, horse reminded me to pause, breathe, find patience, simmer my frustration, submit to the natural order of things, and connect with my greater purpose which was to give voice to this human who had been voiceless for so long. When I felt lost and hopeless, doubting that I had anything to offer, and frantically seeking something to give, horse reminded me of my innate ability to give Ma what all beings need, which was love.

So, I sat with Ma, brushed her hair, manicured her nails, creamed her feet and her hands, ate with her, told her stories, and listened to hers. What transpired over weeks and months and years were minute-by-minute resuscitations. She gained weight, her pale complexion became rosy, the smile returned to her face, and she spoke more expressively. Ma was coming back to life, and I was witnessing her rebirth. In the safe container that my soul held for hers, she opened and allowed her bruised, fraying, and worn-out soul to heal. In the process, mine was doing the same, in a relationship with this mystical horse as our guide and teacher.

Throughout this process with Ma, I recalled the message that came through while I was on Annie's table during my very first craniosacral balancing treatment: "Free her! Let her run free! Let her sing! Let her dance! Let her rage with the fires and flow with the oceans! Let her live."

This message was for me, and now for Ma.

During Ma's passing, horse stayed with me; and when I fell down in the depths of sorrow and heart-wrenching pain, he reassured me to trust in the natural way of life and that I had done all I could. That I gave her the gift that nobody else could—unconditional love, and that allowed her to finally feel as though she had a voice and a choice. When she was ready to go, she did so on her terms, and gave nobody a chance to save to her. She gave herself what she needed, reclaiming her life and her crown like the sovereign queen she was.

Horse told me after Ma passed: "You freed her! You let her run free! You let her sing! You let her dance! You let her rage with the fires and flow with the oceans! You let her live!"

I knew in that moment, that in her dying body her soul came to life, and it was time for me to come to life. That was her gift to me—permission to find my wild roots, abandon all rules of domestication, blaze my own trail, and reclaim my freedom.

After those experiences with Ma and clients like Joanna, I sought opportunities to be up close and personal with horses outside of my healing room. I visited local farms owned by friends. I wanted to be off the horse, as opposed to riding, offering me a chance to interact with the animals naturally and on a level playing field. I learned so much about myself in the process. I was captivated by the relationship between horses and humans. Horses are like humans in that their thoughts, feelings and behaviors are influenced by a combination of biology and past experiences. Like humans, horses are energetically sensitive, easily influenced by the people and environment around them. They can also sense and shift energy within themselves with ease. Horses mirror humans' feelings. If we are anxious, angry, sad, or detached; or if we are not patient or present, the horse will show it all through his actions.

I was particularly enthralled by the idea that because horses are so attuned to feeling and movement, they can detect any internal-external incongruence in humans. They are master bullshit detectors! They can tell if we are presenting false pretenses and where we have separated from our truth. I remember clearly an experience years earlier of spending time in my friend Jodi's barn. I approached a horse who I was told was loving, docile, and warm, yet he bucked and wouldn't allow me near. He wouldn't look me in the eye. What I didn't understand until later is that he sensed in me what I wasn't yet conscious of. He saw my smile as nothing more than the masquerade that it was; the incongruence between my true feelings and my behaviors was too much for him. This taught me that horses desire honesty. They always follow their instincts, knowing only how to be true to themselves in their actions. They can only feel safe with humans who consistently do the same.

My proximity to horses was mirroring the communication skills I present to the world and how I establish rapport with people. I typically went in with smiles blazing, without any discernment, turning up the warmth in an effort to get them to like me right from the start. I became attentive to my body language, seeing that I tended to be hands on and affectionate and while that was genuinely who I was, I learned that when horses aren't understood, it's because humans interfere with their own intentions, and that leads to conflict. I thought about how this is much like human relationships with one another—how we block communication in our human dynamics with our need for control and when that happens, both parties shut down. I thought about my relationships and how much more available others are when I am present, aligned within myself, and open.

The horses showed me where I lacked confidence. Intimidated by their size, I often cowered in their presence, feeling as though I needed to be submissive and didn't deserve to be in their sphere. This allowed me to reflect on other areas of my life where I recoiled and shrunk myself in the presence of people who I believed had more of a right to shine their light and stand tall in their truth.

The more time I spent with horses, I also discovered how well they show humans their unrecognized strengths and gifts, offering feedback for humans' social development, self-regulation, and emotional maturity. They have a keen ability to teach humans about their untapped potential. They possess a fund of wisdom communicated to us through their ways of being.

I learned more about my gifts as an empath from being around horses, particularly in my dreams and journeys. By observing how horses work with their own energy, and noticing how my energy was affected by them, I could identify the various ways that I myself work with energy in my life. Without reminding myself of who I was on an emotional and energetical level and how to work within my energy field, I run the risk of being unaware of how my energy is pushing out into the world reactively instead of responsively. When disconnected from myself, I couldn't see how I was using my energy inefficiently and unproductively, even dangerously at times. When that happens, not only can I not trust myself, but others cannot trust me either. My energetic frequency is low and my vibration in the world is lowered, and much like those erratic and immature horses who are relegated to pasture as they can't be trusted with a job or task of importance, I am useless to the world. Horses were showing me that without an intimate connection with myself, the truth of who I am and what I offer for the world cannot emerge.

I also learned about what actually was happening when people around me—whether friend or client—told me that just being around me could make them feel better. They could be having a horrible day, or be on the brink of suicide, or ready to explode in a fury of rage, and somehow all of that subsides in my presence. I've always known I was a safe container, holding space energetically for people, but it wasn't until I witnessed the same process in horses that I really truly understood the power of my gift. It was almost instantaneous how a horse could transform a bad mood. Countless people will say this, and I witnessed it firsthand for myself. The horse seems to be mindlessly doing its thing, yet it's quite purposefully listening and feeling, calmly, peacefully, and lovingly holding space for the feelings and emotions of the human and then the magic happens as the rage or angst or sadness is replaced with calm, peace, comfort, and hope. The human is more relaxed and open, and their energy can move freely now as blockages have been removed. Clients have told me they don't understand what happened; that they feel so radically different and see the world almost as if the world around them changed. It was transmutation at its finest, and horses reaffirmed my trust in my gifts.

And for horses, empathy and intuition aren't remarkable, magical, or supernatural; in fact, horses remind us that these are ordinary states of being conscious, grounded, and completely present. The noticeably natural mindful stance of horses intrigued me. They live in the here and now, without care of past or future, and this moment-to-moment awareness allows them to connect deeply with their inner world and instincts, as well as being completely attuned to their environments and what's happening around them. They have minimal distress, as they trust in the natural unfolding of life, and they respond as needed. Similarly, they answer the call of their needs, eating when hungry, resting when tired, and even scratching when they have an itch. They don't seek permission from an external source, they source it for themselves.

Horses showed me where I was still trying too hard and striving. Watching them take effortless action towards being the horses they were meant to be reminded me of the Taoist wisdom on non-striving and acceptance. Witnessing the horses freely in their element, releasing the need to conform, abandoning the conditioning in exchange for authenticity that allowed them to move with grace and elegance, reminded me how constant striving for self-improvement was a misuse of my energy and effort.

Surrounding myself with horses also offered me greater experiential knowledge of somatic experiencing and bodywork. The key difference between prey animals and humans is that horses may experience pain that interrupts their nervous system, but the distress is localized to the present moment. They lack the cognitive ability to overthink and analyze the meaning of the pain and how to prevent it in the future. The horse simply cannot project into the future. If something that once frightened them reappears, then they will react again. But they don't sit around waiting for it and worrying about whether it will show up again. In studying this distinction between horses and humans, I learned a critical fact about trauma: The painful event in and of itself isn't what causes suffering or trauma. It's the fear about the pain that creates the trauma, and the choice to remain paralyzed by fear is what is the enemy. This was a profoundly essential discovery that would inform my own healing as well as my approach as a healer.

Then I had my first riding experience; and as I swung my legs over the massive back of Winston, rose to a straight spine, and embraced the magnitude of the experience of being 10 feet off the ground, I realized I was held up by nothing other than faith. As my legs clung to his underbelly like a small child wrapped around her mamma, I placed all of my trust in him—this massive being who could literally end my life in an instant. He and I spoke, a loving conversation in which he asked me to not only trust him, but more importantly to trust myself. I asked him to show me the way when I couldn't see one myself, help me to know trust again, and remind me of the power that I possess to face my fears and release them in to the wind, embracing only faith and an unrelenting inner knowing guided by spirit. I asked him to protect me and strengthen me so that I never again let them break my spirit, dull my shine, or tame my wild.

As we rode, I remembered the feeling of running like the wind. I remembered being there before, at a much earlier time in my life, when I saw the world through his eyes, through our eyes. I heard his words again, so clear:

"When you whisper in my ear, you breathe life into my heart. When you trust me with your power, I can gently strip away all of my defenses. When you show me that I've lost my way, I can finally see the signs for home. When you look at me, I can see hidden parts of my soul through your eyes. When you invite me to relax and find freedom in our movements, I am reminded to walk my path with grace and gratitude for the magical elements of beauty and spirit all around me. When you allow my hands to grace your body as a conduit of life force energy, I learn that peace is an energetic language and the quieter I become, the more I can hear. When we connect heart to heart, I am reminded of the ultimate truth of existence which is that we are all ONE."

Dance of Liberation

Remembering horse's prophetic words were all I needed to empower me to take flight as the woman I was before the world told me who to be: a medicine woman with inner and outer eyes wide open to see with clarity and deep intuition brandishing her sword of truth and authenticity as she runs free as a fierce wild mare.

I just have to remember who I am, what is my medicine, and that I have the fortitude to lovingly deliver it into the world. And when I feel alone, all I have to do is call upon and connect to the power and strength of the collective.

I made these vows to Allegra Topanga as I entered what was clearly a brave new world that would require me to put my newly acquired skills to the test. It was the reason for my quest, my rebellion. I still had Lola's parting words from Maine fresh in my heart: *Go out in the woods, go out! If you don't go out in the woods, nothing will ever happen and your life will never begin.*

Those profound words taken from *The Wolf's Eyelash* from Clarissa Pinkola-Estes (the myth behind the classic Little Red Riding Hood story) encapsulated my own story: the heroine learns the true wisdom of the wolves—unless we go out, rebel, experience the world with our intuition as our guide, life never actually begins.

Rebellion is a natural state of asserting our thoughts, beliefs, and opinions into the greater conversation of the culture. "Don't go out," they say. Fuck the rules! It was time to create my own. I now saw freedom as the remarkable difference between working hard to create a life that is your truth, and working hard to fit in to a life that you have been programmed to believe you should want. I knew that the world had been waiting for my rebellion, for my busting out of the cage to challenge, disagree, and unmute the loud inner chatter of my spirit that was dying to be heard. My voice was relevant. The world needed to ingest my medicine and gifts—to hear my song, listen to my stories, and witness my dance.

Now broken open and free, it was time to dance, but differently. No longer bound by external choreography, I now felt spirit coursing through me allowing my body to move authentically, unbridled, wild and free. Conscious and ecstatic dance mirrored the universal, ceremonious, and moving prayers of reverence that had been used throughout history. Being alive is dancing! It was time to give my body permission to unapologetically tell its story.

So much of my life had been disciplined and militant, selfless and sacrificing—everything from the Catholic School experiences to the Mommy-and-Me playgroups at Gymboree in which I was taught that the best moms were the ones who stifled their own needs, aimed to please their husbands and children, spoke softly and slowly, and behaved prudently and prudishly. My yoga practice also started to feel too linear and rigid. I learned that a perfect Vinyasa class had five Sun Salute A series, three Sun Salute B series, every pose was held for five breaths, no more no less. Even choreographed Nia classes felt too structured and controlled. I followed every rule even when it didn't feel "right" to me. I had lived in a state of contraction. Every action in my life had been motivated by fear.

Not anymore.

My vision quest showed me that I had the choice to move toward what I wanted as opposed to running away from what I didn't want, and that was a game changer. I now chose to run toward anything that made me feel whole and healthy. All my choices were motivated by the intention of aligning with my truth and my mission of living life authentically.

One Dance Tribe

"The dance is strong magic. The dance is a spirit. It turns the body to liquid steel. It makes it vibrate like a guitar. The body can fly without wings. It can sing without voice. The dance is strong magic: The dance is life."

— Pearl Primus

Dance was one way I had been practicing living out loud, but now it was time to kick up the volume another notch. I no longer wanted to be bound by structure and choreography. It was time to establish my own paradigms and practices; time to reclaim my free spirit so I could live life out of the box, like the jovial gypsy child who marched to the beat of her own drum on the streets of the Bronx. Like horse, it was time to surrender to each moment and allow my own instincts and intuition to take the reins, following nothing but spirit.

Once I made that decision, an opportunity to practice presented itself. I attended a One Dance Tribe retreat, a gathering of teachers, spiritual leaders, healers, and artists, from around the globe in a transformational conscious dance event, and as my fairy-knotted mane flew in the breeze as

I ran free, I felt open; a clear channel for shakti energy—the divine force that is the essence of the world and all beings—the feminine energy of creation, of destruction, of all matter. I felt my vibration heighten and a bliss that I once knew as a child. As I moved, I was that pure, graceful yet fiery child once again. That's when I realized that we dance to remember.

At that retreat, I had the privilege of experiencing the Dance of Liberation—a potent blend of movement-based therapy with ancient shamanic tradition and ceremony. In the dimly lit sanctuary of the iconic Garrison Institute, a former 1920s seminary and monastery along the Hudson River, I wrapped a silky purple bandana around my eyes to obscure any trace of light and connect with my inner vision. The rhythm of my breath matched the resonance of ambient flute music reverberating from the speakers, sending cascades of vibration through my body and filling it with juicy, life-force prana. Winged animals, gliding through an orange and yellow sky, appeared in my third eye as the sounds of drums and rattles emerged. Within seconds, beautiful images of snakes slithering rhythmically and panthers prancing fused with my being. We moved as one.

I daringly surrendered and began to undulate sensually and ecstatically. Channels opened. As my heart opened and led the way, an urgent craving for space and freedom, for beauty and sacred sexuality in its purest expression, began to flow. The surge of primal energy within me joined the planetary pulse through all of existence. Every cell danced in a state of harmony. All beings were influenced by my swaying. The birds knew which direction to fly in relation to my movements. The circadian rhythm of the planet aligned with me, because of me. I became aware that I exist because of it. Our movements together connected me to a time of simplicity, of oneness with nature, to the pure essence that exists in all dimensions.

My body took the shape of the trees, of every animal that's ever walked or flown on this planet. My heart lit the way for the creation of life, shining the way for others to come. In this sacred dance, I understood that I create the circle, I enter the circle, I am the circle. My legacy is to create an opening for life, to celebrate the sacredness of the land, the elders, their stories, the songs, the collective wisdom, to propagate the planet with love. I felt part of a communion of souls destined to evolve and co-create in a mission of love, our walking story woven with the fabric of hidden relics and ancient wisdom that have been excavated along the path to freedom. In the spinning of the wheel, the circle of life, one love is always what we return to. Coming home. As my body continued to move like sensual stardust sprinkled on the landscape, I felt myself sharing the wisdom … *Become it. You are it. Own it. Trust it. Creation becomes out of passion and sensual gracefulness for yourself. Feel it. And so it is. Touch every particle of matter with sensuality, and the mundane becomes magic. Have the courage to surrender to the ecstatic bliss. Let go, and dance.*

In those moments of immense clarity and connection with myself and all of creation, I truly experienced what the shamans have always known—that dancing, singing, storytelling, and silence really are the four universal healing salves! Yes, I have all the medicine I need within me. Yes, Shamanism emerged millennia ago in indigenous societies to serve the healing needs of the tribes and help them move through collective challenges and hardships. Yes, it is my dharma to apply the potent ancient medicine that I am privileged to carry within me into our modern times.

As I heard so clearly in my Dance of Liberation these words of a Cherokee poem:

To dance is to pray

To pray is to heal
To heal is to give
To give is to live
To live is to dance

That Dance of Liberation energized my mission of empowering others on their own journeys. I see now that dance is synonymous with change and how we navigate between control and chaos, struggle and ease, power and vulnerability, and fear and trust. By stepping into this dance in the darkness, Allegra Topanga was unleashed and untamed as a radiant embodied being. The feral foal was back, unbridled and running free.

How was I different once the music ended that day? I sashayed away knowing that sometimes the boldest movements we can make are the ones that take the least effort. I had become more comfortable with my vulnerability and resilient in my strength. I understood the difference between fear-based control of the ego, versus the free-form, love-based power of the spirit.

Yet another truth emerged from that day forward. So much of my journey until then was about discovering my inner gifts and abilities that connected me to higher planes of existence. I discovered a reality beyond that which my eyes could perceive. I had connected with alternative realms, otherworldly states of consciousness, and had daily mystical experiences of connecting with Source. Yet I had limited awareness of my own human flesh for so long. I was skilled with how to ascend, but I had been a novice at grounding.

Much like telling a story, consciously dancing as a fully embodied spiritual being was a way for me to assemble myself into one cohesive narrative. I can now see all the parts, and all the experiences that created this story as a whole. I can see all the mishaps and all of the successes and own all of it as a necessary part of the dance. The outcome of the dance, much like the outcome of the story, doesn't matter; what matters most is the story of the journey. The story itself has its own soul. On the dance floor that day, I was moving into my story with all of its joys, wisdom, and grief. Now I just need to choose this every day, to ask myself this question upon waking:

Do I have the discipline and courage to be a free spirit?
... which really means:
Will I bravely choose to be myself at all costs?

Releasing Allegra Topanga on that dance floor seemed to open a portal to the elders and ancestors who came before me, but most noticeably was a strong sense of myself as an elder. Like in the journeys with Natalie all those years prior, seeing myself as the woman in the cloak, with long flowing silver hair representing the depth of accumulated experiences, I knew who I was, and who I am now: the one who carried within a deeply held spirituality and a calm presence who teaches, offers wisdom and principles through her personal stories to bring a sense of balance and harmony to the community. I am now confident that I had a responsibility to bring the elements of ancient tradition, knowledge, ritual, and ceremony to the modern world.

Ironically, the wisdom that I have accumulated on this healing journey came because of the courage to venture out into the unknown to unlearn all that I was conditioned to believe. The truth is that although people in my life were telling me that I changed, I hadn't really changed at all. It's just that the medicine in me was hidden for so long out of fear. All that changed is that I finally found the audacity to be who I truly am.

And my sense of how my mission was to unfold was affirmed in a sacred path card reading with Parashakti, the creator of the Dance of Liberation.

"Kristy, your soul is going through a rite of passage, preparing you for your next chapter as a sacred leader. It is critical to purify your vessel so that spirit can work through you. Practice discernment by saying no to all that isn't in alignment with your truth. Trust and follow your intuition at all costs. Root down and ground to allow for the embodiment of your next chapter of your service in life to really come to its fruition, as you shed the old skin like a snake. Aho! Kristy, you are a medicine woman!"

As the retreat ended, Parashakti came to me, placing inside of my palms a gray suede pouch with fringes and an amber bead at the folded closure. "For you, a beautiful and true medicine woman, may you never forget your medicine."

I knew in that moment that it was time to introduce Allegra Topanga as a wise mentor and elder. During a time when the therapy and coaching industries were flooded with programs and frameworks that emphasized mindset shifting and behavioral changes, with no mention of trauma, or returning to our roots and intuition, it was so clear to me why millions of people, many of whom were showing up on my couch, continued to struggle despite getting "help." It was time for a paradigm shift; and Allegra Topanga was called forth to radically change the personal development game by offering a holistic mentorship approach rooted in ancient wisdom and soulful science that would teach modern seekers at all ages and stages how to shift from outsourcing guidance to discovering and trusting their own inner wisdom. In this way, every person can restore and protect their natural essence and actualize the fullest extent of their potential. Everyone has a right to reclaim their sovereignty. It's time for all humans to be rewilded!

My vision was crystal clear now: I would guide others on their journeys using the light of my wounds. Though my story is intimately personal, I believe it is intensely relatable. After all, the experience of being human is fundamentally a heroine's journey and living life is a vision quest to discover truth and return to our essence. As the natural creators, women possess a fundamental spiritual and psychological connection with all of creation. Regardless of our culture or background, we come from a long line of ancestors who lived in accordance with the natural cycles and rhythms of the Earth, and lived in relationship with animals, plants, and spirits. As modern times have uprooted us from these essential connections, the consequences for most women have been dire. Like the domesticated animals and cultivated lands on the verge of extinction, woman's inner fires have been extinguished. Rewilding is critical for restoring our vital connections in order to reclaim the power of womanhood

And on that brilliant, sun-drenched day, as she soared about the lush green meadows surrounding the majestic old monastery on the Hudson, Allegra's Rewilding Coaching program was conceived.

A Brave New World

*J*ust as I embraced this braver, truer interior version of me, the outside world started to change at lightning speed. A lethal virus began infecting people like wildfire, and fear spread even more rapidly than the disease. Ominous as things sounded in the media, I wasn't scared of the COVID-19 pandemic. If my decades-long vision quest taught me anything, it was how to dance between trust and fear. I knew to surrender to the higher purpose of what was unfolding. No stranger to discomfort, I now trusted that times of uncertainty presented possibilities. I possessed all that I needed to experience the excitement that this pregnant pause had to offer the world.

Arriving home from One Dance Retreat was unlike my previous experiences of integrating back into life following a retreat. Due to the coronavirus, I was regarded as a leper because I had been out in public. Before entering my own home, I had to leave my luggage outside to air out, remove my clothes at the door, and shower immediately to detoxify. It was neither the warm welcome I had envisioned, nor a quiet opportunity to contemplate all I had experienced on my trip. What was happening in my environment and around the world was surreal, actually. Yet in a strange way, it felt oddly comfortable and familiar. A year prior, I had what some might call a premonition, a deep knowing that something epic was afoot for all inhabitants of the world, a massive catastrophic shift for all living beings. It came in the form of a dream:

The world outside my four walls was in chaos, the village was full of sick and dying people who were quarantined. I met up with my group to cook meals and prepare remedies for the people, and ran in shifts to deliver them. I felt the adrenaline rush through me almost as quickly as my feet ran up and down the stairs of this hostel. My friend appeared in front of me, bleeding from his neck. I covered him with a burgundy blanket, hummed sweetly and softly in his ear, and held him in my arms until there was no more blood, and the wound became nothing but a scar. Then a little brown-eyed girl with long blonde pigtails approached and asked, "Can you help me find my bicycle? And maybe you can find someone to play with me? I'm so lonely." I reached for her hand, as I knew exactly where to lead her to find her bicycle. The father of the little girl appeared. "You need to stay with my daughter. She is sick. She needs your medicine." The girl and I sang and danced, made crafts, and told stories together. Then she curled up on my lap and fell asleep peacefully. I felt something inside of her. I reached my hands inside of her body, and I removed a bundle of fear from inside of her stomach, lungs, and heart. I put the fear in a pouch and ran downstairs to feed it to the animals who by this time were starving. The girl's father found me, thanked me profusely for saving his daughter, and asked, "Who are you?" "I am Allegra Topanga."

Upon waking from this dream, I wrote in my journal:

It's time for a change, a shift. I sense something big is about to happen for all of humanity, for all beings. The planet can't be sustained at the pace it is going. I feel like the Earth is spinning off its axis, and the planets are out of alignment. Collectively, all the energy of the universe is out of order. There is a massive energetic cyclone moving at lightning speed creating universal chaos that will soon be felt right in our own backyards, and deep within our bones. In our daily lives we are moving too fast, too furiously, too disconnectedly, and too detached. We have no sense of an inner world, just a preoccupation with an outer world; a fixation on material wealth and acquisitions, with minimal time for human relationships. A completely lost sense of the interconnectedness of all of humanity, that we are all one. A lost sense of the sacredness of families, of family time, of the sacred ceremony of dinners, and other rituals. Of the importance of a tribe. Of the importance of going back to basics—growing, gathering, and cooking food, sharing in community, storytelling and shared wisdom from the elders. Forgotten are the simple yet profoundly meaningful moments. In its place are machines, modern conveniences, overscheduled itineraries, outsourced jobs, and bodies as empty vessels devoid of spirit. A society that has too much and too little at the same time. A society with everything and nothing at the same time. Mother Earth's limited resources cannot sustain the exponential explosion of the population and extortion of reserves. I feel Mother Earth's fatigue in my own bones. She needs time to stop, reset, and receive, and she will soon be calling "time out." Hopefully, we listen like obedient children. Life as we know it will come to a screeching halt. Hopefully, we will all contemplate the deeper meaning. Nobody will be immune from experiencing this period of darkness, and the light awaits only those who make it to the other side. Change is imminent, and the catalyst is on its way. I welcome the winds of change.

In the days that followed, as I somehow had known, things drastically worsened in the world. Thousands more were hospitalized, hospitals were at or above capacity, emergency medical ships were summoned into nearby New York harbor, and even more people were dying. People rushed the stores to overstock on groceries and toiletries (who could forget the toilet paper memes?). Parents became teachers for their kids as schools closed. People worked from home or lost jobs. Many small businesses closed their doors permanently because of huge financial losses. All of humanity was in a mandatory quarantine, except for first responders who were working round the clock to keep people alive.

I took comfort in the truth that led me to know of this event in the first place and knowing what this event truly represented. I trusted that my family would be healthy, and that sickness wasn't an option for us, especially as I had been diligent about boosting not just our physical immunity with vitamins and healing foods, but our energetic immunity such that the frequency of illness had no resonance within us. I knew by now that I didn't have to make others' fear a part of my story. I could create my own reality based upon my own truths.

Although the world was slowing down, I'd never heard so much noise. The collective fear was unbelievably loud; and by this point in my vision quest, I knew that meant I had to get quiet. I sought refuge in the place in which I felt most alive and most myself—nature, running to the place where the water flows freely, the sun radiates its warming light, the birds sing their cheerful calls, the breeze whispers to the tree branches. I sat amongst it all, in connection with it all, and breathed . . .

. . .taking in awareness, acceptance, surrender, grace, trust, openness with each inhale

...releasing resistance, doubt, fear, conditioning, limiting beliefs with each exhale

My breath was my bait, luring me back to my inner truths, the wisdom of my guides, and the sanctuary of my body. My breath was the neutralizer that allowed my body to again become a clear channel, an instrument for the dance and song of spirit to course through as a prayerful offering to raise the vibration of the planet.

. . . As I breathe, I create expansion . . .

. . . I empty so I can feel full . . .

. . . My music becomes clear, and everything unnecessary passes through . . .

. . . Only what's divine remains . . . then I can truly be a conduit for spirit to work through me, for me, for the world.

As I sat in stillness a few days upon returning home, I felt the energy of eagle overhead reminding me to fly above the storm, that I have the freedom and courage to look ahead, that the circle of life is perfectly in balance so there is nothing to fear. I went into my meditation space, reached for my shamanic drum, and sat in the middle of the floor in front of my ceremonial altar. I closed my eyes and hummed my song as I drummed— the same lullaby I "made up" over 35 years ago when I was a scared little girl, alone, sitting on the floor of her room.

This is what I do now when the demons of fear threaten to consume me: I pause, connect with my sensations, allow the energy to move— making space for my intuition to speak—and I can hear the whispers of the soothing song emanating from deep within the cave of my heart. And the scary world transforms into a magical land of love and laughter, where I dance with the trees and horses, and take flight with the birds. In singing my song, I am calling upon my own medicine. I trust that I am abundant, complete, and enough; lacking in nothing, needing nothing. All my soul needs for its evolution is for me to live, just as I am, as an infinite source of love. This became my mantra as I navigated this new world. It requires flexibility, adaptability, and resiliency; all of which I now possessed. I am free to live and ride the waves of life's tides knowing that most of the time, the way things unfold is often so much more magical than my most meticulously predetermined plans.

As for the power animals, numerology, and oracle cards, they are only showing me what already exists in me. They don't teach me anything that I don't already know. I am no longer a seeker. As a source, I am plugged into my inner wisdom and intuition. We can all do this. We can trust that in any situation, we have all we need inside of us, and that even in the most trying of times, and when experiencing pain, we can take action to create expansion and growth, instead of creating suffering. We can see the possibility in all situations and focus on what we actually have control over. By being our own power source, we can manifest the energy of creation to take an undesirable or challenging circumstance and turn it into something for good and for growth. As a result, we can experience freedom, peace, love, and joy even in challenging times. And this leads to a natural cycle of life, using the death of the old to give life to something new.

I now knew another truth: that growth is achieved when we fully live; not when we run away and retreat on journeys to mystical inner worlds connecting with animals, fairies and spirits; or catching glimpses of alternative planes of existence during profound meditations; or finding the proverbial heaven while ecstatically dancing and striving for spirituality. I knew now that my spiritual gifts had little to do with diving inside of a chrysocolla rock or shapeshifting into purple light beaming out of my crown chakra and blasting me into the stars or astral traveling in dreams.

Floating in the clouds isn't living; and basking in angelic light only blinds us from seeing what is actually real in front of our eyes. Feeling safe in the enchantment of the non-physical world, while still shunning my actual physical reality like the plague wasn't enlightenment or living spiritually. Living is staying right here, right now, climbing through the unfathomable murky troughs of pandemic disease and collective chaos; smelling and tasting the sludge, rooting our toes in it, drenching our bodies in it, rubbing it in deeply to each and every layer of our flesh, and seeing that life in the actual trenches could be as magical as the places we go to escape for reprieve.

Every day that we are alive is a vision quest, as we venture into the harsh and unforgiving world witnessing beauty amidst atrocities, forging ahead courageously while starving for truth. It's a battle, yet we have been trained as warriors.

It was time to let my life be my guru and find the strength to sit at its feet and be taught. Wisdom comes when I stop searching and start living; and in living authentically in my full human potential, bringing spiritual practices into the most ordinary moments. It is seeing that life can be a magical adventure in which our choices can manifest our wildest imaginings, and inspiring others to do the same. I finally understood what it meant to truly serve the world as a healer.

As the melody of my song breathed life into this realization, and the memory of shapeshifting into a raven consumed me, I just knew that it was time to create something new. It was time to share my story.

Deliverance

The long, heroic adventure through the light of my wounds has been a reclamation. Every leg of the journey has bestowed precious gems.

Meditation revealed my dark and light shadows. Yoga showed me connection and equanimity. Shamanism revealed my medicine and reminded me to believe. Craniosacral balancing and Reiki unveiled my psychic gifts and the need to trust my intuitive power. Dancing unleashed my wild and reminded me of my fiery grace. Writing gave me my voice and reminded me to express it at all costs. Horses empowered me with purpose and reminded me to freely trailblaze. Collectively, all of it brought me back home to myself, to pure love, to my wild.

I now carried a medicine bag packed with cumulative knowledge gleaned from the elements of Mother Earth, the ancestors and elders who came before me, and the richness of wisdom of my own life experiences guided by intuition and spirit; and now was the time to open it and share it with the world through storytelling, dance, song, meditation, writing, creating and communion with others and the Earth. This was the moment I had been preparing for, and I felt ready.

On a crisp twilight evening that early spring in 2020, I went outside to sit by a pond to allow the wisdom of these truths to penetrate me. As I sat, I admired the magnificent long-legged gray crane who had flown in with its broad wings and slender neck. The small boulder alongside the pond became its dance floor, as its feet, legs, and body moved rhythmically. Though cranes are known to dance as a part of their mating ritual, this crane seemed to find joy in his solo performance. It was as if the pandemonium of the world choreographed his frisky tango.

I thought about how the Japanese refer to the crane as the "bird of happiness," revering these majestic animals as symbols of peace, hope, and healing. In Japanese mythology, it is said that the wings of the crane carried souls up to heaven; and legend has it that if one folded 1,000 origami cranes, one's wish would be granted by the gods. The legend of 1,000 origami cranes was popularized by the story of Sadako Sasaki, a Japanese girl who at the age of two was exposed to radiation from the atomic bomb of Hiroshima during World War II; and by the age of 12 diagnosed with leukemia, she began folding origami cranes during her lengthy hospital stays.

Watching the crane tango with life, I thought about Sasaki's story of transmuting her fear into love. Despite her impending death, she aligned with the energy of creation to give birth to something that could bring hope and inspiration to so many. She chose to live while she was still physically alive, finding hope and love in the shadows of death's door, and in the process giving her soul more experiences for its evolution. She lived her truth, and her truth lives on to this day in her story.

The privilege of witnessing this crane's graceful dance taught me about this process we call 'healing.' I had spent years believing that the healer's journey is one of inevitable strife and suffering; and I approached *the work* like I approached all other things in my life—with all my power and might, pushing out and pulling in, to the point of exhaustion. I expended so much energy on fighting the ego, trying to obliterate it to just feel the good parts of me that I knew were hiding. But battling the ego—a fundamental part of myself that cannot even be destroyed as its vital for the survival of the human—was creating even more inner opposition, division, and turmoil. Trying to get rid of our ego by vehemently driving it into submission isn't healing! I learned to instead embrace and befriend my ego like a fragile child, caring for it by respectfully teaching it boundaries and offering it unconditional love and acceptance. And instead of scolding it when it overstepped, or focusing on its well-intentioned mistakes, I just had to focus my efforts on strengthening my true inner voice so that both ego and true self would learn their respective places in my life.

That's where the freedom comes in—from giving up the fight and realizing that there are no enemies within the self. All parts deserve to be seen and heard, and we get to decide whether to hold on to or let go of what they share. True liberation comes from letting in, letting move through, and then letting go. Surrendering to the dance. This is a conscious, deliberate intentional way of living in which make the choice to let go of all that is not our truth, while embracing all that is and sharing that with the world. Surrendering is a spaciousness that allows for both enjoyable and uncomfortable sensations and feelings to tango together as partners; and the dance is organically choreographed by the raw material of life's magical moments.

I see now that healing is a softer process; it's not forceful, procedural, or systematic. It's a gentle, rhymical, and cyclical process of unveiling, unbecoming, and unlearning; a peaceful letting go and surrendering of all that no longer serves, and all that we no longer are, and gracefully and gratefully loving it away. It's a caring level of honesty that allows us to recognize when the ego is trying to overstep and when the voice of our true self has been muted. In the process, the parts of ourselves that had been cut off or banished into the shadows are invited to emerge, to be cared for, and to be integrated so that we may become whole. And then we can settle in and accept ourselves right as we are with all that we have.

Healing is wholeness. It is a conscious choice to examine my life through the light of my wounds; and like orienting a kaleidoscope towards the light, looking into the depths to see the changing symmetrical patterns formed from the myriad of colorful pieces of my life experiences, I can see the inherent beauty that reveals itself in each go round. I have the choice to use this beauty to choreograph my own radiant life.

These were precisely the lessons that I could now apply to these uncertain times. Each day is a true heroine's journey in which we are all encountering the enemies of isolation, loss, pain, demons, and doubt that can be rattling and threatening. But for me, I can't *un-see* what I have seen. I can't *un-know* what I now know. Each day I make the choice to meet the challenges head on with equanimity such that I can know when to draw my sword of love and truth, trust when to lay it down, and courageously walking the path as a spiritual being in this human vessel, welcoming each encounter as a necessary teacher for my soul's evolution. No fear, only trust.

Thriving in this world demands that we uncage ourselves and live naturally and authentically, courageously following our innate wisdom, and returning to the essential magic and medicine that our truest selves have always known but lost. Like any animal navigating the wild, we must return to our most primitive inherited senses to "read" both the visible and invisible landscapes with nothing but our instincts as our compass. We must be rooted in ancient wisdom in order to rise in these modern times.

In the same way that the crane showed up to share his story with me, I was ready to share mine, confident that this was my personal responsibility to best support the outer world as a guide and healer. I knew now that if I wanted to inspire others to have the courage and the audacity to know themselves, heal themselves, free themselves, see themselves as whole and complete, and above all else, to love themselves, then I had to share my experiences of doing the same. My rewilding was my legacy.

As a sacred storyteller, the truthfulness of my narrative is the bridge that connects us all. My story is my origami crane; and my life is the creative expression of the alchemy from fear to hope, trust, and love. And as the crane's tango came to a simmer, and it sat in stillness on the rock regally stretching its neck with poise and self-assurance, it was time to stretch my own neck out of hiding behind excuses, shame, and doubt.

Preparing for the final stages of labor, I reached for my pen and journal on my desk in front of the window. My eyes caught a glimpse of the majestic crane perched on a rock beside the pond. He waited, he watched, and when the time was right, he entered the water with ease, gently scooping up his meal, and he returned to the rock as the fish dangled from his beak. He savored it, not with fear that it would be his last, but with trust that there would always be more. He knew his place in the landscape of the world; his identity was distinctly clear, and his actions were his living story, his truth. And when he finished his meal, he outstretched his magnificent wings, and flew away into the unknown to continue his journey.

As I followed his ascension with my eyes, I reflected on my vision quest for truth, recapitulated in the soaring expanse of the wings of that crane. The girl, always a seeker, always knowing there was more, always believing

265

there was nothing else worth doing in her life other than finding what was on the other side of the veil they wrapped her in; held back by fear, she was forced to source knowledge from the books, teachings, and institutions that were invested in keeping the wool over her eyes. She studied every letter, committed to memory every word, as her fearful ego exalted while her spirit was dying a slow insidious death. Just as her body had collapsed, falling into the arms of death, the truth within her still had a pulse. She mustered every bit of strength to let what was ready to go die, so that her true spirit could finally live. She knew she must leave, no longer was peaking and peering out of the cave an option. It was time for her to make her way back home. She had to venture out of the illusory world she knew and into the vast unknown; where the knowledge of books and reason had no meaning, for the path was one that could never have been written about and could never be explored within the confines of the mind. This was radical trailblazing, with intuition as the only useful guide; and she would see and feel things that have never been written about, things that others couldn't see, trading mundane for magic with every touch of her hand. She was pure alchemy. Yet she could also root deeply, and trust in herself as the source. Each encounter on her quest changed her so profoundly that she died and was reborn each and every time, bringing her closer and closer to home.

And here she was now, ready to shift from working on herself, to putting her work out in the world, in the energy of creation, letting her life be the innovation. The story of her heroic vision quest adventure has the potential to become her living legacy, passed down to those who come after her, seeking in the same way that she had. She recognized the seekers well, she wanted to teach them how to discover the truth, how to trade comfortable and ordinary, for mystical and magical; and when they accepted her invitation, she would school them with the knowledge of their own spirits, guiding them out of the heavy layers of numbing armor that had shielded them, so they can feel and see and remember. She would summon their true selves with her song, and the vibration will shatter the layered veil even more. With spirit coursing through her, she will guide them into the darkness of their shadows, to discover the light of their wounds, and they would learn that what they thought was a breakdown was really a breakthrough—the point in which they descend into the depths of darkness to rediscover their light, slaying with their golden sword of truth the illusory veil that once shrouded their vision, and they see, finally, the beauty and love that was waiting there all along. She will honor them as sacred, until they remember the divinity within themselves. They will learn to source themselves, never again needing to seek outside. And then, they emerge as exquisite winged-ones ready to soar.

As the pen released from my fingers, I looked out the window witnessing the hawks circling above the pond, following each other in a reverent dance. Seduced by their joy and ecstasy, my body began to move rhythmically. I accepted the invitation to dance. With my wings outstretched in freedom, playfulness, lightness, with my song emanating from my heart, I allowed my body to write the story.

I saw a vision now, a beautiful, majestic mountain. Its rough edges, pointed peaks, and steep cliffs are softened by the warmth of the sun gleaming its rays of light all around in a protective halo. The light illuminates the highlighted earth, revealing unexpected strands of auburn, gold, and rust. There is movement now, and another shadow is casting, as Allegra Topanga arrives. She lays, her skin grazing the soil like lips of a lover plump with desire, with craving, with sensual lust, brushing against the one for whom she is ravenous. She melts into her lover's essence, they become one.

She summons the sun, further ignited by its power. The air envelops her like a blanket, and empowers her wings. Ignited, full, strong, connected, in this magical union of earth, fire, metal, and air, she moves. And with each slow and graceful movement, the earth responds with excitement as its parts awaken. She twists and gyrates, slides and rubs, tantalizing the earth with her every breath-infused rhythm. The rhythms are soft, steady, flowing, melodic bringing harmony to her lover. She breathes deeper, longer, as she is further ignited, feeling the breath of all of existence that she has awakened. She pulses, she penetrates, she rolls, she glides swiftly as the tides and currents of distant oceans respond in kind and the planet is uplifting with each breath, with each chant, with each moan, her song of exaltation, she releases... and releases... and releases.... pure bliss is felt from her flow. She has brought the treasure.

Deliverance.

As my consciousness brought me back into the room, as I jovially moved through the house, I heard the voice of my boys asking, "Mommy why do you dance all the time?"

Taking their hands and arms in mine and leading them to join in the dance, "To get conscious, awaken my heart, liberate my spirit, and evolve my soul. To deliver all of me to this great universe. To see the magic. To surrender. To excavate the stories inside of me. To hear the voice of love and quiet the voice of fear. To share love. To create a portal through which I can connect to all realms. To connect to my authentic self while rooting in the natural Earth. This is my medicine, my healing elixir for the world. I dance to remember my roots, rekindle my instincts, and reclaim my sovereignty."

"Mommy, can you tell us the story about the time when you were little and you were scared?"

"Of course, sweeties, let's go outside and sit all together under that beautiful tree. These stories are for the land, too."

I smiled confidently, picked up my medicine bag, and headed out into the woods, held by all who came before, and with the next generation close behind, so my life could finally begin.

And . . . so it is... Aho!

A Note from Allegra Topanga

"There's nothing to writing; all you do is sit down at a typewriter and bleed."

My children's eyes widened as Hemingway's quote rolled off my tongue as they questioned, "Mommy why did it take you so long to write your book?"

As the light of the first day of the new year dawned, and I hit "send," ushering off another set of edits bringing me so close to the finish line, tears poured and my heart exploded with pride as my boys cheered me on. At 12 and 10 they can't possibly understand that writing this book has been the most difficult thing I have ever done, with only sore nipples of breastfeeding two babies back to back over six years being a close second. Like nursing little fledglings, nourishing my story has been nothing short of both draining and dignifying.

The way I see it, a memoir is a collection of living truths that have been accumulated as one moves through the stories of their life and recognizes that each circumstance has been a grand metaphor for something deeper. It's a documentation of an awakening in which one catches a glimpse of light peeking out from the shadows of a place they never before knew existed. It's a depiction of the map they followed to courageously venture out of the comforts of home and into the unknown territories of their soul to excavate the buried relics of truths of who they are and why they came. It's a celebration of their fortitude and perseverance as they encounter teachers along the way who inevitably challenge them to feel what before they only knew how to repress and suppress. It's a blueprint for how to renter the world as a changed person with a new view, as they can't un-see what they have seen. It's an invitation for others to find the courage to embark on the same heroic adventure, with the comfort of knowing they aren't alone, as they are held closely by the heroines who came before them.

My children have witnessed the sleepless nights, the crying, the isolation, the frustration; and the joy, the pride, the excitement, and the relief as this journal-baby's growth progressed through its developmental stages.

Writing this story has been my most profound therapy, elaborate movement practice, treasured achievement, and miraculous rebirth. Like my children, the soul of this story chose to come through me, and like conscious parenting, in allowing their journeys to organically unfold, I have birthed my own power, purpose, and potential.

I was finally ready to make this debut. I had this calling for so long, but it had been terrifying to consider being so exposed. As an awakened adult, shame still tried to call the shots, telling me that I was still unworthy and that my story had no value. Shame tried to tell me that people would laugh, ridicule, judge, and abandon me for speaking my truth. Shame told me that nobody would even care enough about me to read my story, or that I would come across as weak, desperate, unsuccessful, and unprofessional. Shame told me that I was an unskilled imposter incapable of communicating her story effectively or meaningfully for others. I was terrified that I would be misunderstood and that others wouldn't "get" it. Yet I also worried that I would be completely understood, and that others will get it, get me, see me, and then I wouldn't be able to hide anymore. Shame also told me that my story didn't really matter and didn't deserve for the world to hold space for its existence. I was terrified that as I spoke my truth it would hurt others, incriminate them, make them feel attacked or defensive. I spent years keeping parts of my story hidden in boxes and compartmentalizing feelings. But I quickly learned that compartmentalization is just a fancy word for fear; and the stories that we protect the most are the ones that hold the most power for our healing.

Shame told me never to take off my mask, for the blemishes revealed underneath would make people shudder. Shame silenced me for too long.

I am strong enough to write what previously terrified me, courageous enough to share it for the good of the collective, and compassionate enough to treat myself with love and kindness as I unravel the intricate web of stories that formed the fabric of my being.

Healing is writing, and writing is healing. As I write my story, I am rewriting my nervous system—as each story is excavated from within, I am pruning outdated neural pathways, and each word represents new synaptic connections. With each revelation comes a process of making sense of events in my life, allowing critical connections to organically be made so that the events can be integrated, and the feelings can be assimilated into the whole of my being. With every 'because...', and 'so...,' and 'now I realize . . .' cause and effect is being understood within a timeline of my personal and collective histories, and meaning is made from my memories. With this insight, my perspectives shift, old paradigms are released, healthy belief systems are

273

created, and harmony can be restored within my being. I am rewriting the code for the energetic patterning of my mind, body, and spirit. I am writing the curriculum for my soul's evolution.

Writing has offered me a safe space of solace in which to pause, to take the time and space to be with myself in ceremony with my journals-- my most trusted and loyal friends. It offered me a unique opportunity to learn how to hold space for my own vulnerability without needing to fix anything or solve any problems. Writing gifted me with the appreciation for the intricate complexities of what it means to be human, by expanding my field of awareness and supporting the cultivation of a higher level of compassion for myself and others. In telling my story, I was handed an opportunity to give language to all the feelings and emotions that I carried—everything from the joy to the pain to the sadness to the brokenness and despair, it all had a place to land. My wounds finally had a place to speak, to share their wisdom and their light; and as I allowed their words to flow without interruption, I was reacquainted with my spirit.

The words are the rhythm, the melody, an energy all their own. Like tiny pulses of electricity, their frequency ignites me, and as my hands dance an intimate waltz with the paper, magic is created. I close my eyes; I don't even need to see my partner. I just need to allow my hand to move organically; a conscious dance, an ecstatic expression of connection with spirit, and true oneness from within and with all.

Writing is a movement practice that crafts words as sacred microcosms of energetic potential, manifestations of authenticity and truth, just waiting to connect in resonance with a reader. There is a beautiful connection between the writer and reader, and between the words and all of existence, yet the experience is so much bigger than the words.

I have always valued stories, and people's life stories in particular--what moves them, what inspires them, what makes their soul feel alive, what cracks them open and expands their consciousness. I crave people's stories, especially the ones that they don't even know exist within them, yet I somehow can always feel within them. The stories that inspire me are of ordinary, everyday, raw material of humanness. The tales of uncomfortable life experiences that bring people to their knees in grief, in despair, and agony. I'm moved as I hear the enormous strength that it takes to be uncomfortable, to get brutally honest with oneself while staring in the mirror, to hold space for the vastness of one's own feelings and emotions, and to offer that same unconditional love and support for others even when it's hard. I'm exhilarated by stories filled with genuine authenticity, hearing about those who can remain grounded and giving even as life offers them privilege and success. I am in awe of those who can fail gracefully, even as they mop up puddles of tears, even when they believe they can't go on; I cheer for them when they eventually rise. I seek to acquire knowledge from those whose stories are an admission of their humbleness, knowing that they will always be students. I am intrigued by those who can show up in everyday life amidst screaming kids, work demands, financial strain, laundry, cooking, errands, housecleaning, and still find moments of magic in all of that humdrum; sparks of magic that cause them to pause, look up, and say a prayer of gratitude for all of it. I long to hear stories of those who are courageous enough to stand out from the crowd, dare to be different, and blaze their own trails. I am captivated by those who are brave enough to remove their masks, and I find what's underneath to be mesmerizing and stunningly beautiful.

Storytelling is a sacred ceremony—a celebration of my communication with my spirit, and my soul's communion with others. Every moment of life

275

is actually a story that is unfolding, and writing is a way to capture those moments, like a photograph. And the beauty of it is that the words are all my own—it's my perceptions and feelings, the way that I experienced these moments. People in my life may see them differently or remember them differently, but that doesn't matter. This is my journey, and this is my journal.

My story is a living, breathing, being that I birthed into the world from a womb of love. And each day since my breath conceived her, I have carried her in my womb, watching her grow, change, and transform; a becoming, full of potential and possibility. Our relationship has been a powerful teacher--I have sat with her, talked to her, confided in her, loved her, honored her, valued her as my most prized possession. Other times I yelled at her, judged her, scrapped her, and shamed her. She spoke to me often, reminding me that she came through me, like a child, and asked me to see her, love her, admire her unconditionally as a beautiful expression of my own soul.

She begged me not to leave her, and in return she would never let me down. She always invited me to go deeper; to take risks by going to places that I wouldn't dare to go before, fueled by the courage that comes when I surrender and let love take the reins. She asked me to promise to not hold back, not censor anything, not keep anything locked away, for she had immense admiration for my raw vulnerability. And, she reminded me that she was a safe place for me to explore my feelings, make mistakes, and express my opinions. She looked me deep into my eyes and said, 'Do not be afraid; for shame, fear, doubt, and guilt do not have a place here.'

She offered me refuge as I teased apart thoughts, beliefs, and ideas that roused strong emotion. She provided feedback and insights that helped me to see matters clearly and with a fresh perspective. She energized me to have an open mind and open heart.

She provided a space to build my legacy with the raw material of my gifts of creating order, structure, and guidance-- behaviors that were once motivated by fear now had a place in my medicine bag. She gave me the confidence to be a sharer of knowledge, and a mentor and guide for others using my life as my teachings.

She convinced me to see that it is the wounded ones who offer the greatest teachings for the world; that in the telling of my story, in the courageous expression of the universal feelings that all humans feel yet most bury, I will inspire a movement that will heal even the ones carrying the heaviest of ancestral burdens and the loudest fearful cries for the future. She reminded me that my awakening has the potential to awaken all of humanity.

When she felt like she was dying and couldn't go on anymore, she asked me to breathe life back into her; and in exchange for this resuscitation, she would show me my magic. And she did, each and every time. With every edit, as she read her words back to me, sharing her story reminded me of my gift of alchemizing fear into love. The voice that once so strongly convinced me to be conservative and constricted, neurotic and uptight, now only spoke words of freedom and love.

My authentic voice has clear rhythm and acoustics and is melodious and lyrical. A voice that rouses respect. A voice that comes from my Higher Self, from Source, who wants my soul to expand and evolve. This voice encourages me to be still, calm, peaceful so that I can hear all that it has to offer me. The voice reminds me that I have so much to offer for this world, and so it shows me my gifts, reminds me to look around in awe as if everything were sacred and magical. It reminds me to offer myself the same love and compassion that I so freely offer others. It reminds me that all experience is good and necessary, and that change is a natural part of life. It reminds me that I have everything right within myself. And it shows me that it doesn't have to be loud and forceful to be impactful.

Knowing that my purpose is to guide others on their own journeys catalyzed my quest to expose the truths of my wounds that up until then I had once rendered deplorable. My experiences were beautiful gems to explore, not hideous demons from which to hide.

My wounds were the womb that could birth my story and true voice into this world to be expressed responsibly for truth, conscious healing, creation, and sharing unconditional love. I seek to share it as my personal evolution to inspire a collective revolution, in the same way as my ancestors had. And where I feel choked and restricted, I will send my breath, awaken my voice, sing my song, dance my dance, and write my story, for I know that what we don't speak, we store. As Albert Camus reminds us, "The only way to deal with an unfree world is to become so absolutely free that your very existence is an act of rebellion."

Doing the work of healing is a life-long journey. It's more than a yoga class, new-age philosophy book, seated meditation, or weekend retreat. All of those practices are wonderful, but they alone can't wake you up. And more so, sometimes those well-intentioned practices become easy ways of bypassing the real work, the real nitty gritty of the awakening which is staring at yourself, looking honestly at all of yourself—the pain, the wounds, the mistakes, the hurt you received, the hurt you caused, the excuses, the self-sabotage, the patterns and habits, all of it. And each time you grow through it, and you make it out of the dark and into the light, and you think you have reached a place of peace and enlightenment, bam, something happens again and the cycle just repeats forcing you to level up each time. If we want to ascend, we must be willing to descend time and time again. Part of the awakening process is the realization that you aren't really ever completely awake! And *that's the messy, ugly, exhausting, truth about healing and awakening and rebirth. And all that means, is that there will always be a story to tell.*

I definitely don't have it all figured out. I'm no guru, no expert, no spiritually ascended master. It doesn't matter how many retreats I've ventured on, how many certifications that I've accumulated, how many times I've gotten up into a shoulder stand (the answer is zero, by the way), how many vivid and magical Shamanic Journeys I have had, or how many minutes I can remain still in meditation. All that matters is that I show up authentically with my story as my offering to the world.

This book is only the beginning. When the pen is in my hand, and my innermost musings, memories, and mysteries flowing from my soul form delicately woven patterns on the page, I find freedom and the audacity to authentically live out loud. And as my voice sings and my spirit dances, I am rooted in the richness of experiences that have been the curriculum of my soul's evolution; and I ascend with the wisdom of those experiences and the ones of those who came before me, as my fuel to rise with my mind as a sharp tool, my body as a sacred vessel, and my heart as a trusted compass.

As a sacred storyteller, my medicine is in my stories, as an elder my purpose is offering its potent wisdom to generations after me. My stories are my legacy, my celebration of life, my healing, and my wholeness, as I unapologetically reclaim my freedom and light. The heroine horse has been emancipated.

In sharing my story, I am modeling what it means to do the work. It would be so easy for me to encourage others to heal, while silently opting out myself. But changing the world demands that we start by changing ourselves from the inside out first.

Rewilding is your birthright. My wish for you is that you will be inspired to embark on your own radical rebellion of remembering the roots of your truest self, rekindling the flames of your deep instinctual knowing, and reclaiming the sovereignty to blaze your own trail. The vitality of future generations depends on you to live as if someone left the gate open.

You are what the world has been waiting for.

Let her run free.

Xoxo

A. T.

Acknowledgments

This book was a true birthing experience following a labor of love catalyzed by an intense and often painful incubation period; and I would not have been able to endure without the love and support of so many.

To my mother, thank for showing me the depths of love that a parent can have for a child. I am forever grateful for your endless hard work and sacrifice without complaint, late nights spent worrying, holding my hair and rubbing my back, trusting me when I said I had "the tingles," and devoting yourself to being my mother. It was always you and me against the world. I know why I chose you, and I remain honored to be your daughter. My boys are beyond blessed to have you in their lives. They will always love your chicken cutlets better than mine, and I will too. Every day, I still miss my "mommy."

Dominick, my story isn't one without you. It is easy to feel gratitude for you, as you have been my protector right from the start, believing in me even when I didn't believe in myself. You nourished me while I was inside the chrysalis; and the beautiful union of our hearts gave me the fortitude to birth myself into the world and step into the power that had always resided within me. We have loved together, and now we heal together. I am holding space with love and admiration, as you have done for me. I hope that however each of our journeys unfold, you find joy and peace, and allow yourself to be all that you have been destined to become. Don't fear your depths, it's where you will find all that you have been searching for.

To my beautiful boys, Antonio and Gianni, my little Buddhas, my greatest teachers, who endured nights of shitty take-out, rushed bedtime stories, clouds of burning sage, and incessant ramblings of my innermost thoughts, as I neared the final descent of this book from the birth canal. I hope that my story inspires you to wake up, dive deep, hurt radically, love fiercely, and live authentically. It's what you have taught me. May this book serve as your permission slip to be courageously wild. Saddle up—you've got trails to blaze! Just remember—I love you with all my heart and soul, and I love being your mamma. The world needs you just as you are, never change.

To Gina Mazza, so much more than my patient editor, dear trusted friend, and loving sister, you have been a nourishing midwife during the birthing of my story. Your encouragement, unwavering support, and love have meant everything to me. You have been my most healing therapist, as your hours of listening and genuine understanding allowed me some of the most profound realizations. Your brilliant words of wisdom anchored me so I could learn to let go and surrender. Thank you for so deeply "seeing" me in ways that no one ever could. You have held my life in your hands, honored it as sacred, and helped me to set it free. I love you.

To all of those who walked before me and beside me as guides, the way-showers: Sheila Pearl, Natalie Deeb, Annie Samojedny, Matilde Agar, Pam G, Pat Nast, Donna Brickwood, Eve Fogler, Paul Alexander ("Alex"),

Lola Manekin, Caroline Kohles, Winalee Zeeb, Britta von Tagen, Irene Zimmerman, Debbie Rosas, Parashakti, Jennifer Lucero-Earle, Tina Finkelstein, Laura Parker, and every magnificent horse who taught me how to ride between worlds. I love and respect each of you immensely. You have been, and always will be, my North Stars.

To ML, thank you for only ever wanting me to be myself. IFE.

To my dearest "framily," you all know who you are, you have shown me nothing but unconditional love even when I was MIA and you feared me dead. You have always believed in me even when I struggled to believe in myself. I love you all beyond words.

To C.J., it was you who channeled for me the clear direction from spirit, "Kristy, the world needs to hear your voice!" Your gifts are undeniable. I see you, I believe in you. Now all you gotta do is see for yourself.

Ultimately, this book, and my rewilding, have been made possible by each and every beautiful and unique child, teen, adult, parent, and family who ever stepped foot in my office entrusting their story to me, while listening to mine. My heart swells with gratitude; for in seeing you, I have seen the depths of myself. And in witnessing your journeys, I found the strength to continue mine. Together we have healed and together we have grown. Your light has been a reminder that we are all connected on this spiritual journey back to the stars. I feel incredibly honored to be a part of your story. I have been in awe of each of you, as you rediscovered your roots as you worked to rise. Thank you for the reminder that it is heroic to be human.

About the Author

Known as the modern-day medicine woman, Dr. Kristy Vanacore has been a prominent trailblazer in the field of holistic psychology for two decades. She has developed an innovative approach to mind-body-spirit healing by integrating science with ancient wisdom to reconnect modern seekers with their roots, instincts, and natural freedom.

In her private practice, Kristy combines evidenced-based therapeutic techniques such as Mindfulness-based Stress Reduction, Acceptance and Commitment Therapy, Cognitive Behavioral Therapy, Dialectical Behavior Therapy, Family Systems Therapy and Parent Coaching; somato-emotional release practices like Yoga, Conscious Dance, Authentic Movement,

Nervous System Rebalancing, and Craniosacral Balancing; Energy Therapy such as Reiki Shamanic Healing practices; and functional medicine.

Kristy's life mission has been creating an innovative center for collective healing and community. To date, thousands of families from all over the world have received support through individual coaching, empowerment groups, wellness retreats, and classes. Kristy regularly consults with schools, hospitals, rehabilitation centers, and retreat centers. She is frequently invited to speak locally and nationally about topics such as rebirth of parents, rewilding for families, mindfulness for children, mindful parenting, empowerment and resiliency for children and teens, health and wellness for families, meditation and spiritual development. Kristy also created a professional development mentorship for aspiring healers and world servers.

As a sacred storyteller, Kristy astutely shares the wisdom of the elders through both oral and written tradition. She has seen evidence that excavating one's story is key to becoming a whole being. To that end, she integrates writing into her coaching as an effective part of her clients' healing journeys.

Kristy frequently writes blogs, articles for various publications, as well as collections of poetry. Kristy lives with her family in Connecticut and can be found online at www.kmvgroup.org.

CPSIA information can be obtained
at www.ICGtesting.com
Printed in the USA
LVHW031950020322
712397LV00002B/165

9 781945 026881